ISBN: 9798620712199

Copyright © 2020 by Rick Lyon
www.CosmicCreations.BIZ
ricklyon135@gmail.com

By offering this book in a workbook format, we encourage you to use this to conduct your own presentation at a religious institution of your choice. Study the material. Anticipate potential questions from the group. Practice the presentation out loud to train your mind and mouth to work together. Find a place, set a date and time, promote the class everywhere you can in every way you can. Be prepared. Dress well but comfortably. Remember that you are an ambassador of the Kingdom of Heaven. Arrive early. Greet everyone when they arrive. This will help remove the butterflies and jitters. Pray for our heavenly Father to help you and give you the words he wants you to say. Ask the angels and your Indwelling Spirit to help you. Feel free to modify the instructor introduction and the farewell sections to suit your own thoughts but please leave the other content as is. This material is copyrighted. Space is provided to record your notes and comments after each section.

ACKNOWLEDGEMENTS:

A significant amount of this material has been derived from *The Urantia Book* and the christian Bible plus other religious texts. We encourage you to go further in this process of finding God and discovering who he really is by visiting:

www.urantia.org
and any online resource for the Bible

The God of Jesus

A Personal Introduction to the Real God of Love

Rick Lyon

A Workbook

By Rick Lyon

Edited by Susan Lyon

The God of Jesus Course Outline

The God of Jesus

BEGINNING COURSE SURVEY:

I believe that God is: _____

Who is God? _____

What is God?_____

Where is God? _____

God should:_____

_____

Why did God. . ._____

_____?

What has God done for me? _____

_____

What have I done for God?_____

_____

My personal thoughts about God: _____

_____

I am taking this course because . . . _____

_____

The one thing I most hope to learn:_____

_____

_____

TABLE OF CONTENTS

≈The God of Jesus≈

Dedicated to our heavenly Father, Jesus, and my beloved Indwelling Spirit

Lesson One

The God of Jesus

Course Introduction

Ezra, a backslidden Jew, was charmed by Jesus' teachings and asked him to help him come back to the faith of Israel. He expressed his hopelessness by saying, "I want to be a true son of Abraham, but I cannot find God." Said Jesus: "If you truly want to find God, that desire is in itself evidence that you have already found him. Your trouble is not that you cannot find God, for the Father has already found you; your trouble is simply that you do not know God. Have you not read in the Prophet Jeremiah, 'You shall seek me and find me when you shall search for me with all your heart'? And again, does not this same prophet say: 'And I will give you a heart to know me, that I am the Lord, and you shall belong to my people, and I will be your God'? And have you not also read in the Scriptures where it says: 'He looks down upon men, and if any will say: I have sinned and perverted that which was right, and it profited me not, then will God deliver that man's soul from darkness, and he shall see the light'?" And Ezra found God and to the satisfaction of his soul. Later, this Jew helped build the first Christian church in Syracuse.

Hello everyone and thank you for attending this course. My name is Rick Lyon and the name of this course is "The God of Jesus". I chose this title to spark interest and peak your curiosity. While today we may have questions about who God is or what God is, by the end of this course I hope that you realize the truth that there is no mystery to God; only things that we don't know or cannot know yet. We will get into that pretty quickly.

[Make copies of page V and hand out to students. Briefly review it.]

[Make copies of page VII. Seal in envelopes for students to take home and return. DO NOT OPEN them. Return them to the students at the end of the course unopened.]

During our discussions, please do not use terms such as "I disagree" or "You are wrong" or any similar phrase. We are here to learn from each other and for that to happen we all need to feel safe about sharing our opinions, floating ideas, presenting questions, or exploring the concepts discussed. Nobody on this planet knows the absolute truth so I ask that none of us presume to think we do. While we may express different ideas or opinions, please do not attack anyone else's opinions or beliefs or desire to learn even if you think they are wrong. Sometimes exploring a wrong thing leads to the right thing. Although I don't think anything we discuss will prove to be that irritating to anyone's soul or intellect, let's be loving and courteous in our actions and reactions to each other. Secondly, we are in no hurry here. So try to listen to what someone is saying rather than trying to formulate your response while they are saying it. If there is a pause of silence as we absorb what someone says, that is ok. Don't fear silence when it is due to the contemplation of some new idea or concept. You will hear many Bible quotes within the presentations but I won't always take the time to identify them. Lastly, let the Spirit of Truth and the spirit of God that indwells each of us to lead us in this effort.

[Spontaneous prayer to open]

Instructor Introduction

[EXAMPLE] First, let me introduce myself:

Again, my name is Rick. I recently moved to South Bend, Indiana, after retirement from a steel mill. I am originally from Crawfordsville which is about three hours south of here. I grew up and later lived on the family farm which has been in our family 160 years or so.

I have worked for God for many years; mostly in the past 25 years or so. I have given some presentations, led workshops and hosted study groups every Wednesday evening. I have taught some online courses about "Our Relationship With God", "The Crisis at Capernaum" about the feeding of the 5000, "Jesus, the Master Teacher" and others. I have written a few books that are available on Amazon. One is "A New Revelation of Jesus" which is written as a first person account of the life and teachings of Jesus as if told by Jesus himself. Another is a series of four books that are a collection of frequently asked questions about God, heaven, angels, religion, Jesus, science, philosophy, and cosmology called "FAQ's with the Facts". That series took me twelve years to finish.

I feel led to do this course although I always nervous about doing such things but when you offer yourself as a tool for God, great things can and do happen. I learned the hard way not to do things like this myself but to let God use me to do them. So, hopefully I won't get in the way too much and I pray that God gives me the words he wants said and shows me what he wants done.

I don't know of a time when I didn't know God even as a small boy. Sometimes I feel left out by the fact that I never experienced that emotional explosion of suddenly finding God and conversion. But, somehow I just always knew God to be real and present in my life. I do recall confirming my choice to give my life to God and to wholeheartedly do his will to the best of my ability. I have gone from being shy about my relationship with God to being confident and bold about it. I take offense when people say things about my heavenly Father that are not true. I hurt whenever I see someone who doesn't know that God loves them and places great value on them and trust in them. Yes, God trusts you, depends on you, and needs you.

In the late 1970's, I got a totally unexpected phone call that even today I don't know why I got it. That phone call was from an organization somehow related to Billy Graham. I had gone to a Billy Graham Crusade so that is probably how they got my name. They were having a play at a local church called "Heaven's Gates and Hell's Fury" or something like that. It was a terrible play but they asked me to be a counselor. I heard myself saying "Yes!" and not only "Yes" but enthusiastically saying: "Yes!" One side of my brain was saying "yes" but the other side of my brain was saying: "What the heck are you doing?"

I had never done anything like that before and had no clue how to do it. But, I was determined to represent God the best I could. I wrote out the prayer I wanted to start with. I wrote out all the great things I wanted to say. I practiced until I knew it well. I was sure that I was ready to do the best I could. If you notice, you see where this is headed. The first night I found myself oddly confident but that isn't me. When the play was over and my group of ten teenagers gathered around me, I totally forgot everything I wanted to say. I tried to read the prayer I wrote and fumbled it. I tried to recall all the vast wisdom I wanted to say but couldn't. Gradually, my group of ten drifted politely away and there I was all by myself. You probably noticed that so far it was all about "I" rather than God.

The next night, I told God in probably the first truly sincere prayer of my life that I couldn't do this. If he wanted it done he would have to do it but I offered to be the tool for him. You see, up to this point in my life I knew God or so I thought but I didn't want to bother God with my problems. He has enough to do without worrying about me. But this day, I sincerely asked for God's help. That night, when a different group of ten people gathered around me, I didn't have any notes but I felt prepared. I wasn't really confident but I had peace about it. As I started to speak, I could see people looking back at me. Again there was this kind of left brain right brain thing where I was listening to me speaking but not really doing the speaking is the only way I can describe it. I could see the look on the faces revealing their genuine interest in the words being spoken and they were truly paying attention. When it was over, the person most surprised by what came out of my mouth was me. That night, instead of standing alone at the end, people came up and thanked me. But I knew it wasn't me who just did that. And my life changed that night and today I still thank God for it and remind myself of it. I remind myself to be the instrument for the work God needs done.

God is truly omnipotent, all powerful, but he is not omnificent—meaning that he does not personally do all that is done or needs to be done. God is a great delegator. He never does anything that someone else can do. If God did everything then there would not be anything for us, the angels, or the other spiritual beings to do. Offer yourself to serve God and man, to be the tool God uses to do his will and great things will happen. You will be amazed at what you can do and will do.

This presentation began many years ago as a paper I wrote and submitted to one of those online places where you post your writings hoping to get some notice as a writer or to enlighten the world. It evolved into a series of YouTube videos I never finished. Then I thought about finding a small church to lead and base my ministry on this. Then it became an idea for a book but after moving to South Bend, I felt led to try to present it here to you today. I hope you are led to enjoy it and benefit from it. I admire people who can speak extemporaneously but I never found that skill myself and as I get older that gets even harder. So forgive me for mostly reading from my presentation.

So, why a class on getting to know God? Doesn't everybody, especially those who attend this or any other church already know God? We probably do in varying degrees. I know you because I just met you. I know my wife much better than I know you because I have communicated much more with her than I have with you. Our relationship with God is the same way. Some of us have just found God and others have known him all our lives. The best way for you to know God is to communicate with him through prayer and worship. The more you communicate with God the better you come to know him and discover God's will, and the more you come to know God, the more you will love him.

Another reason to get to know God is so you can help those who don't. That is, sharing the gospel and being an ambassador of the Kingdom of Heaven. Knowing God is the most important relationship you can have or ever will have. Our relationship with God is eternal. As we will see in coming weeks, it is the most personal and intimate relationship you can possibly have with anyone else. Knowing God should be our highest ambition; worshiping God our greatest joy.

Recently, a popular NFL quarterback claimed to be an atheist. While that explains why he played so poorly against the 49ers, it also reveals the way a lot of people who don't really know God feel <u>about</u> God. After a recent school shooting, this quarterback asked: "If God is real why does he allow such terrible things to happen?" Unfortunately, there was nobody in his life to give him the correct answer to this question and worse, some said that this person would come to know God is real when God strikes him down in anger for denying him. This almost confirms that his fears about God are true.

In the book "The Shack" a young girl's dad tells her an Indian legend about how a waterfall was created. Legend has it that God, the Great Spirit, demanded a beautiful princess to sacrifice herself, to kill herself, by jumping off a cliff. In return, God would heal her tribe of a devastating illness that was killing them. The waterfall was created from the tears of the princess. Missy, the daughter, asked why the princess had to die. As anyone who is a parent can relate, her dad did a poor job of explaining it and made the mistake of comparing it to the crucifixion of Jesus. As a result, the girl asked three questions: "Was Jesus' dying real or legend?"; "Why is God so mean?"; and "Will God ever make me jump off a cliff?" How do you think this girl, had she grown up to be an adult, would feel about God? How did this childish legend, which we all know is not true, turn her away from God at such an early age?

Missy's dad missed a perfect opportunity to reveal the truth about God and lead his daughter to know God as her loving heavenly Father; to feel safe, secure, and loved by him. Perhaps, the dad himself didn't know who God really is. As ambassadors of the Kingdom of Heaven and teachers of the gospel, it is our responsibility to reveal the truth about God to every individual person—to lead them to become aware of the fact that all people are children of God; the truth of the Fatherhood of God and the brotherhood of man.

Jesus made it plain that he had come to establish personal and eternal relationships between man and God and that our personal relationship with God should take precedence over all other relationships. And this intimate spiritual fellowship is with all people of all ages and all races. The rewards in this life are spiritual joy and divine communion and in the next life, they are eternal life and progress in knowing God and becoming like him; to achieve Paradise and discover the full purpose of our life.

God is not mean, vengeful, filled with wrath, or anxiously waiting to strike you down for disobeying.

At Magadan Park, Jesus told Nathaniel: Never permit yourself for one moment to believe that the God of love directed your forefathers to go forth in battle to slay all their enemies—men, women, and children. Such records are the words of men, not very holy men, and they are not the Word of God. On the one hand we tell people that God is love, the father of all men, and we should love God but then we tell them that God is a mean angry ogre that you don't want to offend. Jesus told us to love our enemies. We preach a God that was so unloving and unmerciful that he demanded the death of his own innocent son to pay for our sins. Jesus himself never once suggested anything like that. So, which God do you believe in? The God of the ancient past or the God of Jesus?

All of us have heard of men named Aristotle, Plato, and Socrates. To medieval scholars Aristotle was "the Philosopher." In reputation and influence he clearly surpassed all others; in *Dante's Inferno* he is called: "the master of those who know." In the 13th-century Thomas Aquinas blended Christian theology with the philosophy of Aristotle creating what was called Aristotelianism, which soon became established as the new dogma. For the next three hundred years, Aristotle's authority went almost unchallenged in medieval Europe and his influence was felt in every area of intellectual activity.

Aristotle's philosophy was given so much respect that it was often followed without questioning. In fact, it became wrong to question it—that it should be accepted without question or debate. The philosophy of Aristotle was accepted to such a degree that this loyalty and acceptance began to impede philosophic progress stifling the very concept of original and unorthodox thinking that Aristotle preached. Aristotle preached that we should, as we say in modern language, think outside the box and question everything. Ironically, it became blasphemous to question this idea of questioning. Such dogmatic adherence to this philosophy eventually brought about a negative reaction and outright rejection of the Aristotelian worldview and this rejection of what was once unquestionable was a prime motive in the intellectual and scientific revolution that erupted in 16th-century Europe that ended the Dark Ages.

Students of Aristotle did little to help their own cause by stubbornly defending the least defensible parts of Aristotle's philosophy just because it became wrong to question it. In 1624 the Parliament of Paris decreed that "on pain of death no person should either hold or teach any doctrine opposed to Aristotle."

Are we ever guilty of defending the least defensible parts of our beliefs in order to protect and preserve outdated truth from the past? Do we ever hold onto things we no longer really believe just because we are afraid to publicly question them or embrace new truth we have discovered? Are we afraid to search for truth for fear of where it may lead?

Some people, who are afraid of truth and where truth may lead them, believe that if one of their cherished beliefs is determined to be wrong then all they believe is wrong. That belief in and of itself is wrong.

Thomas Hobbes said in 1651 that "Scarce anything can be more absurdly said in natural philosophy than that which now is called Aristotle's Metaphysics; nor more repugnant to government than much of that he hath said in his Politics; nor more ignorantly than a great part of his Ethics." He said this about a philosophy that a few centuries earlier was beyond questioning or criticism. It wasn't that Aristotle's philosophy was bad or wrong but the fact that it became wrong to question that philosophy led to its rejection. What was wrong was that the philosophy failed to grow and progress as society and knowledge advanced.

I think there is a great lesson in this for all of us today. If people fail to grow, fail to progress, fail to learn, fail to be willing to discover truth wherever it may lead, they die intellectually and spiritually. And the death of religion on this world would be so much more catastrophically devastating to mankind and civilization than the loss of Aristotle's philosophy but most importantly it would delay the onset of that world that Jesus promised us; a world where there is no more death, no more tears, no more disease, where the lion will lay down with the lamb, where all men will love one another as Jesus loves us. I use the word "delay" because the gospel of Jesus shall not fail but our lack of personal growth and progress as individuals can delay it.

In all the trials and tribulations of this world, religion is not the problem. Religion is the solution. Nearly all the problems in our families, schools, businesses, politics, and even religious institutions can be reasonably attributed to the lack of religious wisdom and spiritual progress. But we must find the true religion of the spirit, become the true church, and then boldly live our lives according to that spirit (God's will), teach it to our children, and share it with the world. We are key players in Jesus' plan. We are the leaders on this world, the world of the cross, the home planet of Jesus of Nazareth. If we fail in the mission God has given to us, we may become the greatest trophy in the Lucifer rebellion. Earth is the primary battleground in the war between good and evil. While there is no physical bloodshed on this spiritual battleground, the carnage is much worse and long lasting. In the wars that plague our material world, death may be followed by resurrection into the spiritual life. In this war between good and evil, those who die a spiritual death are dead for eternity.

Who's side are we on in this battle? Do we have the courage to go forth bravely as did the Apostles? Do we have the loyalty and faith to fight the good fight for truth, beauty, goodness, righteousness and morality? Aristotle's philosophy, once thought to be the absolute truth, was uplifted and enlightened by new thoughts and new ideas. However, his influence never entirely disappeared. In recent decades, there has been a renewed appreciation of the many deep insights of his philosophy—basically, an openness to new ways of thinking, the courage to question truth in order to find more truth, a willingness to explore the scientific, intellectual, and spiritual elements of life; and the desire to seek the greatest of all human knowledge. In this course we will learn what that is.

≈*The God of Jesus*≈

People are rejecting all religions in greater numbers than ever before. Many see this as a war on religion by materialists and secularists but, I believe, it really is the failure of the religious organizations to meet the spiritual, intellectual, and emotional needs of the people. The religions of today have failed to mature along with the people. The teachings from the past have been frozen into dogma, just as the followers of Aristotle did. Our spiritual ministry is restrained by fear rather than being unleashed to grow in truth, progress is enlightenment, and increase in service. It is our failure to know the truth and to live the truth and be set spiritually free by the truth. Jesus said, "Know the truth and the truth shall set you free." The exploration of truth is not to be feared but encouraged.

Just as Aristotle's philosophy became stale and dogmatic because his followers failed to live what they taught, so do the religions of today fail to inspire the people because the members fail to live the very truths they proclaim. They fail to grow intellectually from experience by recognizing the partnership of religion as the study of God and science as the study of God's creations. They can only progress spiritually through prayer, worship, and living the religion **of** Jesus rather than a religion **about** Jesus; by following Jesus and striving to learn what he taught about God and everything else. Everything Jesus taught and did are of great value to each of us and to all of us. We cannot live the life of the human Jesus because he lived 2000 years ago but we can live the teachings of the divine Jesus because they are alive with the truth, beauty, and goodness of God. Everything he did in his human life was in agreement with the will of the Father in Heaven. Everything he did, he did because he placed such a high value upon all men and women, from sinner to saint, rich and poor, old or young.

The failure of religion to embrace scientific discoveries or offer rational alternatives to many scientific theories has created a conflict between religion and science when in fact the two are inseparable. This has enabled critics of religion to justify their rejection of religion. Even though science acknowledges the physical existence of the universe it fails to acknowledge the spiritual experience of the people who live in it. Science recognizes complexity of creation but fails to acknowledge the need for a creator; that there is some intelligence behind the design of everything from the smallest microbe to the largest galaxy of the universe. I like the term "Purposeful Creation" meaning that everything was created with a purpose and for a purpose. When religion rejects the scientific evidence of creation it is no wonder that science rejects religious proof of the creator.

Religious teachings lose their creative and life-giving power when stagnant truth becomes a boundary line of self-righteous exclusiveness that demands unquestioned loyalty in the face of dynamic truth. Material things do not contemplate the existence of other material things. Machines do not think, create, dream, aspire, idealize, hunger for truth, thirst for righteousness, or personally relate to one another. Contrary to what Disney shows in their movies, the cars out in the parking lot are not out there chatting and asking each other where the best gas is sold. Machines do not motivate their lives with the passion to serve other machines or choose as their eternal goal the task of finding Henry Ford and striving to be like him. Machines are never intellectual, emotional, aesthetic, ethical, moral, or spiritual. Even the world's most powerful computers can only do that which a human mind programs them to do. A mechanism or machine might deteriorate, but it can never progress. A machine cannot grow and this proves that you, the mind and personality and spirit that inhabit your physical material body, are not a machine. The you that inhabits that body is in fact created in the image of God, striving to be like God in all we do. The physical body is made from dust and to dust it shall return. Much like the shell of an egg contains a chick from conception to birth, your body is the shell that supports the spiritual embryo from material conception to your spiritual birth.

Some day you will learn to seek truth as well as fact, to expand your soul as well as your mind. Even now you should learn to water the garden of your heart as well as to seek for the dry sands of knowledge. Books are valueless after the lessons are learned. No chick may be had without the shell, and no shell is of any worth after the chick is hatched. But sometimes when the error is so great, it's sudden correction by revelation would be fatal to those slowly emerging truths which are essential to its experiential uplift and enlightenment. When children have their ideals, do not dislodge them; let them grow. And while you are learning to think as men, you should also be learning to pray as children.

Divine truth is a spiritual and living reality. You can know the truth, and you can live the truth; you can experience the growth of truth in your soul and enjoy liberty by the enlightenment of your mind. It is absolutely true that "You can know truth and the truth will set you free, spiritually free." We should not imprison truth in formulas, codes, creeds, or cultures. Static truth is dead truth, and only dead truth can be held as dogma or traditions that are barriers to your spiritual growth and progress. Remember the little girl Missy? That story of the Indian tradition was a huge barrier to her spiritual growth and her relationship with God. Living truth is dynamic. What you believe to be true today is different from what you believed ten years ago and what you believe ten years from now will be different from what you believe today. That is dynamic truth; that is growth and progress whether it be intellectual or spiritual.

Aristotle's concept of the universe, became increasingly vulnerable to attack as scientific knowledge advanced. His account of nature remained the accepted belief long after it had been substantially undermined by advances in astronomy, mechanics and elsewhere. Those things that were true to Aristotle became untrue as human knowledge advanced and philosophy and wisdom grew from the darkness of the past to the light of the present. Are we repeating these same mistakes of the past in our religions of today? Is the God we often speak of really the God we have faith in?

If we suddenly lost power and found ourselves in a dark room but one of us had a flashlight, who would lead us out of darkness? The one with the light. Let us not turn away and abandon our brothers and sisters who are lost in confusion and darkness but rather let us lead them from spiritual darkness because we have the light of truth. As Jesus said, do not hide our light under the bushel but let our light so shine as to lift up all people and raise up all religions. Use this light of truth to bring spiritual progress to our family, friends, and neighbors. Be a ten talent servant of God by taking this spiritual treasure that we have been given and multiplying it by factors of ten. When God said to go forth and multiply I think he meant to have children but also to bring more adult children to God.

Use your life as an example of the way we all should go. Do something with the talents, knowledge, and faith that God has given you. Don't let fear keep you from growing in your relationship with God and each other. Don't be afraid to pursue truth and follow wherever it leads. Know the fact that at Pentecost, Jesus sent a helper, his Spirit of Truth, to help us know truth and be set spiritually free to love God and serve mankind; to recognize that we are citizens of God's grand cosmic civilization, that God loves us individually and that God is the Father of all and that all men and women are our brothers and sisters; recognize the fatherhood of God and the brotherhood of man. In Judaism, God is the Lord God of Israel but in reality and in truth, God is the Lord God of you. He is your own personal God; the God of individuals as well as nations; the God of men as well as women and children.

Make note of your thoughts, questions, comments here:

_____

_____

_____

_____

_____

_____

_____

_____

_____

_____

_____

_____

_____

Lesson Two
The Concepts of God

Let's begin by briefly looking at the history of the growth of the concepts of God in the Jewish minds of the previous generations before Jesus as they are recorded in the Bible. No doubt you have read these truths in the Scriptures yourself. In 2 Samuel 24:1 where it says: 'And the anger of the Lord was kindled against Israel, so much so that he moved David against them, saying, go number Israel and Judah'? And this was not strange because in the days of Samuel the children of Abraham really believed that Yahweh created both good and evil. But later when we read about these same events in 1 Chronicles 21:1, after the enlargement of the Jewish concept of the nature of God, they did not dare attribute evil to Yahweh; therefore it says: "And Satan stood up against Israel and provoked David to number Israel." This is one example from the Scriptures that clearly shows how the concepts of the nature of God continued to grow from one generation to another. God did not change but as our knowledge of God grows and as our experience with him increases, our understanding of him improves.

God's law is the unchanging reaction of his infinite, perfect, and divine mind. According to James 1:17, in God there "is no variableness neither shadow of changing." Because God is changeless, you can depend on his doing the same thing in the same identical and ordinary way every time whether in the depths of eternity past, now today, or in the eternal future to come. God is the assurance of stability for all created things and beings. He is God; therefore he changes not. However, we are not perfect in our knowledge and wisdom. We do not know all things past, present, and future. So, our understanding of who God is and what he is grows as our knowledge of God increases and our own experience and relationship with him becomes more personal. This is true not only for God the Father, but for all the people we meet in our lives. The more we know them the more we love them.

The concepts of God before the arrival of Melchizedek and his teaching of Abraham consisted mainly of the gods of Egypt, Greece, and the Orient.

In ancient Egypt, around 3100 B.C., the pharaoh was the supreme leader when it came to rituals and religion. Egyptian gods represented various aspects of nature and the people, who relied on nature for their existence, worshiped them and did not want to anger them.

Amun-Ra was considered the king of the gods and goddesses. He became Amun-Ra after being combined with the sun god Ra. He was the father of the pharaohs. His wife was Amunet, their son Khonsu, the moon god. Osiris was the god of vegetation responsible for the flooding and fertility of the Nile River. Osiris was the husband of Isis. They were the parents of Horus. Horus became a pharaoh and later the God of Vengeance. Osiris became god of the underworld or afterlife succeeding Anubis, god the embalmer. Thoth was the god of knowledge and wisdom. He was the arbitrator between good and evil, the controller of both material and spiritual laws.

Just imagine being an Egyptian child and told to say your prayers before bedtime!

The gods of Rome evolved from the gods of Greece. These included Jupiter, the king of the Gods. He was in charge of the sky. Also known as Jove, as in the saying: "By Jove that was bloody good sport." His father was Saturn and his brother Neptune, god of the sea. In Rome it was Jupiter but in Greece it was Zeus who was king of the gods. Pluto was god of the underworld in charge of the afterlife. In Greece this was the god Hades. Apollo was the god of many things but mostly artistic things like music and poetry; probably all the stuff the other gods didn't want to bother with. Then there was Mars, the god of war; Cupid, the god of love; Mercury, the god of money; Vulcan, the God of fire; and Saturn, the god of plenty and peace. Now, realize this is greatly simplified. All these gods overlapped responsibilities so keeping track of who does what was no doubt difficult even for the gods themselves.

The gods of the orient are even more numerous and confusing, at least to me.

The Scriptures reflect the intellectual, moral, and spiritual status of those who create them. Have you not read how the concepts of Yahweh grow in beauty and glory as the prophets make their records from Samuel to Isaiah? And you should remember that the Scriptures are intended for religious instruction and spiritual guidance. They are not the works of either historians or philosophers.

Just think about these concepts of God, how utterly wrong they were, and the significance of the teachings of Melchizedek and the leadership of Abraham in bringing the truth of the one God to mankind becomes evident. Draw a line in the time line of history because this is where it all changed. We see what it was in Egypt, Rome, and Greece. Now let's see what it became as a result of Melchizedek's teachings to Abraham. In Hebrews 7:1-10 we read about Melchizedek.

Let me list some of the names and concepts of God in the times from Abraham up to the life and teachings of Jesus.

1. **Yahweh**—the god of the Sinai clans. This was the primitive concept of Deity which Moses exalted to the higher level of the Lord God of Israel. The Father in heaven never fails to accept the sincere worship of his children on earth, no matter how crude their beliefs or by what name they use for his divine nature.

2. **The Most High**. This concept of the Father in heaven was proclaimed by Melchizedek to Abraham and carried far from Salem by those who believed in this enlarged and expanded idea of God. Abraham left Ur because of the establishment of sun worship, and he became a believer in Melchizedek's teaching of El Elyon—the Most High God. This was a composite concept of God, consisting in the blending of their older Mesopotamian ideas and the doctrines of the Most High.

3. **El Shaddai**. During the early days, many of the Hebrews worshiped El Shaddai, the Egyptian concept of the God of heaven, which they learned about during their captivity in the land of the Nile. Long after the times of Abraham and Melchizedek all three of these concepts of God became joined together to form the doctrine of the creator Deity, the Lord God of Israel.

4. **Elohim**. From the times of Adam the teaching of the Trinity, God the father, God the son, and God the spirit has persisted. The name Elohim recognized the expanding concept of God as a Father with spiritual children in the Son and Spirit.

5. **The Supreme Yahweh**. By the times of Isaiah these beliefs about God had expanded into the concept of a Universal Creator who was simultaneously all-powerful and all-merciful. And this evolving and enlarging concept of God virtually replaced all previous ideas of God in older religions. Coexistent with the Father are the Son and the Spirit, and the revelation of the nature and ministry of these Paradise Deities will continue to enlarge and brighten throughout the endless ages of the eternal spiritual progression of the ascending sons of God—us.

6. **The Father in heaven**. And now, thanks to Jesus, we know God as our Father in heaven. Jesus provides a religion in which the believer is a son of God. That is the good news of the gospel of the kingdom of heaven.

Jesus' human life in the flesh portrays a religious growth from the early ideas of primitive awe and human reverence up through years of personal spiritual communion until he, as a 12 year old, became aware of his divine nature and his oneness with the Father. In one short life, Jesus, beginning as a child, grew and progressed in religious and spiritual experience just as all of us begin here on earth and complete on that day when we stand in the presence of God in Paradise. Jesus progressed from the humble status of a mortal which prompted him to say to the one who called him Good Teacher, "Why do you call me good? None is good but God," to that sublime consciousness of his divine nature which led him to exclaim, "Which one of you convicts me of sin?" I think this demonstrates the pattern of personal religious and spiritual growth in our own lives. The baby Jesus grew from human **to** divine; actually to being both human **and** divine. We too grow from being material humans to spiritual beings.

The Christian Bible is many things and one of those things is a history book. No collection of religious writings gives expression to such a wealth of devotion and inspirational ideas of God as the "Book of Psalms." No other single collection from the Bible covers such a great range of time in history. This "Book of Psalms" is the record of the varying concepts of God by the believers of the Salem religion throughout the Levant and embraces the entire period from Amenemope in Egypt to Isaiah. In the Psalms, God is depicted in all phases of conception, from the crude idea of a tribal deity to the vastly expanded ideal of the later Hebrews, wherein Yahweh is pictured as a loving ruler and merciful Father.

This group of Psalms constitutes the most valuable and helpful assortment of devotional sentiments ever assembled up to the times of the twentieth century. The worshipful spirit of this collection of hymns is greater than that of all other sacred books of the world. In the "Book of Job" we see the various descriptions of God that best preserved the ideas of the real God.

In Palestine the omniscience (wisdom), and omnipotence (all powerful), and omnipresence (the everywhereness) of God was often grasped but seldom did they consider his love and mercy. It was believed that the Yahweh of those times "sends evil spirits to dominate the souls of his enemies"; he prospers his own and obedient children, while he curses and visits dire judgments upon all others. "He disappoints the devices of the crafty; he takes the wise in their own deceit."

In the "Book of Job" we see the first dawning of the mercy of God, saying: "He shall pray to God and shall find favor with him and shall see his face with joy, for God will give to man divine righteousness." Thus was preached salvation, divine favor, by faith: "He is gracious to the repentant and says, 'Deliver him from going down in the pit, for I have found a ransom.' If any say, 'I have sinned and perverted that which was right, and it profited me not,' God will deliver his soul from going into the pit, and he shall see the light." Not since the times of Abraham had the world heard such a ringing and cheering message of human salvation as this extraordinary teaching.

So the remnants of the Salem missionaries maintained the light of truth during the period of the disorganization of the Hebrew peoples until the appearance of Moses, the first of that long line of the teachers of Israel who never stopped as they built, concept upon concept, until they had achieved the realization of the ideal of the Universal Creator Father of all, the greatest concept of Yahweh up to that day.

1. Evolution Of The God Concept Among The Hebrews

The spiritual leaders of the Hebrews did what no others before them had ever succeeded in doing—they deanthropomorphized, de-humanized, their concept of God without converting him into some abstraction that only philosophers could understand. The term "anthropomorphized" means to make something like man. Even common people were able to understand this mature and advanced concept of Yahweh as a Father, if not of the individual, at least of the race.

Man's concept of God was growing. Rather than seeing God as the image of man or the reflection of man's nature and behavior, they began to understand that God was so much more than man; to realize that God is never wrathful, vengeful, or angry. It is true that wisdom does often restrain his love, while justice conditions his rejected mercy. It is true that we often reap what we sow. But the Father is perfect in everything true, beautiful, and good. He always has been and always will be. God does not bring illness and misfortune upon any of his children. God causes the rain to fall upon the just and the unjust. God is no respecter of persons. God changes not but our understanding of him does as these passages reveal.

The concept of the personality of God, while clearly taught at Salem in the days of Melchizedek, was vague and hazy at the time of the Hebrew exodus from Egypt and only gradually evolved in the their minds from generation to generation in response to the teachings of the prophets and spiritual leaders. From Moses to Malachi there occurred an almost continuous growth in the understanding of the personality of God in the Hebrew mind, and this concept was eventually heightened and glorified by the teachings of Jesus about the Father in heaven.

So, let's take a look at what the prophets said about who God is and what God is:

2. Samuel—First Of The Hebrew Prophets

Hostile pressure of the surrounding peoples in Palestine soon taught the Hebrew sheiks they could not hope to survive unless they confederated their tribal organizations into a centralized government. And this centralization of administrative authority afforded a better opportunity for Samuel to function as a teacher and reformer.

Samuel sprang from a long line of the Salem teachers who had persisted in maintaining the truths of Melchizedek in the days of Abraham and as a part of their worship forms. This teacher was a virile and resolute man. Only his great devotion, coupled with his extraordinary determination, enabled him to withstand the almost universal opposition which he encountered when he started out to turn all Israel back to the worship of the supreme Yahweh of Moses' times. And even then he was only partially successful; he won back to the service of the higher concept of Yahweh only the more intelligent half of the Hebrews; the other half continued in the worship of the tribal gods of the country and in the less mature concepts of Yahweh.

Samuel was a rough-and-ready type of man, a practical reformer who could go out in one day with his associates and overthrow a score of Baal temples. The progress he made was by sheer force; he did little preaching, less teaching, but he did act. One day he was mocking the priest of Baal; the next, chopping to pieces a captive king. He devotedly believed in the one God, and he had a clear concept of that one God as creator of heaven and earth: "The pillars of the earth are the Lord's, and he has set the world upon them."

Let me add here that God certainly did not demand or condone such killing of his children. If we realize, understand, or believe that God is the loving father of all his children, then believing that our Father in Heaven would order such a thing cannot be true. Even in the days before Abraham and Moses, the religious law said: "You shall not kill men, women, or children." Never permit yourself for one moment to believe that the God of love, our Father in heaven, directed your forefathers to go forth in battle to slay all their enemies—men, women, and children. Such records are the words of men, not very holy men, and they are not the Word of God.

But the great contribution that Samuel made to the understanding of who God is was his ringing pronouncement that Yahweh was changeless, forever the same being of unerring perfection and glorious divinity. In these times Yahweh was conceived to be an unpredictable God of jealous whims, always regretting that he had done this or that; but now, for the first time since the Hebrews fled from Egypt, they heard these startling words,

"The Strength of Israel (God) will not lie nor repent, for he is not a man, that he should repent."

Stability in dealing with God was proclaimed. Samuel reiterated the Melchizedek covenant with Abraham and declared that the Lord God of Israel was the source of all truth, stability, and constancy.

God has never regretted creating mankind. He never viewed mankind as his one great mistake. He never considered erasing what he had done and starting over. Consider this when you study the story of Noah and the ark. God is not a habit-bound slave to his own perfection, infallible nature, or faultless decisions. God isn't imprisoned or limited by his perfection but his all-powerful nature allows him to create imperfect things, like us, if he chooses to do so. I believe that our imperfection is part of God's perfect plan. The chaos of the material realms is only God's creativity in action. God is not controlled by time so whether it takes a trillion years to create something or if he does it in the blink of an eye, it is all the same to him.

Always had the Hebrews looked upon their God as a man, a superman, an exalted spirit of unknown origin; but now they heard the one-time spirit of Horeb exalted as an unchanging God of creator perfection. Under Samuel's teaching, the God of the Hebrews was beginning the ascent from the idea of a tribal god to the high ideal of an all-powerful and changeless Creator and Supervisor of all creation.

And he preached a new truth of God's sincerity, his covenant-keeping reliability. Said Samuel: "The Lord will not forsake his people." "He has made with us an everlasting covenant, ordered in all things and sure." And so, throughout all Palestine there sounded the call back to the worship of the supreme Yahweh. Ever this energetic teacher proclaimed, "You are great, O Lord God, for there is none like you, neither is there any God beside you."

Before this time, the Hebrews regarded the favor of Yahweh mainly in terms of material prosperity. It was a great shock to Israel, and almost cost Samuel his life, when he dared to proclaim: "The Lord enriches and impoverishes; he debases and exalts. He raises the poor out of the dust and lifts up the beggars to set them among princes to make them inherit the throne of glory." Not since Moses had such comforting promises for the humble and the less fortunate been proclaimed, and thousands of despairing among the poor began to take hope that they could improve their spiritual status.

But Samuel did not progress very far beyond the concept of a tribal god. He proclaimed a Yahweh who made all men but was occupied chiefly with the Hebrews, his chosen people. Even so, as in the days of Moses, once more the God concept portrayed a Deity who is holy and upright. "There is none as holy as the Lord. Who can be compared to this holy Lord God?"

As the years passed, this grizzled old leader progressed in the understanding of God, for he declared: "The Lord is a God of knowledge, and actions are weighed by him. The Lord will judge the ends of the earth, showing mercy to the merciful, and with the upright man he will also be upright." Even here is the dawn of mercy, although it is limited to those who are merciful. Later he went one step further when, in their adversity, he exhorted his people: "Let us fall now into the hands of the Lord, for his mercies are great." "There is no restraint upon the Lord to save many or few."

And this gradual progressive development of the human concept of the character of Yahweh continued under the ministry of Samuel's successors. They attempted to present Yahweh as a covenant-keeping God but hardly maintained the pace set by Samuel; they failed to develop the idea of the mercy of God as Samuel had later conceived it. There was a steady drift back toward the recognition of other gods, despite the maintenance that Yahweh was above all. "Yours is the kingdom, O Lord, and you are exalted as head above all."

The prophets of this age preached a religion of divine power designed to foster a king upon the Hebrew throne. "Yours, O Lord, is the greatness and the power and the glory and the victory and the majesty. In your hand is power and might, and you are able to make great and to give strength to all." And this was the status of the God concept during the time of Samuel. Perhaps here we see the beginning of the erroneous ideas of the messiah that would later lead to the rejection of Jesus.

3. Elijah and Elisha

About the year 1000 B.C., in the tenth century before Christ, the Hebrew nation became divided into two kingdoms. In both of these political divisions many truth teachers endeavoured to stem the tide of spiritual decadence that had set in, and which continued disastrously after the war of separation. But these efforts to advance the Hebraic religion did not prosper until that determined and fearless warrior for righteousness, Elijah, began his teaching. Elijah restored to the northern kingdom a concept of God comparable with that held in the days of Samuel. Elijah had little opportunity to present an advanced concept of God; he was kept busy, as Samuel had been before him, overthrowing the altars of Baal and demolishing the idols of false gods.

In 2 Kings chapter two of the Bible, when Elijah was called away suddenly in a chariot of fire appeared and Elijah went up to heaven in a whirlwind, Elisha, his faithful associate, took up his work and kept the light of truth alive in Palestine.

But these were not times of progress in the concept of God. The Hebrews had not yet ascended even to the ideals of Moses. The era of Elijah and Elisha closed with the better classes of people returning to the worship of the supreme Yahweh and witnessed the restoration of the idea of the Universal Creator to about that place where Samuel had left it.

The inhabitants of Palestine differed in their attitude toward private ownership of land. The southern or wandering Arabian tribes who followed Yahweh, looked upon land as a gift from God to the clan. They believed that land could not be sold or mortgaged. In Leviticus 25:23, Yahweh spoke, saying, 'The land shall not be sold, for the land is mine, and ye are strangers and sojourners with me."

The northern and more settled Canaanites (the followers of Baal) freely bought, sold, and mortgaged their lands. The word "Baal" means owner. Good crops depended on the favor of Baal. The cult was largely concerned with land, its ownership and fertility.

In general, they owned houses, lands, and slaves. They were the aristocratic landlords and lived in the cities. Each Baal had a sacred place, a priesthood, and the "holy women," the ritual temple harlots.

From this basic difference in the regard to land, there came the bitter antagonisms of social, economic, moral, and religious attitudes exhibited by the Canaanites and the Hebrews toward each other. This economic controversy did not become a religious issue until the times of Elijah. From these days the issue was fought out along strictly religious lines—Yahweh vs. Baal—and it ended in the triumph of Yahweh and the subsequent progress toward monotheism.

Elijah shifted the Yahweh-Baal controversy from the land issue to the religious aspect of Hebrew and Canaanite ideologies. He made a moral issue out of the old beliefs about land and launched a vigorous campaign against the Baalites. This was also a fight of the country folk against domination by the city dwellers. It was chiefly under Elijah that Yahweh became Elohim. The prophet began as a land reformer and ended up a religious leader. Baal's gods were many, Yahweh was one—monotheism won over polytheism.

4. Amos and Hosea

A great step in the transition of the tribal god—the god who had so long been served by sacrifices and ceremonies, the Yahweh of the earlier Hebrews—to a God who would punish crime and immorality among even his own people, was taken by Amos, who appeared from among the southern hills to denounce the criminality, drunkenness, oppression, and immorality of the northern tribes. Not since the times of Moses had such ringing truths been proclaimed in Palestine.

Amos was not merely a restorer or reformer; he was a discoverer of new concepts of Deity. He proclaimed much about God that had been announced by his predecessors and courageously attacked the belief in a Divine Being who would tolerate sin among his own so-called chosen people. For the first time since the days of Melchizedek the ears of man heard the denunciation of the double standard of national justice and morality. For the first time in their history Hebrew ears heard that their own God, Yahweh, would no more tolerate crime and sin in their lives than he would among any other people. Amos envisioned the stern and just God of Samuel and Elijah, but he also saw a God who thought no differently of the Hebrews than of any other nation when it came to the punishment of wrongdoing. This was a direct attack on the egotistic doctrine of the "chosen people," and many Hebrews of those days bitterly resented it.

Said Amos: "He who formed the mountains and created the wind, seek him who formed the seven stars and Orion, who turns the shadow of death into the morning and makes the day dark as night." And in denouncing his half-religious and sometimes immoral fellows, he sought to portray the inescapable justice of an unchanging Yahweh when he said of the evildoers: "Though they dig into hell, thence shall I take them; though they climb up to heaven, thence will I bring them down." "And though they go into captivity before their enemies, thence will I direct the sword of justice, and it shall slay them." Amos further startled his hearers when, pointing an accusing finger at them, he declared in the name of Yahweh: "Surely I will never forget any of your works." "And I will sift the house of Israel among all nations as wheat is sifted in a sieve."

Amos proclaimed Yahweh the "God of all nations" and warned the Israelites that ritual must not take the place of righteousness. And before this courageous teacher was stoned to death, he had spread enough leaven of truth to save the doctrine of the supreme Yahweh; he had insured the further evolution of the Melchizedek revelation of the one God in place of many.

Hosea followed Amos and his doctrine of a universal God of justice by the resurrection of Moses' concept of a God of love. Hosea preached forgiveness through repentance, not by sacrifice. He proclaimed a gospel of loving-kindness and divine mercy, saying, as recorded in the book of Hosea: "I will betroth you to me forever; yes, I will betroth you to me in righteousness and judgment and in loving-kindness and in mercies. I will even betroth you to me in faithfulness." "I will love them freely, for my anger is turned away."

Hosea faithfully continued the moral warnings of Amos, saying of God in Hosea 10:10, "It is my desire that I chastise them." But the Israelites regarded it as cruelty bordering on treason when he said: "I will say to those who were not my people, 'you are my people'; and they will say, 'you are our God.'" He continued to preach repentance and forgiveness, saying, "I will heal their backsliding; I will love them freely, for my anger is turned away." Always Hosea proclaimed hope and forgiveness. The burden of his message ever was: "I will have mercy upon my people. They shall know no God but me, for there is no saviour beside me."

Amos brought awareness to the national conscience of the Hebrews the teaching that Yahweh would not condone crime and sin among them just because they were supposedly his chosen people, while Hosea struck the opening notes in the merciful songs of divine compassion and loving-kindness which were so exquisitely sung by Isaiah and his associates. Next came the first Isaiah.

5. The First Isaiah

These were the times when some were proclaiming threats of punishment against personal sins and national crime among the northern clans while others predicted retribution for the transgressions of the southern kingdom. It was in the wake of this arousal of conscience and consciousness in the Hebrew nations that the first Isaiah made his appearance.

Isaiah went on to preach the eternal nature of God, his infinite wisdom, his unchanging perfection of reliability. He represented the God of Israel as saying: "Judgment also will I lay to the line and righteousness to the plummet." "The Lord will give you rest from your sorrow and from your fear and from the hard bondage wherein man has been made to serve." "And your ears shall hear a word behind you, saying, 'this is the way, walk in it.'" "Behold God is my salvation; I will trust and not be afraid, for the Lord is my strength and my song." "'Come now and let us reason together,' says the Lord, 'though your sins be as scarlet, they shall be as white as snow; though they be red like the crimson, they shall be as wool.'"

Speaking to the fear-ridden and soul-hungry Hebrews, this prophet said: "Arise and shine, for your light has come, and the glory of the Lord has risen upon you." "The spirit of the Lord is upon me because he has anointed me to preach good tidings to the meek; he has sent me to bind up the broken-hearted, to proclaim liberty to the captives and the opening of the prison to those who are bound." "I will greatly rejoice in the Lord, my soul shall be joyful in my God, for he has clothed me with the garments of salvation and has covered me with his robe of righteousness." "In all their afflictions he was afflicted, and the angel of his presence saved them. In his love and in his pity he redeemed them."

This Isaiah was followed by Micah and Obadiah, who confirmed and embellished his soul-satisfying gospel. And these two brave messengers boldly denounced the priest-ridden ritual of the Hebrews and fearlessly attacked the whole sacrificial system.

The barbarous idea of appeasing an angry God, of winning the divine favor through sacrifices and the shedding of blood, represents a religion wholly immature and primitive, a philosophy unworthy of an enlightened age of science and truth. Such beliefs are utterly repulsive to our Father. It is an affront to God to believe, hold, or teach that innocent blood must be shed in order to win his favor or to divert the fictitious divine wrath. We will investigate this further in coming sections.

Micah denounced "the rulers who judge for reward and the priests who teach for hire and the prophets who divine for money." He taught of a day of freedom from superstition and priestcraft, saying: "But every man shall sit under his own vine, and no one shall make him afraid, for all people will live, each one according to his understanding of God." This is a message that will bring people back to religion even today.

Ever the burden of Micah's message was: "Shall I come before God with burnt offerings? Will the Lord be pleased with a thousand rams or with ten thousand rivers of oil? Shall I give my first-born for my transgression, the fruit of my body for the sin of my soul? He has shown me, O man, what is good; and what does the Lord require of you but to do justly and to love mercy and to walk humbly with your God?" And it was a great age; these were indeed stirring times when mortal man heard, and some even believed, such emancipating messages more than two and a half millenniums ago. And but for the stubborn resistance of the priests, these teachers would have overthrown the whole bloody ceremonial of the Hebrew ritual of worship.

Following the first Isaiah was Jeremiah.

6. Jeremiah the Fearless

While several teachers continued to preach the gospel of Isaiah, Jeremiah took the next bold step in the internationalization of Yahweh, God of the Hebrews.

Jeremiah fearlessly declared that Yahweh was not on the side of the Hebrews in their military struggles with other nations. He asserted that Yahweh was God of all the earth, of all nations and of all peoples. Jeremiah's teaching was the peak of the rising wave of the internationalization of the God of Israel; finally and forever did this intrepid preacher proclaim that Yahweh was God of all nations, and that there was no Osiris for the Egyptians, Bel for the Babylonians, Ashur for the Assyrians, or Dagon for the Philistines. And thus did the religion of the Hebrews share in the rebirth of monotheism throughout the world during and following this time; at last the concept of Yahweh had ascended to a level of planetary and even cosmic dignity. But many of Jeremiah's associates found it difficult to conceive of Yahweh apart from the Hebrew nation.

Jeremiah also preached of the just and loving God described by Isaiah, declaring: "Yes, I have loved you with an everlasting love; therefore with loving-kindness have I drawn you." "For he does not afflict willingly the children of men."

Said this fearless prophet: "Righteous is our Lord, great in counsel and mighty in work. His eyes are open upon all the ways of all the sons of men, to give every one according to his ways and according to the fruit of his doings." But it was considered blasphemous treason when, during the siege of Jerusalem, he said: "And now have I given these lands into the hand of Nebuchadnezzar, the king of Babylon, my servant." And when Jeremiah counselled the surrender of the city, the priests and civil rulers cast him into the pit of a dismal dungeon.

Next came the second prophet Isaiah.

7. The Second Isaiah

The destruction of the Hebrew nation and their captivity in Mesopotamia would have proved of great benefit to their expanding theology had it not been for the determined action of their priesthood. Their nation had fallen before the armies of Babylon, and their nationalistic Yahweh had suffered from the international preachments of the spiritual leaders.

The young and determined prophet, Isaiah the second, was a full convert to the elder Isaiah's God of justice, love, righteousness, and mercy. He also believed with Jeremiah that Yahweh had become the God of all nations. He preached these truths of the nature of God with such telling effect that he made converts equally among the Jews and their captors. And this young preacher left on record his teachings, which the hostile and unforgiving priests sought to divorce from all association with him. However, their respect for the beauty and grandeur of these teachings led to their being added to the writings of the first Isaiah. And thus may be found the writings of this second Isaiah in the book of that name, embracing chapters forty to fifty-five inclusive.

No prophet or religious teacher from Melchizedek until the time of Jesus attained the high concept of God that Isaiah the second proclaimed during the days of the captivity. It was no small, anthropomorphic, man-made God that this spiritual leader proclaimed. "Behold he takes up the isles as a very little thing." "And as the heavens are higher than the earth, so are my ways higher than your ways and my thoughts higher than your thoughts."

At last there were human teachers proclaiming a real God to mortal man. Like Isaiah the first, this leader preached a God of universal creation and upholding. "I have made the earth and put man upon it. I have created it not in vain; I formed it to be inhabited." "I am the first and the last; there is no God beside me." Speaking for the Lord God of Israel, this new prophet said: "The heavens may vanish and the earth wax old, but my righteousness shall endure forever and my salvation from generation to generation." "Fear you not, for I am with you; be not dismayed, for I am your God." "There is no God beside me—a just God and a Saviour."

And it comforted the Jewish captives, as it has thousands upon thousands ever since, to hear such words as: "Thus says the Lord, 'I have created you, I have redeemed you, I have called you by your name; you are mine.'" "When you pass through the waters, I will be with you since you are precious in my sight." "Can a woman forget her suckling child that she should not have compassion on her son? Yes, she may forget, yet will I not forget my children, for behold I have graven them upon the palms of my hands; I have even covered them with the shadow of my hands." "Let the wicked forsake his ways and the unrighteous man his thoughts, and let him return to the Lord, and he will have mercy upon him, and to our God, for he will abundantly pardon."

Listen again to the gospel of this new revelation of the God of Salem: "He shall feed his flock like a shepherd; he shall gather the lambs in his arms and carry them in his bosom. He gives power to the faint, and to those who have no might he increases strength. Those who wait upon the Lord shall renew their strength; they shall mount up with wings as eagles; they shall run and not be weary; they shall walk and not faint."

This Isaiah spread a far-flung gospel of the enlarging concept of a supreme Yahweh. He rivalled Moses in the eloquence with which he portrayed the Lord God of Israel as the Universal Creator Father of all. He was poetic in his portrayal of the infinite attributes of the divine Father. No more beautiful pronouncements about the heavenly Father have ever been made. Like the Psalms, the writings of Isaiah are among the most sublime and true presentations of the spiritual concept of God ever to reach the ears of mortal man prior to the arrival of Jesus.

In Isaiah 57:15 we read his portrayal of God by the first Isaiah: "I am the high and lofty one who inhabits eternity." "I am the first and the last, and beside me there is no other God." "And the Lord's hand is not shortened that it cannot save, neither his ear heavy that it cannot hear." And it was a new doctrine in Jewish faith when this peaceful but commanding prophet persisted in preaching of God's divine faithfulness. He declared that "God would not forget, would not forsake."

This daring teacher proclaimed that man was very closely related to God, saying: "Everyone who is called by my name I have created for my glory, and they shall show forth my praise. I, even I, am he who blots out their transgressions for my own sake, and I will not remember their sins."

Hear this great Hebrew prophet demolish the concept of a national God while in glory he proclaims the divinity of the Paradise Father, of whom he says, "The heavens are my throne, and the earth is my footstool." And Isaiah's God was none the less holy, majestic, just, and unsearchable. The concept of the angry, vengeful, and jealous Yahweh of the desert Bedouins has almost vanished. A new concept of the supreme and universal Yahweh has appeared in the mind of mortal man, never to be lost to human view. The realization of divine justice has begun the destruction of primitive magic and biologic fear. At last, man is introduced to a universe of law and order and to a universal God of dependable and final attributes and reliable nature. God is not quirky or emotional in his actions and commandments.

And, this Isaiah, preacher of a supernal God never ceased to proclaim this God of love. "I dwell in the high and holy place, also with him who is of a contrite and humble spirit." And still further words of comfort did this great teacher speak to his listeners: "And the Lord will guide you continually and satisfy your soul. You shall be like a watered garden and like a spring whose waters fail not. And if the enemy shall come in like a flood, the spirit of the Lord will lift up a defense against him." And once again did the fear-destroying gospel of Melchizedek and the trust-breeding religion of Salem and Abraham shine forth for the blessing of mankind.

The farseeing and courageous Isaiah effectively replaced the nationalistic Yahweh by his superior concept of the majesty and power of the supreme Yahweh, a God of love, the ruler of the universe, and an affectionate Father of all mankind. Ever since those eventful days the highest God concept in the Occident has embraced universal justice, divine mercy, and eternal righteousness. In superb language and with matchless grace this great teacher portrayed the all-powerful Creator as the all-loving Father.

This prophet of the captivity preached to his people and to those of many nations as they listened by the river in Babylon. And this second Isaiah did much to counteract the many wrong and racially egotistic concepts of the mission of the promised Messiah. But in this effort he was not wholly successful. Had the priests not dedicated themselves to the work of building up nationalism, the teachings of Isaiah would have prepared the way for the recognition and acceptance of Jesus as the promised Messiah by providing a more accurate prediction and realistic expectations of what the Messiah would be.

I suspect that Isaiah was the favorite scripture of Jesus. He quoted it many times and took his title "Son of Man" from these writings for his public ministry.

8. Sacred and Profane History

As a Jewish person searched the Scriptures, they became more confused. An olden seer promised that God would protect and deliver his "chosen people." Amos had threatened that God would abandon Israel unless they re-established their standards of national righteousness. The scribe of Deuteronomy had portrayed the Great Choice—as between the good and the evil, the blessing and the curse. Isaiah the first had preached a beneficent king-deliverer. Jeremiah had proclaimed an era of inner righteousness—the covenant written on the tablets of the heart. The second Isaiah talked about salvation by sacrifice and redemption. Ezekiel proclaimed deliverance through the service of devotion, and Ezra promised prosperity by adherence to the law. But in spite of all this the Jewish people lingered on in bondage, and their spiritual deliverance was delayed.

And all of this false hope led to such a degree of disappointment and frustration that the leaders of the Jews were so confused they failed to recognize and accept the mission and ministry of a divine Son of God when he came to them in the likeness of mortal flesh as the Son of Man.

The Yahweh-Baal struggle ended with the captivity. And so the end of Judah came suddenly. The city was destroyed, and the people were carried away into Babylon. And the captivity shocked the remnant of Israel into monotheism.

In Babylon the Jews realized that they could not exist as a small group in Palestine, having their own peculiar social and economic customs, and that, if their ideologies were to prevail, they must convert the gentiles. From that came their new concept of their racial destiny—the idea that the Jews must become the chosen servants of Yahweh. The Jewish religion of the Old Testament really evolved in Babylon during the captivity.

The doctrine of immortality also took form at Babylon. The Jews had thought that the idea of the future life detracted from the emphasis of their gospel of social justice. Now for the first time theology displaced sociology and economics. Religion was taking shape as a system of human thought and conduct becoming more and more separate from politics, sociology, and economics.

9. The Hebrew Religion

The leaders of the Hebrew religion had taught the Israelites that they were a chosen people, not for special indulgence and monopoly of divine favor, but for the special service of carrying the truth of the one God to all people in every nation. And they had promised the Jewish people that, if they would fulfil this destiny, they would become the spiritual leaders of all peoples, and that the coming Messiah would reign over them and all the world as the Prince of Peace.

When the Jews had been freed by the Persians, they returned to Palestine only to fall into bondage to their own restrictive code of laws, sacrifices, and rituals. And as the Hebrew clans rejected the wonderful story of God as presented by Moses for the rituals of sacrifice and penance, the Hebrew nation rejected the magnificent concept of the second Isaiah for the bondage of rules, regulations, and rituals.

National egotism, false faith in an erroneous vision of the promised Messiah, and the increasing bondage and tyranny of the priesthood forever silenced the voices of the spiritual leaders (excepting Daniel, Ezekiel, Haggai, and Malachi); and from that day to the time of John the Baptist all Israel experienced an increasing spiritual decline. But the Jews never lost the concept of the Universal Father; even to this day they have continued to follow this concept of God.

And so the successive teachers of Israel accomplished the greatest feat in the evolution of religion ever to be effected on earth: the gradual but continuous transformation of the barbaric concept of the savage Yahweh, the jealous and cruel spirit god of the thundering Sinai volcano, to the later exalted and superior concept of the supreme Yahweh, creator of all things and the loving and merciful Father of all mankind. And this concept of God was the highest human visualization of the Universal Father up to that time when it was further enlarged and so exquisitely amplified by the life and teachings of his Son, Jesus of Nazareth.

With that in mind, let us proceed to discover the God of Jesus; who he is, what he is, and how we can become like God in all we think, do, and say.

Make note of your thoughts, questions, comments here:

_____

_____

_____

_____

_____

_____

_____

_____

_____

_____

_____

_____

_____

_____

Lesson Three

Religions In The Times of Jesus

What we will do in this lesson is look at what the top religions of the world in the times of Jesus said about who God is.

I have done research for this presentation and found what I believe to be the most accurate information available but please do your own research if anything I say doesn't feel right or sit well with you. My goal is to highlight the positive aspects of each religion concerning who God is to the different religions. I intend no offense to anyone who is a child of God. The religions of Islam and Sikh did not exist in the times of Jesus and therefore are not included here.

Let me save our discussion of Christianity for our next lesson as Christianity contains more of the teachings of Jesus than the others. Jesus is our greatest first hand source of information about God because Jesus knows God personally.

1. The Forgotten Prophet of Salem

Nearly all of the world's major religions have some original basis in the teachings of Melchizedek to Abraham. Judaism came directly from his teachings and Christianity as a result of that. Even Islam recognizes Adam, Noah, and Abraham. Melchizedek came to prepare the way for Jesus much as John the Baptist did in the days of Jesus. This prophet, Melchizedek, is not well known, I think, because he was a mentor of Abraham and not much was written to create a significant record about this teacher. Instead, such writings have focused on the student Abraham. However, there is quite enough in the Bible and other religious texts to secure his place and importance in history if we care to look.

Melchizedek established a school to train missionaries of this new revelation of God that he brought to the ancestors of Moses. He was the voice of God speaking to Abraham as God actually spoke to Abraham through Melchizedek. Melchizedek was the teacher and mentor of the many prophets that followed Abraham that we studied earlier. He was the teacher and mentor of Abraham and therefore greater than Abraham. He even changed Abraham's name from Abram to Abraham and promised him children as numerous as the stars if he kept the covenant with God. Melchizedek was without beginning or end of days, without father or mother, and a divine teacher. He came from heaven and lived a brief life as a mortal. We will look at what Melchizedek taught Abraham about who God is and what he taught at his school in Salem, the founding city of Jerusalem, and what his missionaries spread throughout the world. From the Christian Bible we read:

In Genesis 14:18 "And Melchizedek king of Salem brought forth bread and wine: and he was the priest of the most high God."

In Psalms 110:4 "The Lord hath sworn, and will not repent, Thou art a priest for ever after the order of Melchizedek."

In Hebrews 7:1 "For this Melchizedek, king of Salem, priest of the most high God, who met Abraham returning from the slaughter of the kings; 2 To whom also Abraham gave a tenth part of all; first being by interpretation King of righteousness, and after that also King of Salem, which is, King of peace; 3 Without father, without mother, without descent, having neither beginning of days, nor end of life; but made like unto the Son of God; abideth a priest continually. 4 Now consider how great this man was, unto whom even the patriarch Abraham gave the tenth of the spoils."

And finally:

In Hebrews 6:20 "Whither the forerunner is for us entered, even Jesus, made an high priest for ever after the order of Melchizedek."

With Melchizedek and Abraham, we see mankind change from believing in the multiple gods of Egypt, Greece, and Rome to the one God, the creator of all things. We see religious ceremonies change from human sacrifice to animal sacrifice—the jump to the true teachings of salvation by faith alone being too much for the people of that day and age. He taught that God is the God of all people and each person. Melchizedek brought the truth of the one God to mankind but also the concept of the Trinity and the universe of spiritual hosts all serving God and man. Melchizedek brought the truth, Jesus was the truth, the living revelation of God, and the Word of God made flesh, that is, mortal. Melchizedek taught that a Son of God would come to live among us, the prophecy of the coming Messiah. And, while his teachings about the Messiah became confused with the people's desire for an earthly ruler, Jesus was the proclaimed spiritual Messiah promised by Melchizedek.

And it should be made plain that all these teachings portraying monotheism were largely derived, directly or indirectly, from the preaching of the missionaries of Melchizedek, who went forth from their Salem headquarters to spread the doctrine of one God—the Most High—to the ends of the earth.

The early teachers of the Salem religion penetrated to the remotest tribes of Africa and Eurasia, ever preaching Melchizedek's gospel of man's faith and trust in God as the only price of obtaining salvation and God's blessings. Melchizedek's covenant with Abraham was the pattern for all the early teachings that went out from Salem and other centers. Our world has never had more enthusiastic and aggressive missionaries of any religion than these noble men and women who carried the teachings of Melchizedek over the entire Eastern Hemisphere. These missionaries were recruited from many peoples and races, and they largely spread their teachings through the medium of native converts. They established training centers in different parts of the world where they taught the natives the Salem religion and then commissioned these pupils to function as teachers among their own people.

The Salem missionaries spread out all over southwestern Asia, through Palestine, Mesopotamia, Egypt, Iran, and Arabia, everywhere proclaiming the good news of the gospel of Melchizedek. In some of these lands their teachings bore fruit; in others they met with varying success. Sometimes their failures were due to lack of wisdom, sometimes to circumstances beyond their control.

2. Cynicism

The residual teachings of the disciples of Melchizedek, excepting those which persisted in the Jewish religion, were best preserved in the doctrines of the Cynics. According to their beliefs:

God is supreme; he is the Most High of heaven and earth. God is the perfected circle of eternity, and he rules the universe of universes. He is the sole maker of the heavens and the earth. When he decrees a thing, that thing is. Our God is one God, and he is compassionate and merciful. Everything that is high, holy, true, and beautiful is like our God. The Most High is the light of heaven and earth; he is the God of the east, the west, the north, and the south.

Even if the earth should pass away, the resplendent face of the Supreme would abide in majesty and glory. The Most High is the first and the last, the beginning and the end of everything. There is but this one God, and his name is Truth. God is self-existent, and he is devoid of all anger and enmity; he is immortal and infinite. Our God is omnipotent and bounteous. While he has many manifestations, we worship only God himself. God knows all—our secrets and our proclamations; he also knows what each of us deserves. His might is equal to all things.

God is a peace giver and a faithful protector of all who fear and trust him. He gives salvation to all who serve him. All creation exists in the power of the Most High. His divine love springs forth from the holiness of his power, and affection is born of the might of his greatness. The Most High has decreed the union of body and soul and has endowed man with his own spirit. What man does must come to an end, but what the Creator does goes on forever. We gain knowledge from the experience of man, but we derive wisdom from the contemplation of the Most High.

God pours rain upon the earth, he causes the sun to shine upon the sprouting grain, and he gives us the abundant harvest of the good things of this life and eternal salvation in the world to come. Our God enjoys great authority; his name is Excellent and his nature is unfathomable. When you are sick, it is the Most High who heals you. God is full of goodness toward all men; we have no friend like the Most High. His mercy fills all places and his goodness encompasses all souls. The Most High is changeless; and he is our helper in every time of need. Wherever you turn to pray, there is the face of the Most High and the open ear of our God. You may hide yourself from men, but not from God. God is not a great distance from us; he is omnipresent. God fills all places and lives in the heart of the man who fears his holy name. Creation is in the Creator and the Creator in his creation. We search for the Most High and then find him in our hearts. You go in quest of a dear friend, and then you discover him within your soul.

The man who knows God looks upon all men as equal; they are his brethren. Those who are selfish, those who ignore their brothers in the flesh, have only weariness as their reward. Those who love their fellows and who have pure hearts shall see God. God never forgets sincerity. He will guide the honest of heart into the truth, for God is truth.

In your lives overthrow error and overcome evil by the love of the living truth. In all your relations with men do good for evil. The Lord God is merciful and loving; he is forgiving. Let us love God, for he first loved us. By God's love and through his mercy we shall be saved. Poor men and rich men are brothers. God is their Father. The evil you would not have done you, do not to others.

At all times call upon his name, and as you believe in his name, so shall your prayer be heard. What a great honor it is to worship the Most High! All the worlds and the universes worship the Most High. And with all your prayers give thanks—ascend to worship. Prayerful worship shuns evil and forbids sin. At all times let us praise the name of the Most High. The man who takes shelter in the Most High conceals his defects from the universe. When you stand before God with a clean heart, you become fearless of all creation. The Most High is like a loving father and mother; he really loves us, his children on earth. Our God will forgive us and guide our footsteps into the ways of salvation. He will take us by the hand and lead us to himself. God saves those who trust him; he does not compel man to serve his name.

If the faith of the Most High has entered your heart, then shall you abide free from fear throughout all the days of your life. Fret not yourself because of the prosperity of the ungodly; fear not those who plot evil; let the soul turn away from sin and put your whole trust in the God of salvation. The weary soul of the wandering mortal finds eternal rest in the arms of the Most High; the wise man hungers for the divine embrace; the earth child longs for the security of the arms of the Universal Father. The noble man seeks for that high estate wherein the soul of the mortal blends with the spirit of the Supreme. God is just: What fruit we receive not from our plantings in this world we shall receive in the next.

3. Judaism

In our first session we discussed how the teachings of Melchizedek came through Abraham to the Hebrew religion. Here is the heart of those beliefs:

In the beginning God created the heavens and the earth and all things therein. And, behold, all he created was very good. The Lord, he is God; there is none beside him in heaven above or upon the earth beneath. Therefore shall you love the Lord your God with all your heart and with all your soul and with all your might. The earth shall be full of the knowledge of the Lord as the waters cover the sea. The heavens declare the glory of God, and the firmament shows his handiwork. Day after day utters speech; night after night shows knowledge. There is no speech or language where their voice is not heard. The Lord's work is great, and in wisdom has he made all things; the greatness of the Lord is unsearchable. He knows the number of the stars; he calls them all by their names.

The power of the Lord is great and his understanding infinite. Says the Lord: 'As the heavens are higher than the earth, so are my ways higher than your ways, and my thoughts higher than your thoughts.' God reveals the deep and secret things because the light dwells with him. The Lord is merciful and gracious; he is long-suffering and abundant in goodness and truth. The Lord is good and upright; the meek will he guide in judgment. Taste and see that the Lord is good! Blessed is the man who trusts God. God is our refuge and strength, a very present help in trouble.

The mercy of the Lord is from everlasting to everlasting upon those who fear him and his righteousness even to our children's children. The Lord is gracious and full of compassion. The Lord is good to all, and his tender mercies are over all his creation; he heals the brokenhearted and binds up their wounds. Whither shall I go from God's spirit? Whither shall I flee from the divine presence? Thus says the High and Lofty One who inhabits eternity, whose name is Holy: 'I dwell in the high and holy place; also with him who is of a contrite heart and a humble spirit!' None can hide himself from our God, for he fills heaven and earth. Let the heavens be glad and let the earth rejoice. Let all nations say: The Lord reigns! Give thanks to God, for his mercy endures forever.

The heavens declare God's righteousness, and all the people have seen his glory. It is God who has made us, and not we ourselves; we are his people, the sheep of his pasture. His mercy is everlasting, and his truth endures to all generations. Our God is governor among the nations. Let the earth be filled with his glory! O that men would praise the Lord for his goodness and for his wonderful gifts to the children of men!

God has made man a little less than divine and has crowned him with love and mercy. The Lord knows the way of the righteous, but the way of the ungodly shall perish. The fear of the Lord is the beginning of wisdom; the knowledge of the Supreme is understanding. Says the Almighty God: 'Walk before me and be perfect.' Forget not that pride goes before destruction and a haughty spirit before a fall. He who rules his own spirit is mightier than he who takes a city. Says the Lord God, the Holy One: 'In returning to your spiritual rest shall you be saved; in quietness and confidence shall be your strength.' They who wait upon the Lord shall renew their strength; they shall mount up with wings like eagles. They shall run and not be weary; they shall walk and not be faint. The Lord shall give you rest from your fear. Says the Lord: 'Fear not, for I am with you. Be not dismayed, for I am your God. I will strengthen you; I will help you; yes, I will uphold you with the right hand of my righteousness.'

God is our Father; the Lord is our redeemer. God has created the universal hosts, and he preserves them all. His righteousness is like the mountains and his judgment like the great deep. He causes us to drink of the river of his pleasures, and in his light we shall see light. It is good to give thanks to the Lord and to sing praises to the Most High; to show forth loving-kindness in the morning and the divine faithfulness every night. God's kingdom is an everlasting kingdom, and his dominion endures throughout all generations. The Lord is my shepherd; I shall not want. He makes me to lie down in green pastures; he leads me beside still waters. He restores my soul. He leads me in the paths of righteousness. Yes, even though I walk through the valley of the shadow of death, I will fear no evil, for God is with me. Surely goodness and mercy shall follow me all the days of my life, and I shall dwell in the house of the Lord forever.

Yahweh is the God of my salvation; therefore in the divine name will I put my trust. I will trust in the Lord with all my heart; I will lean not upon my own understanding. In all my ways I will acknowledge him, and he shall direct my paths. The Lord is faithful; he keeps his word with those who serve him; the just shall live by his faith. If you do not well, it is because sin lies at the door; men reap the evil they plough and the sin they sow. Fret not yourself because of evildoers. If you regard iniquity in your heart, the Lord will not hear you; if you sin against God, you also wrong your own soul. God will bring every man's work to judgment with every secret thing, whether it be good or evil. As a man thinks in his heart, so is he.

The Lord is near all who call upon him in sincerity and in truth. Weeping may endure for a night, but joy comes in the morning. A merry heart does good like a medicine. No good thing will God withhold from those who walk uprightly. Fear God and keep his commandments, for this is the whole duty of man. Thus says the Lord who created the heavens and who formed the earth: 'There is no God beside me, a just God and a savior. Look to me and be saved, all the ends of the earth. If you seek me, you shall find me if you search for me with all your heart.' The meek shall inherit the earth and shall delight themselves in the abundance of peace. Whoever sows iniquity shall reap calamity; they who sow the wind shall reap the whirlwind.

Come now, let us reason together,' says the Lord, 'Though your sins be as scarlet, they shall be as white as snow. Though they be red like crimson, they shall be as wool.' But there is no peace for the wicked; it is your own sins which have withheld the good things from you. God is the health of my countenance and the joy of my soul. The eternal God is my strength; he is our dwelling place, and underneath are the everlasting arms. The Lord is near to those who are brokenhearted; he saves all who have a childlike spirit. Many are the afflictions of the righteous man, but the Lord delivers him out of them all. Commit your way to the Lord—trust him—and he will bring it to pass. He who dwells in the secret place of the Most High shall abide under the shadow of the Almighty.

Love your neighbor as yourself; bear a grudge against no man. Whatsoever you hate do to no man. Love your brother, for the Lord has said: 'I will love my children freely.' The path of the just is as a shining light which shines more and more until the perfect day. They who are wise shall shine as the brightness of the firmament and they who turn many to righteousness as the stars forever and ever. Let the wicked forsake his evil way and the unrighteous man his rebellious thoughts. Says the Lord: 'Let them return to me, and I will have mercy on them; I will abundantly pardon.'

Says God, the creator of heaven and earth: 'Great peace have they who love my law. My commandments are: You shall love me with all your heart; you shall have no gods before me; you shall not take my name in vain; remember the Sabbath day to keep it holy; honor your father and mother; you shall not kill; you shall not commit adultery; you shall not steal; you shall not bear false witness; you shall not covet.'

And to all who love the Lord supremely and their neighbors like themselves, the God of heaven says: 'I will ransom you from the grave; I will redeem you from death. I will be merciful to your children, as well as just. Have I not said of my creatures on earth, you are the sons of the living God? And have I not loved you with an everlasting love? Have I not called you to become like me and to dwell forever with me in Paradise?

4. Buddhism

Buddhism came near to being a great and beautiful religion without God, without a personal and universal Deity. However, certain of their earlier beliefs reflected the influence of the teachings of the Melchizedek missionaries who continued their work in India even to the times of Buddha. According to their beliefs:

Out of a pure heart shall gladness spring forth to the Infinite; all my being shall be at peace with this supermortal rejoicing. My soul is filled with content, and my heart overflows with the bliss of peaceful trust. I have no fear; I am free from anxiety. I dwell in security, and my enemies cannot alarm me. I am satisfied with the fruits of my confidence. I have found the approach to the Immortal easy of access. I pray for faith to sustain me on the long journey; I know that faith from beyond will not fail me. I know my brethren will prosper if they become imbued with the faith of the Immortal, even the faith that creates modesty, uprightness, wisdom, courage, knowledge, and perseverance. Let us forsake sorrow and disown fear. By faith let us lay hold upon true righteousness and genuine manliness. Let us learn to meditate on justice and mercy. Faith is man's true wealth; it is the endowment of virtue and glory.

Unrighteousness is contemptible; sin is despicable. Evil is degrading, whether held in thought or wrought out in deeds. Pain and sorrow follow in the path of evil as the dust follows the wind. Happiness and peace of mind follow pure thinking and virtuous living as the shadow follows the substance of material things. Evil is the fruit of wrongly directed thinking. It is evil to see sin where there is no sin; to see no sin where there is sin. Evil is the path of false doctrines. Those who avoid evil by seeing things as they are gain joy by thus embracing the truth. Make an end of your misery by loathing sin. When you look up to the Noble One, turn away from sin with a whole heart. Make no apology for evil; make no excuse for sin. By your efforts to make amends for past sins you acquire strength to resist future tendencies thereto. Restraint is born of repentance. Leave no fault unconfessed to the Noble One.

Cheerfulness and gladness are the rewards of deeds well done and to the glory of the Immortal. No man can rob you of the liberty of your own mind. When the faith of your religion has emancipated your heart, when the mind, like a mountain, is settled and immovable, then shall the peace of the soul flow tranquilly like a river of waters. Those who are sure of salvation are forever free from lust, envy, hatred, and the delusions of wealth. While faith is the energy of the better life, nevertheless, must you work out your own salvation with perseverance. If you would be certain of your final salvation, then make sure that you sincerely seek to fulfill all righteousness. Cultivate the assurance of the heart which springs from within and thus come to enjoy the ecstasy of eternal salvation.

No religionist may hope to attain the enlightenment of immortal wisdom who persists in being slothful, indolent, feeble, idle, shameless, and selfish. But whoso is thoughtful, prudent, reflective, fervent, and earnest—even while he yet lives on earth—may attain the supreme enlightenment of the peace and liberty of divine wisdom. Remember, every act shall receive its reward. Evil results in sorrow and sin ends in pain. Joy and happiness are the outcome of a good life. Even the evildoer enjoys a season of grace before the time of the full ripening of his evil deeds, but inevitably there must come the full harvest of evil-doing. Let no man think lightly of sin, saying in his heart: 'The penalty of wrongdoing shall not come near me.' What you do shall be done to you, in the judgment of wisdom. Injustice done to your fellows shall come back upon you. The creature cannot escape the destiny of his deeds.

The fool has said in his heart, 'Evil shall not overtake me'; but safety is found only when the soul craves reproof and the mind seeks wisdom. The wise man is a noble soul who is friendly in the midst of his enemies, tranquil among the turbulent, and generous among the grasping. Love of self is like weeds in a goodly field. Selfishness leads to grief; perpetual care kills. The tamed mind yields happiness. He is the greatest of warriors who overcomes and subdues himself. Restraint in all things is good. He alone is a superior person who esteems virtue and is observant of his duty. Let not anger and hate master you. Speak harshly of no one. Contentment is the greatest wealth. What is given wisely is well saved. Do not to others those things you would not wish done to you. Pay good for evil; overcome evil with the good.

A righteous soul is more to be desired than the sovereignty of all the earth. Immortality is the goal of sincerity; death, the end of thoughtless living. Those who are earnest die not; the thoughtless are dead already. Blessed are they who have insight into the deathless state. Those who torture the living will hardly find happiness after death. The unselfish go to heaven, where they rejoice in the bliss of infinite liberality and continue to increase in noble generosity. Every mortal who thinks righteously, speaks nobly, and acts unselfishly shall not only enjoy virtue here during this brief life but shall also, after the dissolution of the body, continue to enjoy the delights of heaven.

5. Hinduism

The missionaries of Melchizedek carried the teachings of the one God with them wherever they journeyed. Much of this doctrine of the one God, together with other and previous concepts, became part of the subsequent teachings of Hinduism. According to their beliefs:

God is the great God, in every way supreme. He is the Lord who encompasses all things. He is the creator and controller of the universe of universes. God is one God; he is alone and by himself; he is the only one. And this one God is our Maker and the last destiny of the soul. The Supreme One is brilliant beyond description; he is the Light of Lights. Every heart and every world is illuminated by this divine light. God is our protector—he stands by the side of his creatures—and those who learn to know him become immortal. God is the great source of energy; he is the Great Soul. He exercises universal lordship over all. This one God is loving, glorious, and adorable. Our God is supreme in power and abides in the supreme abode. This true Person is eternal and divine; he is the primal Lord of heaven. All the prophets have hailed him, and he has revealed himself to us. We worship him. O Supreme Person, source of beings, Lord of creation, and ruler of the universe, reveal to us, your creatures, the power whereby you abide immanent! God has made the sun and the stars; he is bright, pure, and self-existent. His eternal knowledge is divinely wise. The Eternal is unpenetrated by evil. Inasmuch as the universe sprang from God, he does rule it appropriately. He is the cause of creation, and hence are all things established in him.

God is the sure refuge of every good man when in need; the Immortal One cares for all mankind. God's salvation is strong and his kindness is gracious. He is a loving protector, a blessed defender. Says the Lord: 'I dwell within their own souls as a lamp of wisdom. I am the splendor of the splendid and the goodness of the good. Where two or three gather together, there am I also.' The creature cannot escape the presence of the Creator. The Lord even counts the ceaseless winking of every mortal's eyes; and we worship this divine Being as our inseparable companion. He is all-prevailing, bountiful, omnipresent, and infinitely kind. The Lord is our ruler, shelter, and supreme controller, and his primeval spirit dwells within the mortal soul. The Eternal Witness to vice and virtue dwells within man's heart. Let us long meditate on the adorable and divine Vivifier; let his spirit fully direct our thoughts. From this unreal world lead us to the real! From darkness lead us to the light! From death guide us to immortality!

With our hearts purged of all hate, let us worship the Eternal. Our God is the Lord of prayer; he hears the cry of his children. Let all men submit their wills to him, the Resolute. Let us delight in the liberality of the Lord of prayer. Make prayer your inmost friend and worship your soul's support. 'If you will but worship me in love,' says the Eternal, 'I will give you the wisdom to attain me, for my worship is the virtue common to all creatures.' God is the illuminator of the gloomy and the power of those who are faint. Since God is our strong friend, we have no more fear. We praise the name of the never-conquered Conqueror. We worship him because he is man's faithful and eternal helper. God is our sure leader and unfailing guide. He is the great parent of heaven and earth, possessed of unlimited energy and infinite wisdom. His splendor is sublime and his beauty divine. He is the supreme refuge of the universe and the changeless guardian of everlasting law. Our God is the Lord of life and the Comforter of all men; he is the lover of mankind and the helper of those who are distressed. He is our life giver and the Good Shepherd of the human flocks. God is our father, brother, and friend. And we long to know this God in our inner being.

We have learned to win faith by the yearning of our hearts. We have attained wisdom by the restraint of our senses, and by wisdom we have experienced peace in the Supreme. He who is full of faith worships truly when his inner self is intent upon God. Our God wears the heavens as a mantle; he also inhabits the other six wide-spreading universes. He is supreme over all and in all. We crave forgiveness from the Lord for all of our trespasses against our fellows; and we would release our friend from the wrong he has done us. Our spirit loathes all evil; therefore, O Lord, free us from all taint of sin. We pray to God as a comforter, protector, and savior—one who loves us.

The spirit of the Universe Keeper enters the soul of the simple creature. That man is wise who worships the One God. Those who strive for perfection must indeed know the Lord Supreme. He never fears who knows the blissful security of the Supreme, for the Supreme says to those who serve him, 'Fear not, for I am with you.' The God of providence is our Father. God is truth. And it is the desire of God that his creatures should understand him—come fully to know the truth. Truth is eternal; it sustains the universe. Our supreme desire shall be union with the Supreme. The Great Controller is the generator of all things—all evolves from him. And this is the sum of duty: Let no man do to another what would be repugnant to himself; cherish no malice, smite not him who smites you, conquer anger with mercy, and vanquish hate by benevolence. And all this we should do because God is a kind friend and a gracious father who remits all our earthly offenses.

God is our Father, the earth our mother, and the universe our birthplace. Without God the soul is a prisoner; to know God releases the soul. By meditation on God, by union with him, there comes deliverance from the illusions of evil and ultimate salvation from all material fetters. When man shall roll up space as a piece of leather, then will come the end of evil because man has found God. O God, save us from the threefold ruin of hell—lust, wrath, and avarice! O soul, gird yourself for the spirit struggle of immortality! When the end of mortal life comes, hesitate not to forsake this body for a more fit and beautiful form and to awake in the realms of the Supreme and Immortal, where there is no fear, sorrow, hunger, thirst, or death. To know God is to cut the cords of death. The God-knowing soul rises in the universe like the cream appears on top of the milk. We worship God, the all-worker, the Great Soul, who is ever seated in the heart of his creatures. And they who know that God is enthroned in the human heart are destined to become like him—immortal. Evil must be left behind in this world, but virtue follows the soul to heaven.

It is only the wicked who say: The universe has neither truth nor a ruler; it was only designed for our lusts. Such souls are deluded by the smallness of their intellects. They thus abandon themselves to the enjoyment of their lusts and deprive their souls of the joys of virtue and the pleasures of righteousness. What can be greater than to experience salvation from sin? The man who has seen the Supreme is immortal. Man's friends of the flesh cannot survive death; virtue alone walks by man's side as he journeys ever onward toward the gladsome and sunlit fields of Paradise.

≈ The God of Jesus ≈

6. Zoroastrianism

Zoroaster was himself directly in contact with the descendants of the earlier Melchizedek missionaries, and their doctrine of the one God became a central teaching in the religion which he founded in Persia. Aside from Judaism, no religion of that day contained more of these Salem teachings. From this religion comes the following:

All things come from, and belong to, the One God—all-wise, good, righteous, holy, resplendent, and glorious. This, our God, is the source of all luminosity. He is the Creator, the God of all good purposes, and the protector of the justice of the universe. The wise course in life is to act in consonance with the spirit of truth. God is all-seeing, and he beholds both the evil deeds of the wicked and the good works of the righteous; our God observes all things with a flashing eye. His touch is the touch of healing. The Lord is an all-powerful benefactor. God stretches out his beneficent hand to both the righteous and the wicked. God established the world and ordained the rewards for good and for evil. The all-wise God has promised immortality to the pious souls who think purely and act righteously. As you supremely desire, so shall you be. The light of the sun is as wisdom to those who discern God in the universe.

Praise God by seeking the pleasure of the Wise One. Worship the God of light by joyfully walking in the paths ordained by his revealed religion. There is but one Supreme God, the Lord of Lights. We worship him who made the waters, plants, animals, the earth, and the heavens. Our God is Lord, most beneficent. We worship the most beauteous, the bountiful Immortal, endowed with eternal light. God is farthest from us and at the same time nearest to us in that he dwells within our souls. Our God is the divine and holiest Spirit of Paradise, and yet he is more friendly to man than the most friendly of all creatures. God is most helpful to us in this greatest of all businesses, the knowing of himself. God is our most adorable and righteous friend; he is our wisdom, life, and vigor of soul and body. Through our good thinking the wise Creator will enable us to do his will, thereby attaining the realization of all that is divinely perfect.

Lord, teach us how to live this life in the flesh while preparing for the next life of the spirit. Speak to us, Lord, and we will do your bidding. Teach us the good paths, and we will go right. Grant us that we may attain union with you. We know that the religion is right which leads to union with righteousness. God is our wise nature, best thought, and righteous act. May God grant us unity with the divine spirit and immortality in himself!

This religion of the Wise One cleanses the believer from every evil thought and sinful deed. I bow before the God of heaven in repentance if I have offended in thought, word, or act—intentionally or unintentionally—and I offer prayers for mercy and praise for forgiveness. I know when I make confession, if I purpose not to do again the evil thing, that sin will be removed from my soul. I know that forgiveness takes away the bonds of sin. Those who do evil shall receive punishment, but those who follow truth shall enjoy the bliss of an eternal salvation. Through grace lay hold upon us and minister saving power to our souls. We claim mercy because we aspire to attain perfection; we would be like God.

7. Jainism

The third group of religious believers who preserved the doctrine of one God in India—the survival of the Melchizedek teaching—were known in those days as the Suduanists. Later, these believers became known as followers of Jainism. They taught:

The Lord of Heaven is supreme. Those who commit sin will not ascend on high, but those who walk in the paths of righteousness shall find a place in heaven. We are assured of the life hereafter if we know truth. The soul of man may ascend to the highest heaven, there to develop its true spiritual nature, to attain perfection. The estate of heaven delivers man from the bondage of sin and introduces him to the final beatitudes; the righteous man has already experienced an end of sin and all its associated miseries. Self is man's invincible foe, and self is manifested as man's four greatest passions: anger, pride, deceit, and greed. Man's greatest victory is the conquest of himself. When man looks to God for forgiveness, and when he makes bold to enjoy such liberty, he is thereby delivered from fear. Man should journey through life treating his fellow creatures as he would like to be treated.

8. Shinto

This belief contains remnants of the earlier Melchizedek teachings as is shown by the following abstracts:

Says the Lord: 'You are all recipients of my divine power; all men enjoy my ministry of mercy. I derive great pleasure in the multiplication of righteous men throughout the land. In both the beauties of nature and the virtues of men does the Prince of Heaven seek to reveal himself and to show forth his righteous nature. Since the olden people did not know my name, I manifested myself by being born into the world as a visible existence and endured such abasement even that man should not forget my name. I am the maker of heaven and earth; the sun and the moon and all the stars obey my will. I am the ruler of all creatures on land and in the four seas. Although I am great and supreme, still I have regard for the prayer of the poorest man. If any creature will worship me, I will hear his prayer and grant the desire of his heart.'

'Every time man yields to anxiety, he takes one step away from the leading of the spirit of his heart. Pride obscures God. If you would obtain heavenly help, put away your pride; every hair of pride shuts off saving light, as it were, by a great cloud. If you are not right on the inside, it is useless to pray for that which is on the outside. 'If I hear your prayers, it is because you come before me with a clean heart, free from falsehood and hypocrisy, with a soul which reflects truth like a mirror. If you would gain immortality, forsake the world and come to me.'

≈ The God of Jesus ≈

9. Taoism

The doctrine of one God became a part of the early teachings of several Chinese religions; the one persisting the longest and containing most monotheistic truth was Taoism. Some of the basic teachings of its founder are:

How pure and tranquil is the Supreme One and yet how powerful and mighty, how deep and unfathomable! This God of heaven is the honored ancestor of all things. If you know the Eternal, you are enlightened and wise. If you know not the Eternal, then does ignorance manifest itself as evil, and thus do the passions of sin arise. This wondrous Being existed before the heavens and the earth were. He is truly spiritual; he stands alone and changes not. He is indeed the world's mother, and all creation moves around him. This Great One imparts himself to men and thereby enables them to excel and to survive. Even if one has but a little knowledge, he can still walk in the ways of the Supreme; he can conform to the will of heaven.

All good works of true service come from the Supreme. All things depend on the Great Source for life. The Great Supreme seeks no credit for his bestowals. He is supreme in power, yet he remains hidden from our gaze. He unceasingly transmutes his attributes while perfecting his creatures. The heavenly Reason is slow and patient in his designs but sure of his accomplishments. The Supreme overspreads the universe and sustains it all. How great and mighty are his overflowing influence and drawing power! True goodness is like water in that it blesses everything and harms nothing. And like water, true goodness seeks the lowest places, even those levels which others avoid, and that is because it is akin to the Supreme. The Supreme creates all things, in nature nourishing them and in spirit perfecting them. And it is a mystery how the Supreme fosters, protects, and perfects the creature without compelling him. He guides and directs, but without self-assertion. He ministers progression, but without domination.

The wise man universalizes his heart. A little knowledge is a dangerous thing. Those who aspire to greatness must learn to humble themselves. In creation the Supreme became the world's mother. To know one's mother is to recognize one's sonship. He is a wise man who regards all parts from the point of view of the whole. Relate yourself to every man as if you were in his place. Recompense injury with kindness. If you love people, they will draw near you—you will have no difficulty in winning them.

The Great Supreme is all-pervading; he is on the left hand and on the right; he supports all creation and indwells all true beings. You cannot find the Supreme, neither can you go to a place where he is not. If a man recognizes the evil of his ways and repents of sin from the heart, then may he seek forgiveness; he may escape the penalty; he may change calamity into blessing. The Supreme is the secure refuge for all creation; he is the guardian and savior of mankind. If you seek for him daily, you shall find him. Since he can forgive sins, he is indeed most precious to all men. Always remember that God does not reward man for what he does but for what he is; therefore should you extend help to your fellows without the thought of rewards. Do good without thought of benefit to the self.

They who know the laws of the Eternal are wise. Ignorance of the divine law is misery and disaster. They who know the laws of God are liberal minded. If you know the Eternal, even though your body perish, your soul shall survive in spirit service. You are truly wise when you recognize your insignificance. If you abide in the light of the Eternal, you shall enjoy the enlightenment of the Supreme. Those who dedicate their persons to the service of the Supreme are joyous in this pursuit of the Eternal. When man dies, the spirit begins to wing its long flight on the great home journey.

10. Confucianism

What Heaven appoints is without error. Truth is real and divine. Everything originates in Heaven, and the Great Heaven makes no mistakes. Heaven has appointed many subordinates to assist in the instruction and uplifting of the inferior creatures. Great, very great, is the One God who rules man from on high. God is majestic in power and awful in judgment. But this Great God has conferred a moral sense even on many inferior people. Heaven's bounty never stops. Benevolence is Heaven's choicest gift to men. Heaven has bestowed its nobility upon the soul of man; the virtues of man are the fruit of this endowment of Heaven's nobility. The Great Heaven is all-discerning and goes with man in all his doings. And we do well when we call the Great Heaven our Father and our Mother. If we are thus servants of our divine ancestors, then may we in confidence pray to Heaven. At all times and in everything let us stand in awe of the majesty of Heaven. We acknowledge, O God, the Most High and sovereign Potentate, that judgment rests with you, and that all mercy proceeds from the divine heart.

God is with us; therefore we have no fear in our hearts. If there be found any virtue in me, it is the manifestation of Heaven who abides with me. But this Heaven within me often makes hard demands on my faith. If God is with me, I have determined to have no doubt in my heart. Faith must be very near the truth of things, and I do not see how a man can live without this good faith. Good and evil do not befall men without cause. Heaven deals with man's soul in accordance with its purpose. When you find yourself in the wrong, do not hesitate to confess your error and be quick to make amends.

A wise man is occupied with the search for truth, not in seeking for a mere living. To attain the perfection of Heaven is the goal of man. The superior man is given to self-adjustment, and he is free from anxiety and fear. God is with you; have no doubt in your heart. Every good deed has its recompense. The superior man murmurs not against Heaven nor holds a grudge against men. What you do not like when done to yourself, do not to others. Let compassion be a part of all punishment; in every way endeavor to make punishment a blessing. Such is the way of Great Heaven. While all creatures must die and return to the earth, the spirit of the noble man goes forth to be displayed on high and to ascend to the glorious light of final brightness."

This was the state of the world's religions during the times of Jesus 2000 years ago.

Make note of your thoughts, questions, comments here:

_____

_____

_____

_____

_____

_____

_____

_____

_____

_____

_____

_____

_____

_____

Lesson Four
The Parables of Jesus
About God

Jesus taught using many methods. He taught by first asking questions of someone and then answering their questions to him. Sometimes he told stories or spoke directly. His most powerful teaching method was the parable.

Included here are three favorite parables of Jesus. I include them because they say a lot about who God is and what he really is like. Getting to know God personally is our goal here.

On a warm Thursday afternoon Jesus talked to the multitude about the "Grace of Salvation." In the course of this sermon he retold the story of the lost sheep and the lost coin and then added his favorite parable of the prodigal son. Said Jesus:

1. Parable of the Lost Son

"You have been admonished by the prophets from Samuel to John that you should seek for God—search for truth. Always have they said, 'Seek the Lord while he may be found.' And all such teaching should be taken to heart. But I have come to show you that, while you are seeking to find God, God is likewise seeking to find you. Many times have I told you the story of the good shepherd who left the ninety and nine sheep in the fold while he went forth searching for the one that was lost, and how, when he had found the straying sheep, he laid it over his shoulder and tenderly carried it back to the fold. And when the lost sheep had been restored to the fold, you remember that the good shepherd called in his friends and bade them rejoice with him over the finding of the sheep that had been lost. Again I say there is more joy in heaven over one sinner who repents than over the ninety and nine just persons who need no repentance. The fact that souls are lost only increases the interest of the heavenly Father. I have come to this world to do my Father's bidding, and it has truly been said of the Son of Man that he is a friend of publicans and sinners.

"You have been taught that divine acceptance comes after your repentance and as a result of all your works of sacrifice and penitence, but I assure you that the Father accepts you even before you have repented and sends the Son and his associates to find you and bring you, with rejoicing, back to the fold, the kingdom of sonship and spiritual progress. You are all like sheep which have gone astray, and I have come to seek and to save those who are lost.

"And you should also remember the story of the woman who, having had ten pieces of silver made into a necklace of adornment, lost one piece, and how she lit the lamp and diligently swept the house and kept up the search until she found the lost piece of silver. And as soon as she found the coin that was lost, she called together her friends and neighbors, saying, 'Rejoice with me, for I have found the piece that was lost.' So again I say, there is always joy in the presence of the angels of heaven over one sinner who repents and returns to the Father's fold. And I tell you this story to impress upon you that the Father and his Son go forth to search for those who are lost, and in this search we employ all influences capable of rendering assistance in our diligent efforts to find those who are lost, those who stand in need of salvation. And so, while the Son of Man goes out in the wilderness to seek for the sheep gone astray, he also searches for the coin which is lost in the house. The sheep wanders away, unintentionally; the coin is covered by the dust of time and obscured by the accumulation of the things of men.

"And now I would like to tell you the story of a thoughtless son of a well-to-do farmer who deliberately left his father's house and went off into a foreign land, where he fell into much tribulation. You recall that the sheep strayed away without intention, but this youth left his home with premeditation. It was like this:

"A certain man had two sons; one, the younger, was lighthearted and carefree, always seeking for a good time and shirking responsibility, while his older brother was serious, sober, hard-working, and willing to bear responsibility. Now these two brothers did not get along well together; they were always quarrelling and bickering. The younger lad was cheerful and vivacious, but indolent and unreliable; the older son was steady and industrious, at the same time self-centered, surly, and conceited. The younger son enjoyed play but shunned work; the older devoted himself to work but seldom played. This association became so disagreeable that the younger son came to his father and said: 'Father, give me the third portion of your possessions which would fall to me and allow me to go out into the world to seek my own fortune.' And when the father heard this request, knowing how unhappy the young man was at home and with his older brother, he divided his property, giving the youth his share.

"Within a few weeks the young man gathered together all his funds and set out upon a journey to a far country, and finding nothing profitable to do which was also pleasurable, he soon wasted all his inheritance in riotous living. And when he had spent all, there arose a prolonged famine in that country, and he found himself in want. And so, when he suffered hunger and his distress was great, he found employment with one of the citizens of that country, who sent him into the fields to feed swine. And the young man would fain have filled himself with the husks which the swine ate, but no one would give him anything.

"One day, when he was very hungry, he came to himself and said: 'How many hired servants of my father have bread enough and to spare while I perish with hunger, feeding swine off here in a foreign country! I will arise and go to my father, and I will say to him: Father, I have sinned against heaven and against you. I am no more worthy to be called your son; only be willing to make me one of your hired servants.' And when the young man had reached this decision, he arose and started out for his father's house.

"Now this father had grieved much for his son; he had missed the cheerful, though thoughtless, lad. This father loved this son and was always on the lookout for his return, so that on the day he approached his home, even while he was yet afar off, the father saw him and, being moved with loving compassion, ran out to meet him, and with affectionate greeting he embraced and kissed him. And after they had thus met, the son looked up into his father's tearful face and said: 'Father, I have sinned against heaven and in your sight; I am no more worthy to be called a son'—but the lad did not find opportunity to complete his confession because the overjoyed father said to the servants who had by this time come running up: 'Bring quickly his best robe, the one I have saved, and put it on him and put the son's ring on his hand and fetch sandals for his feet.'

"And then, after the happy father had led the footsore and weary lad into the house, he called to his servants: 'Bring on the fatted calf and kill it, and let us eat and make merry, for this my son was dead and is alive again; he was lost and is found.' And they all gathered about the father to rejoice with him over the restoration of his son.

"About this time, while they were celebrating, the elder son came in from his day's work in the field, and as he drew near the house, he heard the music and the dancing. And when he came up to the back door, he called out one of the servants and inquired as to the meaning of all this festivity. And then said the servant: 'Your long-lost brother has come home, and your father has killed the fatted calf to rejoice over his son's safe return. Come in that you also may greet your brother and receive him back into your father's house.'

"But when the older brother heard this, he was so hurt and angry he would not go into the house. When his father heard of his resentment of the welcome of his younger brother, he went out to entreat him. But the older son would not yield to his father's persuasion. He answered his father, saying: 'Here these many years have I served you, never transgressing the least of your commands, and yet you never gave me even a kid that I might make merry with my friends. I have remained here to care for you all these years, and you never made rejoicing over my faithful service, but when this your son returns, having squandered your substance with harlots, you make haste to kill the fatted calf and make merry over him.'

"Since this father truly loved both of his sons, he tried to reason with this older one: 'But, my son, you have all the while been with me, and all this which I have is yours. You could have had a kid at any time you had made friends to share your merriment. But it is only proper that you should now join with me in being glad and merry because of your brother's return. Think of it, my son, your brother was lost and is found; he has returned alive to us!'"

This was one of the most touching and effective of all the parables which Jesus ever presented to impress upon his hearers the Father's willingness to receive all who seek entrance into the kingdom of heaven.

Jesus was very partial to telling these three stories at the same time. He presented the story of the lost sheep to show that, when men unintentionally stray away from the path of life, the Father is mindful of such lost ones and goes out, with his Sons, the true shepherds of the flock, to seek the lost sheep. He then would recite the story of the coin lost in the house to illustrate how thorough is the divine searching for all who are confused, confounded, or otherwise spiritually blinded by the material cares and accumulations of life. And then he would launch forth into the telling of this parable of the lost son, the reception of the returning prodigal, to show how complete is the restoration of the lost son into his Father's house and heart.

Many, many times during his years of teaching, Jesus told and retold this story of the prodigal son. This parable and the story of the good Samaritan were his favorite means of teaching the love of the Father and the neighborliness of man.

2. Parable of the Shrewd Steward

One evening Simon Zelotes, commenting on one of Jesus' statements, said: "Master, what did you mean when you said today that many of the children of the world are wiser in their generation than are the children of the kingdom since they are skillful in making friends with the mammon of unrighteousness?" Jesus answered:

"Some of you, before you entered the kingdom, were very shrewd in dealing with your business associates. If you were unjust and often unfair, you were nonetheless prudent and farseeing in that you transacted your business with an eye single to your present profit and future safety. Likewise should you now so order your lives in the kingdom as to provide for your present joy while you also make certain of your future enjoyment of treasures laid up in heaven. If you were so diligent in making gains for yourselves when in the service of self, why should you show less diligence in gaining souls for the kingdom since you are now servants of the brotherhood of man and stewards of God?

"You may all learn a lesson from the story of a certain rich man who had a shrewd but unjust steward. This steward had not only oppressed his master's clients for his own selfish gain, but he had also directly wasted and squandered his master's funds. When all this finally came to the ears of his master, he called the steward before him and asked the meaning of these rumors and required that he should give immediate accounting of his stewardship and prepare to turn his master's affairs over to another.

"Now this unfaithful steward began to say to himself: 'What shall I do since I am about to lose this stewardship? I have not the strength to dig; to beg I am ashamed. I know what I will do to make certain that, when I am put out of this stewardship, I will be welcomed into the houses of all who do business with my master.' And then, calling in each of his lord's debtors, he said to the first, 'How much do you owe my master?' He answered, 'A hundred measures of oil.' Then said the steward, 'Take your wax board bond, sit down quickly, and change it to fifty.' Then he said to another debtor, 'How much do you owe?' And he replied, 'A hundred measures of wheat.' Then said the steward, 'Take your bond and write fourscore.' And this he did with numerous other debtors. And so did this dishonest steward seek to make friends for himself after he would be discharged from his stewardship. Even his lord and master, when he subsequently found out about this, was compelled to admit that his unfaithful steward had at least shown sagacity in the manner in which he had sought to provide for future days of want and adversity.

"And it is in this way that the sons of this world sometimes show more wisdom in their preparation for the future than do the children of light. I say to you who profess to be acquiring treasure in heaven: Take lessons from those who make friends with the mammon of unrighteousness, and likewise so conduct your lives that you make eternal friendship with the forces of righteousness in order that, when all things earthly fail, you shall be joyfully received into the eternal habitations.

"I affirm that he who is faithful in little will also be faithful in much, while he who is unrighteous in little will also be unrighteous in much. If you have not shown foresight and integrity in the affairs of this world, how can you hope to be faithful and prudent when you are trusted with the stewardship of the true riches of the heavenly kingdom? If you are not good stewards and faithful bankers, if you have not been faithful in that which is another's, who will be foolish enough to give you great treasure in your own name?

"And again I assert that no man can serve two masters; either he will hate the one and love the other, or else he will hold to one while he despises the other. You cannot serve God and mammon."

When the Pharisees who were present heard this, they began to sneer and scoff since they were much given to the acquirement of riches. These unfriendly hearers sought to engage Jesus in unprofitable argumentation, but he refused to debate with his enemies. When the Pharisees fell to wrangling among themselves, their loud speaking attracted large numbers of the multitude encamped thereabouts; and when they began to dispute with each other, Jesus withdrew, going to his tent for the night.

3. The Rich Man and the Beggar

When the meeting became too noisy, Simon Peter, standing up, took charge, saying: "Men and brethren, it is not seemly thus to dispute among yourselves. The Master has spoken, and you do well to ponder his words. And this is no new doctrine which he proclaimed to you. Have you not also heard the allegory of the Nazarites concerning the rich man and the beggar? Some of us heard John the Baptist thunder this parable of warning to those who love riches and covet dishonest wealth. And while this olden parable is not according to the gospel we preach, you would all do well to heed its lessons until such a time as you comprehend the new light of the kingdom of heaven. The story as John told it was like this:

"There was a certain rich man named Dives, who, being clothed in purple and fine linen, lived in mirth and splendor every day. And there was a certain beggar named Lazarus, who was laid at this rich man's gate, covered with sores and desiring to be fed with the crumbs which fell from the rich man's table; yes, even the dogs came and licked his sores. And it came to pass that the beggar died and was carried away by the angels to rest in Abraham's bosom. And then, presently, this rich man also died and was buried with great pomp and regal splendor. When the rich man departed from this world, he waked up in Hades, and finding himself in torment, he lifted up his eyes and beheld Abraham afar off and Lazarus in his bosom. And then Dives cried aloud: 'Father Abraham, have mercy on me and send over Lazarus that he may dip the tip of his finger in water to cool my tongue, for I am in great anguish because of my punishment.' And then Abraham replied: 'My son, you should remember that in your lifetime you enjoyed the good things while Lazarus in like manner suffered the evil. But now all this is changed, seeing that Lazarus is comforted while you are tormented. And besides, between us and you there is a great gulf so that we cannot go to you, neither can you come over to us.' Then said Dives to Abraham: 'I pray you send Lazarus back to my father's house, inasmuch as I have five brothers, that he may so testify as to prevent my brothers from coming to this place of torment.' But Abraham said: 'My son, they have Moses and the prophets; let them hear them.' And then answered Dives: 'No, No, Father Abraham! but if one go to them from the dead, they will repent.' And then said Abraham: 'If they hear not Moses and the prophets, neither will they be persuaded even if one were to rise from the dead.'"

After Peter had recited this ancient parable of the Nazarite brotherhood, and since the crowd had quieted down, Andrew arose and dismissed them for the night. Although both the apostles and his disciples frequently asked Jesus questions about the parable of Dives and Lazarus, he never consented to make comment thereon.

Jesus always had trouble trying to explain to the apostles that, while they proclaimed the establishment of the kingdom of God, the Father in heaven was not a king. At the time Jesus lived on earth and taught in the flesh, the people of earth knew mostly of kings and emperors in the governments of the nations, and the Jews had long contemplated the coming of the kingdom of God. For these and other reasons, the Master thought best to designate the spiritual brotherhood of man as the kingdom of heaven and the spirit head of this brotherhood as the Father in heaven. Never did Jesus refer to his Father as a king. In his intimate talks with the apostles he always referred to himself as the Son of Man and as their elder brother. He depicted all his followers as servants of mankind and messengers of the gospel of the kingdom.

Jesus never gave his apostles a systematic lesson concerning the personality and attributes of the Father in heaven. He never asked men to believe in his Father; he took it for granted they did. Jesus never belittled himself by offering arguments in proof of the reality of the Father. His teaching regarding the Father all centered in the declaration that he and the Father are one; that he who has seen the Son has seen the Father; that the Father, like the Son, knows all things; that only the Son really knows the Father, and he to whom the Son will reveal him; that he who knows the Son knows also the Father; and that the Father sent him into the world to reveal their combined natures and to show forth their conjoint work. He never made other pronouncements about his Father except to the woman of Samaria at Jacob's well, when he declared, "God is spirit."

You learn about God from Jesus by observing the divinity of his life, not by depending on his teachings. From the life of the Master, you may each adopt that concept of God which represents the measure of your capacity to perceive spiritual and divine realities, truths both real and eternal. The finite man can never hope to comprehend the Infinite God except as God is revealed in the personality of the human life of Jesus of Nazareth.

Jesus well knew that God can be known only by the realities of experience; never can he be understood by the mere teaching of the mind. Jesus taught his apostles that, while they never could fully understand God, they could most certainly know him, even as they had known the Son of Man. You can know God, not by understanding what Jesus said, but by knowing what Jesus was. Jesus was a revelation of God.

Except when quoting the Hebrew scriptures, Jesus referred to Deity by only two names: God and Father. And when the Master made reference to his Father as God, he usually employed the Hebrew word signifying the plural God (the Trinity) and not the word Yahweh, which stood for the progressive conception of the tribal God of the Jews.

Jesus never called the Father a king, and he very much regretted that the Jewish hope for a restored kingdom and John's proclamation of a coming kingdom made it necessary for him to denominate his proposed spiritual brotherhood the kingdom of heaven. With the one exception—the declaration that "God is spirit"—Jesus never referred to Deity in any manner other than in terms descriptive of his own personal relationship with the God of Paradise.

Jesus employed the word God to designate the idea of Deity and the word Father to designate the experience of knowing God. When the word Father is employed to denote God, it should be understood in its largest possible meaning. The word God cannot be defined and therefore stands for the infinite concept of the Father, while the term Father, being capable of partial definition, may be employed to represent the human concept of the divine Father as he is associated with man during the course of mortal existence.

To the Jews, Elohim was the God of gods, while Yahweh was the God of Israel. Jesus accepted the concept of Elohim and called this supreme group of beings God. In the place of the concept of Yahweh, the racial deity, he introduced the idea of the fatherhood of God and the world-wide brotherhood of man. He exalted the Yahweh concept of a deified racial Father to the idea of a Father of all the children of men, a divine Father of the individual believer. And he further taught that this God of universes and this Father of all men were one and the same Paradise Deity.

Jesus never claimed to be the manifestation of Elohim (God) in the flesh. He never declared that he was a revelation of Elohim to the world. He never taught that he who had seen him had seen Elohim. But he did proclaim himself as the revelation of the Father in the flesh, and he did say that whoso had seen him had seen the Father. As the divine Son he claimed to represent only the Father.

He was, indeed, the Son of even the Elohim God; but in the likeness of mortal flesh and to the mortal sons of God, he chose to limit his revelation to the portrayal of his Father's character in a way that such a revelation might be understood by mortal man. As regards the character of the other persons of the Paradise Trinity, we shall have to be content with the teaching that they are altogether like the Father, who has been revealed in personal portraiture in the life of his incarnated Son, Jesus of Nazareth.

Although Jesus revealed the true nature of the heavenly Father in his earth life, he taught little about him. In fact, he taught only two things: that God is spirit, and that, in all matters of relationship with his creatures, he is a Father. On this evening Jesus made the final pronouncement of his relationship with God when he declared: "I have come out from the Father, and I have come into the world; again, I will leave the world and go to the Father."

But mark you! never did Jesus say, "Whoso has heard me has heard God." But he did say, "He who has seen me has seen the Father." To hear Jesus' teaching is not equivalent to knowing God, but to see Jesus is an experience which in itself is a revelation of the Father to the soul. The God of universes rules the far-flung creation, but it is the Father in heaven who sends forth his spirit to dwell within your minds.

Jesus is the spiritual lens in human likeness which makes visible to the material creature Him who is invisible. He is your elder brother who, in the flesh, makes known to you a being of infinite attributes whom not even the celestial hosts can presume fully to understand. But all of this must consist in the personal experience of the individual believer. God who is spirit can be known only as a spiritual experience. God can be revealed to the finite sons of the material worlds, by the divine Son of the spiritual realms, only as a Father. You can know the Eternal as a Father; you can worship him as the God of universes, the infinite Creator of all reality and existence.

Make note of your thoughts, questions, comments here:

_____

_____

_____

_____

_____

_____

_____

_____

_____

_____

_____

_____

Lesson Five
The Universal Father

This is the fifth lesson in a series of discussions about God — our heavenly Father; I am going to challenge you a bit during our time together but I hope that both you and I will become closer to God, progress in our understanding and knowledge of God, and strengthen our faith in God.

As we get older we also get wiser. We gain more experience, greater knowledge, and we discover more truth about the things we believe. Our faith may be childlike but our beliefs should not be childish. Belief plus experience becomes faith. Let our beliefs be free to discover greater truth and our hearts and minds open to greater visions of God's glory. Let us be steadfast in our faith but allow our beliefs to grow and expand as we gain experience and knowledge about our heavenly Father. None of us shall know absolute truth until the day we stand in God's presence. For now we must do our best to discern and accept truth as it is revealed to us and as our capacity to understand grows. This is what is meant when people say that truth is dynamic. Yes, there is absolute truth but only God knows all truth and the absolute truth of everything. It wasn't that long ago that the scientific truth was that cutting people to bleed was a cure for disease. What was unquestionable truth then is seen as fairytale medicine today. So, let us be open to progressing from the truth we know today to greater truth tomorrow. The watchword of life is progress.

The Bible is what I call dynamic truth. Dynamic truth is changing or progressing truth. How many of you have read the Bible cover to cover at least once? Each time you go back and read it you find new truth and more truth. You read it before and thought you had all the truth but every time you read it, it seems that someone has gone back and edited it to include more truth because you find things you didn't see before. Did the book change? Did truth change? No, but your understanding grew and your perspective and perception of it grew making the book seem to be alive and growing each time you read it. If ten years ago I gave you a quiz on the truths it contains you would score pretty well but if you took the same quiz today you would score even higher. That is dynamic truth. Truth is truth but your level of knowledge changes and grows to make it dynamic truth.

We are told that we should seek God, find God, pray to God, live our life according to God's will, be like God, and worship God. If that is true then we should first try to understand as much as we can about who God is in order to do all these things. We need to know, love, and admire God before we can trust him, place our faith in him, desire to be like him, and ultimately worship him.

As we studied last week, in the old testament of the Bible God is portrayed as a kingly ruler, a heavenly judge, or perhaps a cosmic policeman; a stern taskmaster, a jealous and vengeful god to be feared. "Fear God" was the cry of the past. In the Old Testament, God is called a loving father fifteen times but in the New Testament, written after Jesus came to reveal God more fully to us, God is called a loving Father two hundred and forty-five times. Remember, God changes not but our knowledge of him hopefully does.

True religion is not a system of philosophic belief which can be reasoned out and substantiated by natural proofs, neither is it a fantastic and mystic experience of indescribable feelings of ecstasy which can be enjoyed only by the romantic devotees of mysticism. Religion is not the product of reason, but viewed from within, it is altogether reasonable. Religion is not derived from the logic of human philosophy, but as a mortal experience it is altogether logical. Religion is the experiencing of divinity in the consciousness of a moral being of material origin; it represents true experience with the eternal realities in time, the realization of spiritual satisfactions.

Religion lives and prospers, not by sight and feeling, but rather by faith and insight. The highest religious experience is not dependent on prior acts of belief, tradition, and authority; neither is religion the offspring of sublime feelings and purely mystical emotions. It is, rather, a profoundly deep and actual experience of spiritual communion with the spiritual influences resident within the human mind. It is simply the purely personal experience of experiencing the reality of God. The seeds of true religion originate in man's moral consciousness, and they are revealed in the growth of man's spiritual insight and the God-hungry mortal mind.

The social characteristics of a true religion consist in the fact that it invariably seeks to convert the individual and to transform the world. Religion implies the existence of ideals which far transcend the known standards of ethics and morality embodied in even the highest social usages of the most mature institutions of civilization. Religion reaches out for undiscovered ideals, unexplored realities, superhuman values, divine wisdom, and true spirit attainment. True religion does all of this; all other beliefs are not worthy of the name. You cannot have a genuine spiritual religion without the supreme and supernal ideal of an eternal God. A religion without this God is an invention of man, a human institution of lifeless intellectual beliefs and meaningless emotional ceremonies. A religion might claim as the object of its devotion a great ideal. But such ideals of unreality are not attainable; such a concept is an illusion. The only ideals susceptible of human attainment are the divine realities of the infinite values resident in the spiritual fact of the eternal God.

There are many religions in the world today and almost all of them have a god as their object of worship and prayer. Those that do not have a supreme spiritual being as their focus are not a true religion. They are a philosophy. Every religion has its own religious text or writings and from many of those we can take some elements of truth about God. Every religion contains some truth about God but no religion contains all the truth about God. I have read several of these texts and I am sure you have too.

At Pentecost, Jesus poured out upon all mankind the Spirit of Truth which is like the Indwelling Spirit of God within us except the Spirit of Truth is the presence of Jesus in our hearts and minds. This spirit helps us to know and accept truth when we hear it and leads us to want to share it with others.

≈The God of Jesus≈

Some of what I am going to share with you in this course comes from a few different religious writings and you will no doubt recognize many of them. You will find that many of them agree with each other. In fact, I think if you really study the major religions they agree much more than they disagree. They tend to agree more about God and faith and less on history and beliefs. But that is okay.

When we go searching for God and seek to discover who God is we should look first at the life and teachings of Jesus because Jesus was the greatest revelation of God to mankind, in fact, the greatest possible revelation of God until the day we actually stand in God's presence.

It is difficult for us to understand but Jesus is divine and human at the same time. When Jesus said, "He who has seen me has seen the Father" he didn't mean that he is the Father. Jesus prayed to and worshiped God the Father and sought the Father's will and chose to do God's will in everything he did. Many times Jesus said, "If it is my Father's will" before doing something. Of the Trinity, the Son is said to be the Word of God, meaning the expression of God. I think that means like the voice of God. Jesus was the Word made flesh; the expression of God made physically visible to us.

Jesus never asked for or allowed anyone to worship him. It is okay to pray to Jesus but worship goes only to the Father. What Jesus meant when he said, "He who has seen me has seen the Father" is that when we study the life and teachings of Jesus, we see a perfect representation of God. Remember the Bette Midler song "What if God was one of us?" Well, if God was one of us he would be just like Jesus because the divine Jesus was just like God and the human Jesus was one of us. Jesus is the ultimate revelation of God to man and in many ways Jesus was the revelation of man to God because through Jesus, God experienced what it is like to be one of us. Sometimes I think of Jesus as the ultimate undercover boss— if you remember that television show. Jesus knows our sufferings and our joys and can share in every experience, every emotion, every good time and every bad time. He understands our strengths and weaknesses, and loves us even more for who we are because he came to experience this life as we do. God himself also knows our sufferings and our joys. He shares in every experience, every emotion, every good time and every bad time, understands our strengths and weaknesses, and loves us even more for who we are because of the mortal life experience of his only begotten son, Jesus, and the spirit gift that God sent to indwell us; to lead and guide us on the path of salvation and to Paradise.

My hope is that this series of discussions will do the same for you—cause you to love God even more because of who he is. God is so much more than we can imagine or understand. He is so much more true, beautiful and good than we can ever realize and perhaps that is what leads to the mystery of God. We should want to know more about God so that our relationship with God is not based on "fear God" but rather "Love God". God is like us in this way: he wants to love and be loved. He does not want to be feared. He wants you to do his will, that is, make good choices and wise decisions, because you trust him and have faith in his love and guidance. The more we know God, the more we will love him.

1. The Universal Father

Let me start here with a big picture preview and introduction of the God of Jesus; who God is and what God is, the mystery of God. The purpose of this big picture overview is to encourage you to contemplate the immensity of God, his omnipresence, omniscience, and his omnipotence. By the end of this class you will, I hope, understand those terms but not only understand them in terms of God but know them in terms of the Father. So, sit back, relax, and bear with me for a bit. Let your mind envision the entirety of all of God's creation, from here with us and on this planet, including all of God's vast wonderous and magnificent creation, all the way up to and including Heaven and Paradise; from today back into the eternal past and into the eternal future. Use your personality to expand your mind and your spirit to embrace these infinitely large concepts of God. Now that I made that sound really scary let me assure you that nothing we learn here is anything that you don't already know in your mind and in your heart. I am just hoping to bring them to your attention.

There is great confusion about the meaning of such terms as God, divinity, and deity. It is exceedingly difficult for us as created material beings with spiritual potential to imagine or even begin to understand a spiritual creator. But even spiritual beings need a place to call home. Heaven is a real place and Paradise is the geographic center of God's creation and the dwelling place of the eternal God himself.

God is beginning-less, endless, timeless, and spaceless. For God, time and space are nonexistent; God can do anything instantly without the barrier of time and God can be anywhere and everywhere as he is not limited by space. We cannot measure the height, width, or breadth of God. The presence of God is infinite. Therefore, it is impossible for us as material beings to begin to visualize anything infinitely large or infinitely old let alone anything that will continue to exist into infinity and beyond, to quote Buzz Lightyear.

God is the source of all that which is divine—spiritual. God is only understandable by us in the concepts of truth, beauty, and goodness; recognized in personality as love, mercy, and ministry; and revealed as justice, power, and sovereignty, and experienced as matter, mind, and spirit.

We all have an irresistible urge to symbolize our concepts of God. We need something visual either materially visible or mentally visual to make God real to us. Some people claim they don't believe in God because they cannot see him. And yet, there are many things they cannot see that they do believe in. Things like love, awareness, moral duty and idealism. We know these are real but they are hard to symbolize, visualize, or define. The cross we wear as a necklace is one form of symbolism of God or the love of God and what Jesus did for us.

When I was a boy in school, I was the only one who believed in life on other planets. Today, nearly everyone including all scientists don't wonder **if** we will find life on other worlds but **when**. At night, when we look up at the stars and suddenly become aware of our cosmic society, we recognize that there must be a First Cause, the one and only uncaused reality. We call that God, the one thing without beginning or end that must have created everything else.

God is the word we use to represent the personalization of Deity, the reality of Deity. For us, everything real must have a name. We have many names for God depending on our religion and our relationship with God. At first, we begin to feel that there is a "higher power" which is a thing or a force or something superior perhaps even material. Then we call him God and consider him a spiritual thing. Then we grow in our personal relationship with him until, with personal experience and loving affection, we call him Father and come to know him as a person and our friend. Ultimately, we recognize him as our father-creator. We discover him as our heavenly Father who we can relate to and interact with; one who loves us and wants to be loved by us.

No matter what word we use to identify God, that word should always recognize his personality. God is also a creator, controller, and upholder of universes; The Universal Father, the First Person of Deity, the man upstairs, the Holy One, and many others. But the name we use is important only to us as we try to symbolize or visualize God in our minds. The name you use indicates your level of experience with God and your personal relationship with him. When Moses asked God his name, God replied, "I AM". Jesus called him Father.

God, is infinite as well as eternal and is therefore limited or restricted only by his own freewill choices. The only thing God cannot do are those things that God has decided not to do, but even God cannot create square circles or produce evil that is inherently good. God cannot do the ungodlike thing.

God—the Universal Father—is the creator of everything and as such he has a personal relationship with every living thing and infinite control over all things material and spiritual. No thing or being exists except in direct or indirect relation to, and dependence upon, God the Father. The physical gravity forces of the material universes are centered in Heaven, Paradise, and God. The Father is the source of and the center for all personality, matter, mind, and spirit.

The first theoretical action of the "I AM" was that of becoming the Father of the Eternal Son and the Infinite Spirit completing the Trinity. Then he created the surrounding heaven with Paradise as the center for this first family to live in. This is our way of looking at the beginning of everything but since God, the Son, the Spirit, Paradise, and Heaven are eternal, there never was an actual beginning or a first thought or first action. These things and beings always have been and always will be. There never was a time when God did not exist; there never was a time when the "I AM" was not the Father of the Son and of the Spirit or the architect of Heaven.

Much of our confusion in our efforts to discover the Father, is caused by the limitations of our own ability to understand what I will call the mystery of God. God is knowable and personal and real and some day we will truly and literally stand in the glorious light of his actual presence but I suspect that only God the Son and God the Spirit truly know the Father as much as any one person can know another; as any child can know their parent. There is no mystery to God or mystery about God but there are things about God that we cannot know at this far distant location from him; far distant geographically and spiritually. We are at the very beginning, the low end if you will, of spiritual existence. God is at the high end. He is the absolute and the ultimate spiritual being. The Son and the Spirit and probably untold numbers of angels and spiritual beings probably know God first hand but we can, at least for now, only know God by faith. At least, that was true until Jesus came to show us the Father and the Father sent a spiritual helper to live or dwell within us as partners in life, mentors in progress, and guides to find our way home to the Father.

To help us better understand the nature and attributes of our Father in later sessions, let us first think about five things that make up our own nature. We are:

1. **Body**. The material or physical organism of man. The living electrochemical mechanism of animal nature and origin. And not to get into this discussion now but when scientists talk about the evolution of man, this is what they are referring to. The animal nature of our physical body but in fact WE, this personality, mind, and spirit thing that lives in the material body, came from God, was created in God's image, and seeks to return to God. Think of this body as the material womb of the spiritual embryo.

2. **Mind**. The thinking, perceiving, and feeling mechanism of the human organism. The total conscious, subconscious, and unconscious experience. The intelligence associated with the emotional life reaching upward through worship and wisdom to the spirit level. Mind seeking the source of all wisdom and knowledge. The mind is the mother of your soul.

3. **Spirit**. We read in 1 Corinthians 3:16 "Do you not know that you are a temple of God and that the Spirit of God dwells in you?" and also in Ezekiel 36:27 "I will put my Spirit within you and cause you to walk in my statutes, and you will be careful to observe my ordinances." The Father sent the divine spirit to dwell, or live, within the human mind. In this text I will refer to this as the "Indwelling Spirit" or "God Within." This immortal spirit is destined to merge with our personality to create our soul as we grow and progress from purely material beings who can only know God through faith to spiritual beings who can stand in the presence of God the Almighty.

4. **Personality**. The personality is another reality that is difficult to define. Our personality is neither body, mind, nor spirit; neither is it the soul. Personality is the one changeless reality in our ever-changing experience; our personality unifies all other associated factors of individuality: body, mind, spirit, and soul. Our personality is a unique gift which the Father gives to each of his children. Each personality is as unique and countless as snowflakes but infinitely more so.

5. **Soul.** The soul is something we often struggle to understand or realize. The soul is our growing and progressing self, expanding through the experiences of life. As we choose to "do the will of the Father in heaven," so does the Indwelling Spirit becomes the father of a new reality in human experience. Our mortal mind is the mother of this emerging reality that we call the soul. Our personality is the womb of conception for the soul. This new reality is neither material nor spiritual—but a combination of the two. This is the appearance of the immortal soul which is destined to survive mortal death and begin the journey to Paradise. The joining of our personality with the spirit, when we make the choice to do God's will and put our faith trust in him, is what gives us eternal life.

The heavenly Father is the father of personality. He bestows personality upon his children and he is the destiny of each personality. Personality is hard to define. We really cannot say what it is but we know it when we see it. Our personality is who we really are minus the material body, the intellectual mind, and the Indwelling Spirit. And this personality is from God, just as the Indwelling Spirit is also from God himself. If we peel away the layers of the onion that makes up who we are, our personality is the core of our being. It is the image of God that we are created in and yet totally unique and individual in all of creation. And having come from God, it seeks to find its way home; to the place where it is loved and longs to be.

Our Father is the God of all creation. He is the beginning, the source, and center of all things and all beings that exist in all eternity past, present, and future. Even the most materialistic scientist must admit that there must be one uncaused cause, one thing that always has been and always will be that everything else came from.

Albert Einstein said, "I'm not an atheist and I don't think I can call myself a pantheist." [Pantheism is the belief in a God without personality]. He continued to say: "We are in the position of a little child entering a huge library filled with books in many different languages. The child knows someone must have written those books. It does not know how. The child dimly suspects a mysterious order in the arrangement of the books but doesn't know what it is. That, it seems to me, is the attitude of even the most intelligent human being toward God." It is claimed that he also said, "The more I study science, the more I believe in God."

First think of God as a creator, then as a controller, and lastly as an infinite upholder. First, God created everything; then he controls and maintains it. If God should fail to do any of these functions, everything would cease to exist—but God never fails. When you use the term "never" in relation to God, that is truly never as in the eternal never.

The truth about God began to dawn upon mankind when the prophet said, in Nehemiah 9:6: "You, God, are alone; there is none beside you. You have created the heaven and the heaven of heavens, with all their hosts; you preserve and control them. By the Sons of God were the universes made." Jesus is the creator of our universe; our creator, our brother, and our friend.

This statement, "you God are alone", I believe answers other great questions we mortals have; these are: "What is my purpose?" "Why am I here?" This is honestly just my own opinion but I think we are here because at some point in the depths of eternity past, God was alone. God needed someone to love and someone to love him. And… here we are. To love God and to be loved by God is our purpose. To be perfect in our lives as God is in his and to love one another as Jesus loves us is the action that results from loving and being loved by God.

God is perfect and the Paradise he lives in is perfect. When people ask, "Why didn't God create everything perfect?" I say, "he did". In Heaven everything is perfect. On earth everything is perfect according to his plan. Our life beginning in imperfection but progressing to perfection is part of God's perfect plan. God does not make mistakes and has no regrets—especially about creating mankind. God loves all his children and takes joy in our joys and suffers in our sorrows but he has no regrets about creating any of us.

God is superbly endowed with the attributes of patience, mercy, and love which are so exquisitely revealed in his spiritual ministry. God administers love to overshadow justice with mercy. God possesses all supreme kindness and merciful affection. Our universe is being forged out between the anvil of justice and the hammer of suffering; but he who wields the hammer is a loving Father of divine mercy.

The confusion and turmoil of our world does not indicate that the Paradise Father lacks either interest or ability to manage affairs differently. The Creator is possessed of full power to make this world a veritable paradise but such an Eden would not contribute to the development of those strong, noble, and experienced characters which God is so surely forging out between the anvils of necessity and the hammers of anguish. Our anxieties and sorrows, our trials and disappointments, are just as much a part of the divine plan as are the exquisite joys and supreme happiness of our lives. Our "metal" is being shaped and tempered, formed and strengthened. Someday we will be perfected and so will this world be a paradise of light and light through mankind's partnership with God.

It is hard for some to accept this idea of a loving all powerful God because the world as we know it, is a dark and confused place a long way from being perfect. But in our imperfection is the struggle to become perfect even as God is perfect. Perhaps that applies not only to us but to our planet as well. May the earth be perfect even as heaven is perfect. But the progress of this world depends on the progress of the individual person on this world. And it is this struggle with imperfection that gives us some things that are extremely valuable that perfect created beings cannot have and that is the experience of failure, a sense of accomplishment, and faith.

Life will become a burden of existence unless you learn how to fail gracefully. There is an art in defeat which noble souls always acquire; you must know how to lose cheerfully; you must be fearless of disappointment. Never hesitate to admit failure. Make no attempt to hide failure under deceptive smiles and beaming optimism. Success may generate courage and promote confidence, but wisdom comes only from the experiences of adjustment to the results of one's failures. Men who prefer optimistic illusions to reality can never become wise. Only those who face facts and adjust them to ideals can achieve wisdom. Those timid souls who can only keep up the struggle of life by the aid of continuous false illusions of success are doomed to suffer failure and experience defeat as they ultimately awaken from the dream world of their own imaginations. And it is in this business of facing failure and adjusting to defeat that the far-reaching vision of religion exerts its supreme influence. Failure is simply an educational episode—a cultural experiment in the acquirement of wisdom—in the experience of the God-seeking man who has embarked on the eternal adventure of the exploration of a universe. To such men defeat is but a new tool for the achievement of higher levels of universe reality.

Faith is knowing less than we can believe. Faith is believing without seeing. Belief based on faith is more valuable than belief based solely on knowledge. It is easy to believe in something that we can see and touch but God is a spiritual being that we as mortal material beings cannot see or physically touch. God is love and like love. Love cannot be seen or weighed in a balance but we certainly can feel it's presence and observe the result of it and conclude the fact that it is real.

We can only discover God through experiences that produce belief and belief, through experience, progresses to Faith. Faith is so much more than mere belief. When someone asks me if I believe in God, I say "Yes! Absolutely, I believe in and trust God but I also know God is real and I have faith in Him." To me, the word belief allows room for doubt—as in: I believe this is true but I could be wrong. But faith leaves no room for doubt because I know and I know now that God is real and that he loves me and I love him. I put all my faith and all my trust in God. I choose to do God's will and live my life accordingly. I often fail. I'm not perfect—only trying to be—and learning from the effort.

Our supreme goal as children of God should be to find the eternal God, to comprehend his divine nature, and to recognize him as the Universal Father—the father of all things. God-knowing individuals have only one supreme ambition, just one consuming desire, and that is to become like God. I had an Orthodox Jewish fellow tell me once that I should be careful about thinking that I can become God because I said that I want to be like God. I assured him that we certainly do not become God or become "a" God but our goal, our mandate from God is to "Be you perfect, even as I am perfect." We are to live our life according to God's will and in that way, when our will becomes perfectly aligned with God's will then we become like God in the way we think and things we do.

At that point, we will be perfect in our life as God is in his. At that point, all our prayers will be answered because all our prayer requests will be only for those things that are the same as what God wants to give us. Imitation is said to be the sincerest form of flattery and I strive each day to imitate God in the way I react to situations and respond to people. Isn't that what we mean when we ask "What would Jesus do?"

Jesus came to show us that this is achievable for us mortals—perhaps not in just one short lifetime as he did—but the possibility of attaining the equivalent of divine perfection is the final and certain destiny of all our mortal struggles here on earth and our eternal spiritual progress. And when we achieve that goal, we shall find ourselves standing in the very presence of God and hearing him say "well done my true and faithful child". Becoming more and more like our Father is our first duty, and should be our highest ambition. Worshiping God is our greatest joy.

This search for God is the supreme challenge and the ultimate adventure for all of God's children. Jesus revealed the Father to us through his life in the flesh and invited us to believe as he believes. Jesus showed us the way we should live our life, the way we should believe and have faith in God, and he showed us the way to salvation — eternal life. He showed us how to live with and treat other people even to the point of loving and forgiving our enemies. This is what he meant when he said "Follow me".

After Jesus died on the cross, he came back to show us that all he said is true. He came back to prove to us that there is life after death and that same resurrection awaits all of us if we "follow him".

2. The Father's Name

The word "God," the idea of God as contrasted with the ideal of God, can become a part of any religion, no matter how immature or false that religion may chance to be. And this idea of God can become anything which those who entertain it may choose to make it. The lower religions shape their ideas of God to meet the natural state of the human heart; the higher religions demand that the human heart shall be changed to meet the demands of the ideals of true religion.

When we meet someone for the first time what is it we usually ask? "Hi, I'm Rick. What's your name?" However, God has never revealed himself by name, only by his nature. "God" is just our word symbol for whoever and whatever God is. The only hint we are given is when God said, "I AM". If we believe that we are the children of this Creator, it is only natural that we should call him Father. But this is a name of our own choosing, and it grows out of the recognition of our own personal relationship with our creator.

Our heavenly Father never imposes any form of title or recognition, formal worship, or slavish service upon us. The one thing that God gave us that is totally unassailable in our life is freewill; the ability and the freedom to choose to love him or reject him. God does not force us to love him or create us in such a way that we have no choice but to love him. We must of ourselves — in our own hearts — recognize, love, and voluntarily worship him. He refuses to force us to love him or demand that we do his will. God gave us spiritual freedom so that we can voluntarily make the choice to love him because we **want** to love him and not because we are **required** to. The affectionate dedication of the human will to the doing of the Father's will is our greatest gift to God. In fact, such a commitment is our only possible gift of true value to the Paradise Father. Our heavenly Father has everything already. He created it. So, what can you give someone who truly does have everything? Yourself. Everything we are and everything we have comes from God; there is nothing which man can give to God except our love and our freewill choosing to do God's will, and such decisions, such commitment, constitutes true worship. Worship is so satisfying to the love-dominated nature of the heavenly Father. Remember how you felt when your child for the first time said, "I love you."?

Jesus, during the course of this final prayer with his apostles, said that he is the revelation and manifestation of the Father's name to the world. The Father in heaven had sought to reveal himself to Moses, but he could proceed no further than to cause it to be said, "I AM." And when Moses pressed him for further revelation of himself, God only said, "I AM that I AM." I don't believe that God meant that his name is "I AM" but rather since God has no specific name he said, "I AM". I AM as in "I AM this." And "I AM that."

When Jesus had finished his earth life, the name of the Father had been so revealed that the Master, who was the Father incarnate, could truly say:

I AM the bread of life.

I AM the living water.

I AM the light of the world.

I AM the desire of all ages.

I AM the open door to eternal salvation.

I AM the reality of endless life.

I AM the good shepherd.

I AM the pathway of infinite perfection.

I AM the resurrection and the life.

I AM the secret of eternal survival.

I AM the way, the truth, and the life.

I AM the infinite Father of my finite children.

I AM the true vine; you are the branches.

I AM the hope of all who know the living truth.

I AM the living bridge from one world to another.

I AM the living link between time and eternity.

In this way, Jesus enlarged the name of God to all generations. As divine love reveals the nature of God, eternal truth discloses his name in ever-enlarging proportions.

Prayer is when we ask God for something. Worship is when we thank God for everything. This worshipful thanksgiving is a gift to God. But, your greatest gift to God is yourself, God's greatest gift to you is that spiritual piece of himself that he sent to live within all of us — the Indwelling Spirit. God knows everything you think, do and say and how you feel because he actually lives within you. Our own personality lives within this temporary physical body and so does this spiritual entity from God. Hard to understand but true.

I think this may also be a good pattern for successful human relationships—friendships, parenthood, and marriage. Truly successful relationships are ones where both people give themselves to each other in whatever relationship they may have. Love means wanting to do good for someone. And when we desire to do something good for a friend, our child, or our spouse, then we show that we love them. We make their needs a priority over our needs and in a true loving relationship we fulfill another person's need to be loved and hopefully in return our need to love and be loved is fulfilled as well.

Once we become truly God-conscious or aware of the reality and presence of God, after we discover his glorious nature, then, based on our personal relationship with him, we will find a name which expresses and describes our concept of "who" God is to us. And so, the Creator becomes known by numerous names in the many cultures and religions of this world, in spirit all meaning the same being but each name standing for the degree of their relationship with God within their own hearts and minds. The prophets of old called him "the everlasting God" and referred to him as the one who "inhabits eternity." Since God is infinite then perhaps the names we can give him are infinite as well. I wonder sometimes if we don't confuse people by using multiple names for the same being. But just as I am called a father, brother, husband, friend, etc. God is all things to all people so it is no wonder that we have many names for God.

On our world where our Lord came and lived and experienced the mortal life as Jesus of Nazareth and revealed God to us through that life, God is generally known by some name that reflects his tender affection and fatherly devotion. So most of us who follow Jesus refer to God as "our Father" or some similar term. I have even known people to call God "Papa" to express an even closer personal relationship with him.

Referring to God as "our Father" reveals the reality of the family of God. I think the term "Father" is a very expressive and appropriate name for the eternal God. He is best known by the name "God" but for me that is more what he is than who he is. However, the name you have given to God is of little importance; the significant thing is that you know him and aspire to be like him.

Sometimes when a person has had an abusive human father, telling them that the Father in Heaven loves them and they should love him is counterproductive. But, it is then up to us to reveal who the heavenly Father really is to that person and demonstrate how a real human father should love his children and teach them how to be loving parents to their future children. As a parent representing the nature of God and his personality to our children, we then teach them how to be loving parents to their children. When Jesus told us to love one another as he loves us, remember that Jesus loves even the little children.

The world needs to see Jesus living again on earth in the experience of spirit-born people who effectively reveal the Master, and thus God the Father, to all men. We do this by doing what Jesus would do and living the way Jesus lived—totally dedicated to doing the will of God. In that way, we can help people realize the vast difference between an abusive mortal father and their loving divine father. Perhaps in this way they can understand God and not blame him for all the earthly hardships they endure.

3. The Reality of God

God is the source of intellectual truth, divine beauty and personal goodness. God and the spiritual world are the true reality. This material world that we call home is only a shadow of this eternal reality. As immensely huge as the material universe of universes is, the spiritual world is exponentially larger. In fact, it is infinitely larger. Scientists make fantastic theories about parallel universes and I say they are right. There is a parallel universe of reality and it is the spiritual universe with Paradise, Heaven, and all the almost numberless spiritual beings that inhabit it. That is the real reality and this world is only the shadow of it. Mortal material life lasts only from 0 to 110 years but our spiritual life is eternal. Our spiritual future is the true reality. That which is permanent is the truly real thing. Material existence comes and goes but our spirit is eternal—permanent and forever.

God himself is the eternal reality, the first reality. God is neither man-like nor machine-like. All too often I think we try to make God like man rather than making man like God. The term for this is anthropomorphism, meaning to make things like man. We tend to look at things unfamiliar and see them as something familiar. This is why we see faces in clouds or in rocks on Mars. Too often has mankind tried to explain God by making God think and act like man rather than trying to make man think and act like God.

The lower religions shape their ideas of God to meet the natural state of the human heart; the higher religions demand that the human heart shall be changed to meet the demands of the ideals of true religion. God is not simply the supreme desire of man, the object of some mortal quest for truth. Neither is God merely a concept of righteousness. The Universal Father is not a synonym for nature. God is the supreme reality, not merely man's traditional concept of supreme values. God is not a focusing of spiritual meanings, neither is he "the noblest work of man." God may be any or all of these things but he is all that and so much more. He is a saving person and a loving Father to all who enjoy spiritual peace on earth, and who crave to experience salvation: survival after physical death.

The reality of God is demonstrated in our experience with the leading of our Indwelling Spirit, the spirit fragment of God himself that lives within us. This Indwelling Spirit was given to us by our Father to help us achieve eternal life and to guide us so that we can find our way home—back to the source of our personality and identity. We can know that God and this Indwelling Spirit are real because we have the intellectual capacity for knowing God—God-consciousness, that is, being aware of God's presence; our spiritual urge to find God—God-seeking; and our personal craving to be like God—the wholehearted desire to do the Father's will. Only a person can know another person. We know for fact that God exists simply because we can ask if he does. Having found God means that God has first found us.

The existence of God can never be proven by scientific experiment or by the pure reasoning of logical deduction. God can be realized only through human experience. However, the reality of God is reasonable to logic, plausible to philosophy, essential to religion, and indispensable to any hope of life after death.

Those of us who know God have experienced the fact of his presence. We hold in our personal experience the only positive proof of the existence of the living God which one human can offer to another. The existence of God is utterly beyond all possibility of demonstration except for the personal relationship between the God-knowing person and God himself. You know God is real because you have experienced him, you have a relationship with him. We cannot convince another person God is real through our own experience. They must experience God for themselves. I cannot convince you that God is real any more than you can convince me that he is not.

4. God is a Universal Spirit

God is "the sovereign, eternal, immortal, invisible, and only true God." Even though we are "the offspring of God," or "created in the image of God" we should not think that the Father is like ourselves in form and physique. We are spiritual beings living in our material body — kind of like a chick living inside an egg. Spirit beings, such as angels, are real, notwithstanding that they, like many other known things, are invisible to our material human eyes. They are just not made of material flesh and blood. They are made of heavenly substance.

Said the seer of old: "Lo, he goes by me, and I see him not; he passes on also, but I perceive him not." We may constantly observe the works of God. We may be highly conscious of the material evidence of his majestic creation and conduct, but rarely may we gaze upon the visible manifestation of God or any other spiritual being, not even the one present within our own mortal shell. Once we shed this material shell and find our spiritual vision, only then can we see our spiritual companions and the angels that watch over us.

The Universal Father is not invisible because he is hiding himself from his children but rather it is our own limited spiritual vision that prevents us from seeing him or others of his heavenly hosts. The situation rather is as God said: "You cannot see my face, for no mortal can see me and live." No material man could behold the spirit God and preserve his mortal existence. The glory and the spiritual brilliance of the divine personality is impossible to approach by material beings. We must shed this material shell of our spiritual embryo before we can see spiritual beings. Imagine being a chick inside an egg. All you see is the inside of the shell. You hear noises and sense temperature and light changes and movements that indicate there is something beyond that shell but you cannot see it or touch it. The chick can decide that the mother hen and a world outside the shell is not real because he cannot see or touch either one. Or, the chick can evaluate his personal experience and have faith in the existence of the mother hen and the world beyond and long for the day when he discards the shell and awakens in the presence of the being he chose to believe in.

While we cannot see God as we exist inside this mortal shell, it is not necessary to see God with the eyes of the flesh in order to know him and see him by the faith-vision of our spiritual mind.

In our experience, mind is joined to matter — our brain resides in our material body. When mortal death occurs, things linked to the material being must die as well. Survival, or what we call life after death, salvation, or "being saved" comes about from the transformation of our material linked mind to one that is spirit linked — a mind that becomes God-conscious and aware of our spiritual sonship with God. Our material intellectual mind changes and eventually becomes spirit taught and spirit led. This evolution of the human mind from matter association to spirit union results in the appearance of our immortal soul. We refer to this as being born again. Material mortal mind is destined to become increasingly material and therefore in danger of extinction; mind that yields to spirit leading is destined to become increasingly spiritual and ultimately to achieve oneness with the divine Indwelling Spirit and the reward for that is eternal life. In today's world some may question whether they want to have eternal life or not after living through this one. But spiritual salvation, life after death is only the beginning of an endless career of adventure, an everlasting life of anticipation, an eternal voyage of discovery.

"God is spirit" and "God is love," and these two attributes of God are most completely revealed to us in the life and teachings of Jesus. While the great God is absolute, eternal, and infinite, he is also true, beautiful, and good. When faced with a choice and we ask "What is God's will?" I think the simple answer to that is to ask: "Is what I am about to think, do, or say true, beautiful or good?" If the answer is "yes" then I think we can be reasonably assured that we are doing God's will. It is really that simple.

5. The Mystery of God

We are at the bottom of the spiritual ladder and God is at the top. God is so much more than we can possibly comprehend from the bottom of the ladder. So, naturally there are many things about God that we cannot know or understand and it is those things we do not know, cannot possibly know, that makes God seem mysterious or that he is hiding from us. Perhaps the greatest of all the unfathomable mysteries of God is the presence of the divine Indwelling Spirit within us. I imagine that this ability of a piece of God, a fragment of his being, to live within us is the most profound mystery of all mysteries. We know it is possible though because we live in here too, and through experience we know it is a truth and a fact.

Our physical bodies are "the temples of God" because a fragment of God lives within us. Therefore, our bodies are truly temples and we should do a better job of maintaining that temple that this spirit is held within. Drugs, alcohol, and other material vices are physical poisons while impatience, anger, ego, and hatred are spirit poisons that foul the temple. Remember this when you read about Jesus cleansing the temple.

In 1 Corinthians 6:19-20 we read: "Do you not know that your bodies are temples of the Holy Spirit, who is in you, whom you have received from God? Therefore, honor God with your bodies."

When we are through down here, when our earthly course has been run, when our trial in the flesh is finished, when the dust of our mortal tabernacle "returns to the earth whence it came"; then the indwelling "Spirit shall return to God who gave it." If we choose salvation, we get to go too. This fragment of God is not yet ours by right of possession. It is a gift from God and it is intended to be one with us if we choose to survive this mortal life.

This creates the question: "What must we do to be saved?" Jesus told us that there really is a simple answer: the wholehearted desire and choosing to do God's will constitutes faith in God and it is by faith that you are saved. Like the woman who touched the hem of his garment as Jesus passed by, it is our faith that saves us. And never ever doubt that God wants you to be saved. He wants you to survive.

God is not sitting up there waiting for you to make mistakes so he can beat you down or punish you. Those are human actions — not spiritual ways. He sent Jesus to show us the way to salvation and he sent his Indwelling Spirit to lead us home. God will do everything in his power to help you except to steal away your freedom to choose or reject salvation. He will do everything in his power to help you achieve eternal life except force it upon you. The one thing you have to do, must do, is choose. And, then, once you choose you must act.

I think you will find that once you choose, you will be driven to act and produce what are called the fruits of the spirit. And the fruits of the divine spirit that blossom in the lives of spirit-born and God-knowing mortals are: loving service, unselfish devotion, courageous loyalty, sincere fairness, enlightened honesty, undying hope, confiding trust, merciful ministry, unfailing goodness, forgiving tolerance, and enduring peace. Our Father requires that we bear much spirit fruit. Remember, much has been given to you; therefore will much be required of you. You may enter the kingdom as a child, but the Father requires that you grow up, by grace, to the full stature of spiritual adulthood.

Such spirit-guided and divinely illuminated mortals, while they yet tread the lowly paths of toil and faithfully perform the duties of their earthly assignments, have already begun to discern the lights of eternal life as they glimmer on the faraway shores of a better world; already have they begun to comprehend the reality of that inspiring and comforting truth, "The kingdom of God is not meat and drink but righteousness, peace, and joy in the Holy Spirit." And throughout every trial and in the presence of every hardship, spirit-born souls are sustained by that hope which transcends all fear because the love of God is felt in all hearts by the presence of the divine Spirit.

The so called mystery of God comes from the difference which exists between the finite mortal and the infinite spirit, the material and the spiritual, the imperfection of man and the perfection of God. God unfailingly reveals himself to every person up to the fullness of each person's capacity to grasp the qualities of his divine being. But even God cannot make a pint hold a quart so our ability to know God is determined by our capacity and willingness to receive his love and feel his presence, not by God's inability or unwillingness to reveal himself. God gives life and love in never-ending abundance. All you have to do is be willing to love and be loved; to accept the gift that God is offering you. The bigger your container, the more you can receive. The more you love the more you are loved.

God is no respecter of persons. Our relationship with God is limited only by our own capacity to receive God's love and to love him in return. We should strive each day to expand that capacity. Each day we should learn to accept more of God's love and to love God more. Each day we should learn to extend that love to others; each day learn to love one more person who shares our journey through this life.

While God's ways may seem mysterious to us, God himself is not a mystery. When we attempt to explain the realities of the spirit world to material-minded people, mystery appears; mysteries so subtle and yet so profound that only by faith can we achieve the recognition of the Infinite Father. Can we fault those who have not experienced God that they find all this hard to believe? Let us pray for every unbeliever to have their own personal experience with God so that they too shall be saved and join us in eternity; join us in the excitement of the ultimate adventure of finding God and becoming like him.

So why does God seem so mysterious? Why does he not just appear before us here today and reveal himself to us? Is God hiding from us?

No. God is unapproachable by mortal beings because he "dwells in a light which no material creature can approach." The immensity and grandeur of God is beyond the grasp of our imperfect mind. He "measures the waters in the hollow of his hand, measures a universe with the span of his hand. It is he who sits on the circle of the earth, who stretches out the heavens as a curtain and spreads them out as a universe to dwell in." "Lift up your eyes on high and behold who has created all these things, who brings out their worlds by number and calls them all by their names"; and so it is true that "the invisible things of God are only partially understood by the things which are made." The person created cannot fully understand their creator. The creator must always be something greater than the thing created. Today, and as we are, we must accept the reality of God from the fact of the existence of his diverse creation, and also through the revelation of his son, Jesus.

We cannot see God until we complete our transformation from material to spiritual beings and actually arrive in Paradise. I suspect that even if we could be teleported into the presence of God that we would not know we were there. We would still only be able to see what our material eyes can see or feel that which our skin can feel. We might know we were there because the spirit within us would surely be jumping for joy at being home again.

6. Personality of the Universal Father

If your mind isn't already overloaded, let us consider the subject of the personality of God; that is, does God have a personality? Is he a person? Is God truly someone that people can relate to and come to know and love in the way that we know and love other people—even more so?

We should not permit the immensity and magnitude of God to blind us to his loving personality. "He who planned the ear, shall he not hear? He who formed the eye, shall he not see?" The Universal Father is the greatest of all personalities; he is the origin and destiny of all personality throughout all creation. God is both infinite and personal.

Everything we love about God, is the result of his divine personality. God is much more than our concept of personality but it is also true that he cannot possibly be anything less. He cannot be anything less than an eternal, infinite, and perfectly true, beautiful and good personality.

The great Greek philosopher Rodan had recently become a disciple of Jesus through the teaching of one of John the Baptist's associates who had conducted a mission at Alexandria. Rodan was earnestly engaged in the task of harmonizing his philosophy of life with Jesus' new religious teachings, when he came to Magadan hoping that the Master would talk these problems over with him. He also desired to secure a firsthand and authoritative version of the gospel from either Jesus or one of his apostles.

This Greek did not believe that God is a person or has a personality. He contended that the Father in heaven is not, cannot be, a person as man is a person. While it may be difficult to prove that God is a person or a personality, Rodan found it still more difficult to prove he is anything less.

Rodan claimed that the existence of personality requires the capacity for communication between beings of equal status; beings who are capable of sympathetic understanding of each other. Said Rodan: "In order to be a person, God must have a capacity for communication which would enable him to be fully understood by those who seek to communicate with him. But since there is nobody equal to God, then in terms of equality, God is alone in the universe. There are none equal to him; there are none with whom he can communicate." Or so Rodan believed.

Let me point out before we get too deep into this discussion that it is not important **what** we believe God is as long as we know **who** God is. And I think that the fact that we can ask who God is, adds to the argument that God is a personality. Looking back at the example I gave earlier about the cars in the parking lot, they are not out there communicating with each other. They may have traits, but they do not have personality.

We know that God does communicate with man, and therefore he must be a person according to Rodan's own definition. The Greek philosopher rejected this on the grounds that God does not reveal himself personally; that he is an invisible mystery. However, our own personal experience with God reveals that God is knowable by us and if God was not a personality, we could not know him and he could not know us. Rodan had his own personal experiences with God, but he contended these experiences only proved the *reality* of God, not his *personality*.

Eventually however, Rodan came to believe in the personality of the Father, by the following steps of reasoning:

1. The Father in Paradise does enjoy equality of communication with at least two other beings who are fully equal to himself and wholly like himself—the Eternal Son and the Infinite Spirit. In view of the doctrine of the Trinity, the Greek was compelled to concede the possibility of personality of the Universal Father based on this.

2. Since Jesus was equal with the Father, and since this Son of God obviously had personality and a personal relationship with his earth children, this was proof of the fact, and demonstration of the possibility, that God, along with the Son and the Spirit, are persons with personality and this forever settled the question regarding the ability of God to communicate with man and the possibility of man's communicating with God.

3. That Jesus was on terms of mutual association and perfect communication with man; that Jesus was the Son of God. That the relationship of the Son with the Father indicates equality of communication and mutual sympathetic understanding; that Jesus and the Father were one. That Jesus maintained at one and the same time understanding communication with both God and man, and that, since both God and man comprehend the meaning of Jesus' communications, both God and man possess personality if the definition is the ability to share communication. That the personality of Jesus demonstrated the personality of God, while it proved conclusively the presence of God in man. That two things which are related to the same thing are related to each other.

4. That personality represents man's highest concept of human reality and divine values; that God also represents man's highest concept of divine reality and infinite values; therefore, that God must be a divine and infinite personality, a personality in reality although infinitely and eternally greater than man's concept and definition of personality, but nevertheless always and totally a personality.

5. That God must be a personality since he is the Creator of all personality and the destiny of all personality. Rodan had been tremendously influenced by this teaching of Jesus, "Be you therefore perfect, even as your Father in heaven is perfect."

Rodan concluded that God is a person but he is also superhuman, transcendent, supreme, infinite, eternal, final, and universal, and that, while God must be infinitely more than a personality, he cannot be anything less. He accepted Jesus as the personal revelation of the Father and the satisfaction of all logic, reason, and philosophy as proof of the personality of God.

While we cannot physically see God, we can know him as a person; by faith accept that God so loves the world that he provides for our salvation and our eternal spiritual progression; and that he "delights in his children." God is a perfect, eternal, loving, and infinite Father personality.

God is truly and everlastingly a perfect personality, a person who can "know and be known," who can "love and be loved," and one who can be our friend and we can be his. Through our life, by the way we live it, we should teach others about our friendship with God. If we think God is a pretty cool guy, a good person, then we should go about teaching friendship with God to others.

Even though God is infinitely large and present in all places throughout the universes, this does not in the slightest diminish his capacity to everlastingly maintain personal connection with every one of his creatures. He cares about the sparrow and literally knows the number of hairs on your head. Which in my case may not be that hard to count.

The idea of a personal god becomes a measure of the maturity of any religion that has a god. There are some religions that don't have a personal god. Primitive religions have many personal gods, and they were fashioned in the image of man. To deny the personality of God leaves us only the choice of two philosophic dilemmas as Einstein described them: materialism or pantheism.

A material body is not required to have personality in either man or God. This error is shown in both extremes of human philosophy. In materialism, since man loses his body at death, he ceases to exist as a personality; in pantheism, since God has no body, he is not, therefore, a person.

Personality is not simply an attribute of God; it represents the totality of the complete unified infinite nature of our heavenly Father. Personality is in fact the revelation of the reality and nature of God.

God, being eternal, universal, absolute, and infinite, does not grow in knowledge nor increase in wisdom. He cannot get bigger or older or more real or more powerful or more loving because he is already perfect. We do all these things because we are imperfect. We are still "in the making." Therefore, our knowledge and understanding and our relationship with God does grow and increase. Our concepts of God grow even though God himself does not. There is nothing bigger than infinity nor older than eternity.

God does not acquire experience, as we do, but he does, enjoy sharing in our increasing knowledge and our growing experiences. Have you ever invited God to share an experience with you? Try it sometime when you see something beautiful or experience something enjoyable and see what happens.

The absolute perfection of God would cause him to suffer the awful boring limitations of perfection were it not for the fact that the Universal Father directly participates in the personality struggle of every imperfect soul of his creation. Our Father does experience the experiences of every spirit being and every mortal creature who are a part of the Father's ever-expanding never-ending divine experience. I believe that God does grow in his experience through us sharing our experiences with him and he becomes more personal to us as we get to know him more and more. Perhaps this is another reason why God needs us as much as we need him.

It is literally true: "In all your afflictions he is afflicted." "In all your triumphs he triumphs in and with you." His divine spirit is a real part of you. The Universal Father realizes all the individual experiences of the forward struggles of every entity, being, and personality of all creation. And all this is literally true, for "in Him we all live and move and have our being."

7. Personality in the Universe

God is to science a cause, to philosophy an idea, to religion a person, even the loving heavenly Father. God is to the scientist the primal force of the universe — even though they refuse to call him God. To the philosopher God is a theory of unity of mind and spirit, to the religionist God is a living personal spiritual experience; a father and a friend. Our current understanding of who God is grows and expands only by our own spiritual progress and that knowledge will become fully complete only when the day comes when we finally stand in the presence of the living God in Paradise.

Man comprehends things from the finite to the infinite; God looks from the infinite to the finite. Man possesses the lowest type of personality; God, the highest. Mankind could not begin to understand the divine personality until it was revealed in the life and teachings of Jesus.

Some degree of moral equality and spiritual harmony is essential to the friendship between two persons; a loving personality can hardly reveal themselves to a loveless person. In order to know God, we must be wholly dedicated to the effort. Halfhearted, partial devotion to finding God and knowing God will not be successful.

The more completely man understands himself and appreciates the personality of his fellows, the more he will crave to know the original personality, and the more earnestly such a God-knowing human will strive to become like the original personality. You can argue over opinions about God, but experience with him and in him exists above and beyond all human controversy and mere intellectual logic. The God-knowing person describes his spiritual experiences, not to convince unbelievers, but for the encouragement and satisfaction of other believers. This is one reason why church attendance and spiritual fellowship with others is so important — to strengthen yourself and those around you. "Preaching to the choir" is good practice for preaching to others about the Fatherhood of God and the Brotherhood of Mankind.

Since our mind is aware of the existence of the universe, it is safe to assume that the universe was created by something with a mind and that it is managed by a personality. Our mind can only perceive the minds of other personalities. If our mind can experience the universe, then there must be a divine mind and an actual personality somewhere in that universe. Jesus' earth life was the perfect demonstration of the realization and revelation of the personality of God in a truly human experience.

8. Spiritual Value of Personality

When Jesus talked about "the living God," he was referring to God as a personal Deity — our Father in heaven. He is not suggesting the possibility that God might be dead, or the possibility that God could die, but rather teaching us that God is a real and personal being — a living and loving organism. Interactions can be had between nonpersonal things, but not communication. Communication between a parent and child, as between God and man, cannot be enjoyed unless both are persons. Only personalities can communicate with each other and our communication with God is through the presence of his divine gift, our Indwelling Spirit. Through this presence of God within us, we are never alone. God knows what we are going through and he hears our prayers. He shares our tribulations but I think it is too often overlooked that he also shares our joys and accomplishments..

Our relationship with God is not like the relationship that a drop of water might find with the ocean. On this planet we are one in seven billion. In the universe, we are probably one in several trillion people on several billion worlds but we are not lost in the ocean of God's love. Our relationship with God is 24/7. It is a one on one relationship. Our unity with God, our closeness to God, grows by our desire to share our life with him and to be more like him. Such a sublime relationship can exist only between personalities.

Communication is the key to any personal relationship. We are close to our parents when we are little because we communicate with them every day and we depend on them. But when we get married we communicate more with our spouse than with our parents. So we grow closer to our spouse and more distant from our parents. Think about your best friend in high school and compare your relationship with them then versus today. Our relationship with God is the same. If you talk with God daily or even are blessed to be in constant communion with God then you become closer to God. If you only turn to God in times of trouble then you may feel that God is not listening because you have grown distant from God. You are not sharing your life with God. This is why prayer is important. This is why it is important to be mindful of God's nearness and constant presence because anytime you need to talk with him he is only a thought away.

Truth might be possible apart from personality, beauty may exist without personality, but goodness — human or divine — is possible only by personality. Only a *person* can love and be loved. Only a personality can be true, beautiful, and good.

We cannot fully understand how God can be changeless, all-powerful, and perfect, and at the same time be surrounded by an ever-changing and apparently imperfect universe. But we *know* such a truth in our own personal experience since we all maintain our own personality in spite of the constant changing of both ourselves and our environment. Personality is the one thing about us that never changes. I think this explains the changelessness of God. God changes not because he is the perfect personality.

The reality of God cannot be grasped by mathematics, logic, or philosophy, but only by personal experience with a personal God. Neither science, philosophy, nor theology can prove the personality of God. Only our own personal experience can lead us to the realization of the existence of God. This is why we cannot prove to someone else that God is real because that can only happen when they personally experience God for themselves. We only truly believe that which we convince ourselves is true.

One of the greatest thrills for me is the knowledge that each day, in this life and the next, we grow in our knowledge of God and how he loves us. We all love the Father more because of his loving nature than for his amazing powers. We might be right to fear an all-powerful God but how much better it is to be loved by a personal loving Father. I think I would love God just as much if he were not so great and powerful, as long as he is so good and merciful. We love God more for who he is than what he is. We love God because we have come to know him and the more we know him the more we love him. We love God because first he loves us. If you take away anything from my humble efforts here today, please know that God loves you—each and every one of you as an individual—and God loves you unconditionally and he wants you to love him. God loves you and would never do anything to hurt you. Don't let anyone tell you otherwise.

In our next section we will consider the nature of God.

Make note of your thoughts, questions, comments here:

Lesson Six

The Nature of God

This is the sixth in a series of discussions about God—our heavenly Father—who God is and what God is? During our time together I hope that both you and I will become closer to God, progress in our understanding and knowledge of God, and strengthen our faith in God. The more we know about God the more we will love him.

We are told that we should seek God, find God, pray to God, live our life according to God's will, to become like God, and worship God. If that is true then we should first try to understand as much as we can about who God is. So, let's explore the nature of God. You've heard someone say "It's in my nature" or "It's in my DNA"; Nature being the basic unchangeable characteristics of something.

In our journey together it will prove helpful, to study certain characteristics of the divine nature which make up the character of God. The nature of God can best be understood by the revelation of the Father that Jesus of Nazareth so perfectly revealed in his teachings and in his superb mortal life in the flesh. The divine nature can also be better understood if we recognize and remember that we are the children of God. We should look up to the Father in Paradise as a true spiritual Father.

The nature of God can be studied in a revelation of supreme ideas. The character of God can be seen as supreme ideals, but the most enlightening and spiritually satisfying of all revelations of the divine nature is the religious life of Jesus, both in the human Jesus and the divine Jesus—the son of man and the son of God. If the mortal life of Jesus is the revelation of God to man, we may enlighten ourselves and increase our understanding of the nature and the character of our heavenly Father by studying the life and teachings of Jesus.

In our efforts to learn about God, we are tremendously handicapped by the limited capacity of our intellectual mortal mind to understand eternal spiritual things. We are seriously handicapped by the limitations of language for there are no words which can express the infinity and grandeur of God. Therefore, we must rely upon our own spiritual nature and personal experience to even begin to know God. All our efforts to enlarge our understanding of God would be all but hopeless except for the fact that we are indwelt by the spirit of God and the Spirit of Truth and the Holy Spirit. Because I think very few people understand this magnificent gift that God has given every one of us let me pause to cite a couple of specific Bible verses—even though I said I wouldn't.

We all know John 3:16 but let me remind you of First Corinthians 3:16 that says, "Do you not know that you are the temple of God, and that the Spirit of God dwells within you?" First Corinthians 6:19 says, "Do you not know that your body is the temple of the Holy Ghost which is in you?" This truth can be found repeatedly throughout the Bible and other religious texts in nearly all religions past and present around the world. Our mortal body is the temple, the dwelling place of God's spirit; a piece of God himself that helps us and guides us. Some people find it plausible to believe that people can be possessed by evil spirits. Can it be that difficult to know that the spirit of God lives within us? With this in mind, let us ask for help and guidance from all our spiritual helpers in our search for God. Let us cheerfully undertake this journey to discover and become closer to God.

1. The Infinity of God

Let's start with the big stuff—the infinity of God. God is all powerful—omnipotent. God is everywhere—Omnipresent and God is all knowing—omniscient. There is no limit to God. God is infinite. God is the great and only I AM.

"Touching the Infinite, we cannot find him out. The divine footsteps are not known." "His understanding is infinite and his greatness is unsearchable." The blinding light of the Father's presence is such that to his lowly creatures he apparently "dwells in the thick darkness." That is kind of like having one of those tactical flashlights the police use shining in your eyes. All you see is the bright light surrounded by what appears to be blackness. Not only are his thoughts and plans unsearchable, [God that is, not the policeman] but "he does great and marvelous things without number." "God is great; we comprehend him not, neither can the number of his years be searched out." "Will God indeed dwell on the earth? Behold, the heaven and the heaven of heavens cannot contain him." "How unsearchable are his judgments and his ways past finding out!"

The Universal Father is the God of all creation, the source and center of all things and beings. God is a creator, a controller, and the upholder of all things. The truth about God had begun to dawn upon mankind when the prophet said: "You, God, are alone; there is none beside you. You have created the heaven and the heaven of heavens, with all their hosts; you preserve and control them. By the Sons of God were the universes made. The Creator covers himself with light as with a garment and stretches out the heavens as a curtain." Only the concept of one God in the place of many gods enabled mortal man to realize the Father is the divine creator and infinite sovereign controller of universes.

"There is but one God, the infinite Father, who is also a faithful Creator." "The divine Creator is also the source and destiny of immortal souls. He is the Supreme Soul, the Primal (or original) Mind, and the Unlimited Spirit of all creation." "The great Controller makes no mistakes. He is resplendent in majesty and glory." "The Creator God is wholly devoid of fear and enmity. He is immortal, eternal, self-existent, divine, and bountiful." "How pure and beautiful, how deep and unfathomable is the supernal Ancestor of all things!" "The Infinite is most excellent in that he imparts himself to men. He is the beginning and the end, the Father of every good and perfect purpose." "With God all things are possible; the eternal Creator is the cause of causes."

God is fully aware of both his own infinity and eternity; likewise he fully knows his perfection and his power. The Father constantly and unfailingly meets the needs of all his creations and all his children. The great God knows and understands himself; he is fully aware of all his attributes of perfection. God is not a cosmic accident; neither is he a cosmic experimenter. We may engage in adventure; we may experiment; we may practice; but the Universal Father sees the end from the beginning, and his divine plan and eternal purpose embraces and comprehends all the experiments and all the adventures of all his children—both mortal and spiritual children. Nothing is new to God, and nothing ever comes as a surprise to him.

God inhabits the circle of eternity. He is without beginning or end of days. To God there is no past, present, or future; all time is present at any given moment; something so fantastic that we can only imagine such a thing in sci-fi movies.

The Universal Father is absolutely and without qualification limitless in all his powers, abilities, and character. He is infinitely true, infinitely beautiful, and infinitely good and so he is infinitely perfect in every way. And it is His infinite spiritual perfection that prevents all direct personal communication with imperfect material beings—us. This is why we cannot speak directly to God today in our present form. However, our heavenly Father has bridged this gap; First, through His Son, Jesus Christ. Being both man and god, Jesus can communicate with both of us. Jesus came to reveal God to us but he also revealed us to God. Jesus revealed to God—and to us—the perfect person that we can potentially become. Although Jesus is perfect in divinity, he exposed himself to the imperfection of our mortal lives by living a life of the very flesh and blood of which we are made, becoming one of us and one with us. In this, God becomes man. Jesus is literally the Son of God and the Son of Man. When we read that God knows our pains and our joys it is because Jesus came and experienced them for himself—kind of like that TV show "Undercover Boss". Jesus was the ultimate undercover boss.

Secondly, there are various orders of angels and other celestial hosts who guide and watch over us and often minister to us and serve us.

And third, as mentioned previously, there is the spirit of God that dwells within us, the actual gift of the great God himself sent to help us adjust our thoughts and actions to be more in tune with God; guiding us to choose to do Gods will. This gift is sent to us without announcement and without explanation. In endless profusion they descend from the heights of glory to grace and indwell the billions of humble minds of those mortals who possess the capacity to know God.

In these ways and probably in ways we are not aware of, does the Paradise Father lovingly and willingly modify, dilute, and reduce his infinity and perfection in order that he may be able to draw nearer to his mortal children. And so, through these manifestations of God—Jesus, angels, and the Indwelling Spirit—is the infinite Father able to enjoy close personal contact with each and every one of us individually and, as we say, 24/7.

All this he has done and now does, and evermore will continue to do, without in the least detracting from the fact and reality of his infinity, eternity, and power. These gifts of God, the Indwelling Spirits, are limitless. He will never run out of them. There will always be one for every one of his mortal children, on this world and all others in the universes. To understand God's infinity, we need to realize that just as the old song says that even after all the time that has passed, we have no less days to sing God's praise than when we first began. That is the definition of infinity and eternity. When God gives us something or does something it does not in any way reduce God or use up his power or energy for God is limitless, endless, eternal, and infinite. No matter how many worlds God decides to create or how many people inhabit this world or others, there is no less love or watchcare for the trillion trillionth one than when he first began. And these things are absolutely true, regardless of the cloud of mystery that surrounds them, or the impossibility of our understanding them.

Because our Father's plans are infinite and eternal, it is impossible for us to ever grasp or fully understand these divine plans and purposes. We can glimpse the Father's purposes only now and then, here and there, as they are revealed in the outworking of the plan of salvation and spiritual progress. We cannot understand the significance of infinity, but the infinite Father does most certainly fully understand and lovingly embrace all of his children. From our point of view on this speck of sand floating in space, it is difficult for us to see a plan or believe that God is in control but let me assure you that there is in the mind of God a plan which embraces every creature of all his vast domains, and this plan is an eternal purpose of boundless opportunity, unlimited progress, and endless life. And the infinite treasures of such a plan are yours — if you choose to accept them!

God is divine, eternal, and infinite in all that he is and does. We, being material beings, are finite beings. Infinite means endless. There is nothing bigger than infinity but finite things have limits. We are finite beings living within God's infinite being just as the earth is a finite material thing in an infinite universe. God's infinite being and personality must contain within it all finite human personality. Therefore, it is now understandable and literally true that: "In Him we live and move and have our being." That fragment of the Universal Father which indwells every mortal man *is* a part of the infinity of God, the Father of all Fathers, the Universal Father. God not only dwells within you but also within all those around you; ALL those around you. If God is the Father of all then all people you meet, ALL people you meet, are children of God and your literal, not just spiritual, brother or sister.

God first loved you. God loved you as a Father before you were born of a woman and before you are born of the spirit. God loves you today unconditionally and forever. Nothing you have done, are doing, or ever will do can cause God not to love you. We understand this because, as mortal parents, we love our imperfect children even when they misbehave. As the young Jesus told his mortal father Joseph, the heavenly father cannot love us less than our mortal parents love us. God loves his people, all people, but more importantly, he loves you, you individually and uniquely, because you are his child—a child of God.

The Apostle Paul said: "I am persuaded that neither death, nor life, nor angels, nor principalities, nor powers, nor things present, nor things to come, nor height, nor depth, nor anything else shall be able to separate us from the love of God."

Our love should be just as binding and bonding upon our relationships with each other as it is with our Paradise Father. Love one another as Jesus loves us. Love our Father in heaven as our Father loves us.

If we truly believe that God is the father of all people then we must believe in the brotherhood of all mankind. If we believe in an all-loving and merciful God who loves all his children, then in our efforts to be perfect as God is perfect, we too should be all-loving, merciful, and forgiving of our brothers and sisters around the world—even those who we may believe are our enemies, those who think or act differently, and those whose behaviors make them difficult to love.

When we look upon the people of this world with our material eyes, we see the colors of black, brown, red, white, or yellow. We see various Christians, Muslims, Jews, Buddhists, and others. But with our spiritual vision, we see only the children of our Father in Paradise and yet I suggest that it is our material vision that is blind and our spiritual vision that is 20/20. We know too that whatever kindness or harm we do to the least of these, we do also to our Father.

2. The Father's Eternal Perfection

God is perfect. The olden prophets understood the eternal, never-beginning, never-ending, circular nature of the Universal Father. God is literally and eternally present throughout all his universe. He inhabits the present moment with all his absolute majesty and eternal greatness. "The Father has life in himself, and this life is eternal life." Throughout the eternal ages it has been the Father who "gives life to all." There is infinite perfection in His divine integrity. "I am the Lord; I change not." He is the Father of lights—meaning, I believe, that he is creator of all the stars in the sky—and in all his cosmic activities there "is no variableness neither shadow of changing." He "declares the end from the beginning." He says: "My counsel shall stand; I will do all my pleasures" "according to the eternal purpose which I purposed in my Son." Thus are the plans and purposes of God like himself: eternal, perfect, and forever changeless.

"Whatsoever God does, it shall be forever; nothing can be added to it nor anything taken from it." The Universal Father does not repent of (or change) his original purposes of wisdom and perfection. His plans are steadfast, his counsel unchangeable, and his actions are divine and perfect. "A thousand years in his sight are but as yesterday when it is past and as a watch in the night." The perfection of divinity and the magnitude of eternity are forever beyond the full grasp of our mortal mind.

From our point of view the actions of a changeless God may seem to change as we deal with our day to day trials and triumphs; but underneath the surface and beneath all outward signs and indications, there is still present the changeless purpose, the everlasting plan, of the eternal God. The perceived imperfection of this world is part of God's perfect plan—a plan of overcoming imperfection by our choices, our decisions, and our faith; growing and progressing eventually becoming as perfect in our realm as God is in his realm—or at least trying to be. We struggle in this life because it is the overcoming of imperfection, the learning how to do unto others as God would do unto them, the rejection of sin, and the embracing of the Father's will that makes us able to stand, as perfected beings, in the presence of an eternally perfect father sometime in the future. Is it not the task of a loving father to teach his children the perfect path in life? I have heard it said that the greatest affliction of life is to have never been afflicted. We all know rich people who are unhappy with their wealthy and materially perfect life.

In our realm—our daily life here on earth—perfection may seem to be a relative term and indeed it is. When we are told to "be you perfect even as God is perfect" this does not mean that we can be as perfect as God but that we should strive to be as perfect in our life as God is in his. God's perfection is undiluted, absolute, and perfect. The actions of God may vary from time to time or place to place and cause us to see what **we** believe is imperfection—that is chaos and confusion—but that does not lessen the fact that everything God does is perfect according to his plans and his will and from his perspective.

Jesus showed us that living the perfect mortal life is possible—although it may be hard to imagine that any of us can hope to achieve that level of perfection in just one short lifetime as he did, it is certainly possible—just as Enoch and Elijah did. Now, all of you are sitting there saying "but I am not a prophet like Enoch and Elijah". You can be and in fact are a modern day prophet when you witness to others and live your life according to God's will. This is why it is so very important for you to know God and continue to know more about God—so you can live in a way that demonstrates God's love and cause people to want what you have—to cause the materially wealthy emperor to be jealous of your spiritual riches. And so that you may speak with confidence and authority when you teach and lead others to God. Few persons live up to the faith which they really have. Unreasoned fear is a master intellectual fraud practiced upon the evolving mortal soul. The majority of impoverished souls are truly rich, but they refuse to believe it.

God's personal perfection is not based on his righteousness but rather in the perfection of the goodness of his divine nature. He is final, complete, and perfect. There is no thing lacking in the beauty and perfection of his righteous character. And the whole scheme of living is centered in the divine purpose of our progressing to the point of sharing the Father's divine perfection so that someday we may be with God and be of service to God.

God is eternally and infinitely perfect, he cannot personally know imperfection as his own experience, but he is fully aware of all the imperfectness that we experience. The personal and liberating touch of God overshadows our hearts and surrounds all of us. In this way, as well as through the life of Jesus and the spirit that indwells us, does the heavenly Father actually participate in our experience *with* immaturity and imperfection in this mortal life.

Evil is not a part of the divine nature of God. Our Father did not create evil but his awareness of our mortal experience *with* evil and all of man's imperfection, error, sin, and iniquity are most certainly a part of God's ever-expanding realization of the children of time and moral responsibility—that's us again. Is this not like we are as mortal parents in that we don't actually commit the mistakes of our children but we are painfully aware of their mistakes and share in the consequences?

≈The God of Jesus≈

3. Justice and Righteousness

God is righteous, therefore, is he just. "The Lord is righteous in all his ways." "'I have not done without cause all that I have done,' says the Lord." "The judgments of the Lord are true and righteous altogether." The justice of the heavenly Father cannot be influenced by the actions of his children, "for there is no iniquity with the Lord our God, no respect of persons, no taking of gifts."

How futile it is to appeal to God to change his plans, his way of doing things, so that we can avoid the just consequences of our actions when they oppose his wise natural laws and righteous spiritual mandates! "Be not deceived; God is not mocked, for whatsoever a man sows that shall he also reap." True, even in the justice of reaping the harvest of wrongdoing, this divine justice is always tempered with mercy. It is God's infinite wisdom that determines the proportions of justice and mercy which shall be delivered in any given circumstance. The greatest punishment (in reality an inevitable consequence) for wrongdoing and deliberate rebellion against God is death—spiritual death as opposed to physical death because physical death is survivable—that is salvation. The final result of wholehearted sin is spiritual death. In reality, such sin-identified individuals have destroyed themselves by their willful embrace of iniquity. The consequences of sin and iniquity are always delayed until the fullness of love and mercy have been met.

When the sin-identified person has been judged and all hope of salvation is gone, the sentence is finally confirmed and their fate is sealed. There is no resurrection from such a fate; it is everlasting and eternal.

Such attitudes of evil can survive in the universe only because of God's mercy pending the justice and fairness of his judgment of the individual. Evil and sin themselves are not real "things". They are the absence of something. In school one of the most interesting things I learned in science class is that there is no such thing as cold. Cold is only the absence of heat. Cold is measured by the amount of heat available. The complete absence of heat is called "absolute zero". The measurement of heat is called temperature. The less heat there is, the colder it is. We can feel heat or the lack of it. I think evil is similar in that it is the absence of goodness. We can feel goodness and therefore we can measure our actions or the actions of others by the amount of goodness they contain. So when someone says that they were overcome by evil—as if evil is a real thing—that is not true. What they experience is a lack of goodness; a failure to choose goodness; a failure to choose the way of God. God's will is truth, beauty, and goodness so the more true, beautiful, and good we are the more we are in tune with God's will. A truly evil person is one in which no goodness can be found.

Let's interrupt this program to consider the differences between error, evil, sin, and iniquity because these are the potholes in the highway to Heaven. We find it difficult to fully comprehend the significance or grasp the meanings of error, evil, sin, and iniquity.

Just like Lucifer, Satan, and the Devil are not the same being, error, evil, sin, and iniquity are not the same thing. Rather are they levels of evil in both cases.

God has given us the freedom to choose between doing his will or not, between choosing right or wrong, between good or bad. In order to create this ability to choose, God created imperfection in contrast to perfection. And it is this contrast between perfection and imperfection that creates the potential for evil. The conflict between truth and falsehood creates potential for error. In order to have this freedom, we must have the potential of slavery of sin. We can only choose one thing if we have the two opposing realms of sin and righteousness. The persistent choice of God's will leads to the Kingdom of Heaven but when rejected leads to the pit of sin and iniquity.

Error is when we make a mistake due to the lack of knowledge or understanding; when perhaps our intentions are good but we do the wrong thing. Fortunately, God judges us on our intentions, not our errors. Evil is when we choose to do the wrong thing perhaps out of anger, revenge, or hurt feelings for example. Sin is when we deliberately choose to do something we know is wrong but we do it anyway. The key word here is "deliberately". Sin is what can have long term, even eternal, consequences. Iniquity is the irreversible habit of sin; when a person has rejected God intentionally and forever. The wages of sin are death, eternal spiritual death, and so it is with iniquity also. We all make errors and sometimes commit evil but when these cross the line into deliberate willful choices then we are in real serious trouble. But even sin can be forgiven. However, I doubt that any iniquitous person can change their ways. Old habits are hard to break. It requires a great and noble character, having started out wrong, to turn about and go right. All too often one's own mind tends to justify continuance in the path of sin when once it is chosen. The fear of whatever led to the sin often becomes a prideful fear of changing to good. The loss of personal self-worth can make changing our ways seem to be not worth the effort. When sin becomes iniquity, that is, a sinful habit or way of life, then it is virtually impossible to repent and seek forgiveness.

The apostle Peter never fully believed that he could be forgiven until he met his Master after the resurrection and saw that he was greeted and loved just as before the experiences of his tragic denials. But, his denial of Jesus was caused by fear and weakness. Therefore, it was forgiven and forgotten by Jesus.

Jesus led men to feel at home in the world; he delivered them from the slavery of the law and taught them that the world is not fundamentally evil. Jesus did not share Paul's pessimistic view of humankind. The Master looked upon men as the sons of God and foresaw a magnificent and eternal future for those who chose survival. He saw man positively, not negatively. He sees most men as weak rather than wicked, more distraught than depraved. But no matter what their status, they are all God's children and his brethren.

Jesus taught people to place a high value upon themselves in time and in eternity. Because of this high estimate which Jesus placed upon men, he was willing to spend himself in the unremitting service of mankind. And it was this infinite worth of the finite mortal that made the golden rule a vital factor in his religion. You should never fail to be uplifted by the extraordinary faith Jesus has in you.

"The spirit of the life of Christ Jesus has made us free from the law of material living and the temptations of evil and sin." "This is the victory that overcomes the flesh, even your faith."

The mission of Christ Jesus is one of creation and spiritualization. Christ devotes himself to the effective execution of the Father's plan of mortal ascension to Heaven through spiritual progress but also to the rehabilitation of rebels and wrongdoers. Forgiveness is yours if only you ask for it and turn away from of error, evil, and sin. Go and sin no more.

Having started out on the way of life everlasting, having accepted the assignment and received your orders to advance, do not fear the dangers of human forgetfulness and inconsistency. Do not be troubled with doubts of failure or by perplexing confusion. Do not falter and question your status and standing, for in every dark hour, at every crossroad in the forward struggle, the Spirit of Truth will always speak, saying, "This is the way." And Jesus says: "Follow me!"

This was kind of a detour from our topic but perhaps it does increase our understanding of who God truly is and what he is really like.

4. The Divine Mercy

God is merciful. Mercy is simply justice tempered by that wisdom which grows out of perfection of knowledge and the full recognition of the natural weaknesses and environmental handicaps of his children. "Our God is full of compassion, gracious, long-suffering, and plenteous in mercy." Therefore "whosoever calls upon the Lord shall be saved," "for he will abundantly pardon." "The mercy of the Lord is from everlasting to everlasting"; yes, "his mercy endures forever." "I AM the Lord who executes loving-kindness, judgment, and righteousness in the earth, for in these things I delight." "I do not afflict willingly nor grieve the children of men," for "I AM the Father of mercies and the God of all comfort."

God is by his personal nature kind, compassionate, and everlastingly merciful. And never is it necessary that any influence be brought to bear upon the Father to call forth his loving-kindness. You don't need to bargain with God in order to receive favor from Him or have your prayers answered. Our need is wholly sufficient to insure the full flow of the Father's tender mercies and his saving grace. Since God knows all about his children, it is easy for him to forgive them. The better a man understands his neighbor, the easier it will be to forgive him, even to love him.

Only infinite wisdom enables a righteous God to minister justice and mercy at the same time and in any given situation. The heavenly Father is never torn by conflicting attitudes toward his children; God is never a victim of confusion or doubt.

Mercy is the natural and inevitable result of our Father's goodness and love. The good nature of a loving Father could not possibly withhold the wise ministry of mercy to each and every one of his children. His justice and divine mercy together are what we call *fairness.* God is infinitely and always fair in everything he does.

Divine mercy creates fairness in the relationship between perfection and imperfection. Mercy is the justice of righteousness moderated to take into consideration the situations of mortal life; the righteousness of eternity modified to meet the highest interests and welfare of the children of God. Mercy is not a conflict or reduction of justice but rather an understanding of the demands of justice, as it is fairly applied as the consequences of our actions. Mercy is the justice of God wisely and lovingly poured out upon all men and women who need it.

5. The Love of God

"God is love"; therefore his only personal reaction toward the affairs of men and angels is always a reaction of divine love and affection. The Father loves us so much that he bestowed life upon us. "He makes his sun to rise on the evil and on the good and sends rain on the just and the unjust."

It is wrong to think that God must be bribed or coaxed into loving his children. God does not need sacrifices or payments in order to love you in exchange because "the Father himself loves you." It is because of his Fatherly affection for you that God sent his son to show you the way to live and the way to salvation and to prove to you that there is life after mortal death. The resurrection of Jesus proves that. God loves you so much that he sent a piece of himself to dwell within you to guide you and to help you adjust your mind's thinking and your spirit's doing to match the will of God. He sent prophets to tell us what we should do and the ways we should go. God sent his word in the form of a book to give us the intellectual knowledge and spiritual insight. God's love is universal; "whosoever will may come." He would "have all men be saved by coming into the knowledge of the truth." He is "not willing that any should perish." **Not one—Not you**.

God is not the great antagonist we are sometimes led to believe. God is your greatest fan. He is cheering you on, rooting for your success, doing all that he can to help you. God is the first to reach out his hand when you need saving from the disastrous results of some foolish transgression of the divine laws. God's love is by nature a fatherly affection; therefore does he sometimes "chasten us for our own profit, that we may be partakers of his holiness." Even during your fiery trials remember that "in all our afflictions he is afflicted with us."

God is divinely kind to sinners. When rebels return to righteousness, as with the prodigal son, they are mercifully received, "for our God will abundantly pardon." "I AM he who blots out your transgressions for my own sake, and I will not remember your sins." How many of us have said, "I forgive you but I won't forget what you did?" God is not like that. He not only forgives—he forgets. He expunges the record of our misdeeds.

After all, the greatest evidence of the goodness of God and the supreme reason for loving him is the indwelling gift of the Father—the spirit within you who waits patiently for the hour when you both shall be eternally made one and your eternal soul is born. Though you cannot find God by searching, if you will submit to the leading of the Indwelling Spirit, you will be unerringly guided, step by step and age by age, until you finally stand in the presence of the Paradise Father.

How unreasonable it is that you should not worship God because the limitations of human nature and the handicaps of our material being make it impossible for us to see him. Between God and us there is a tremendous distance. There is a great gulf of spiritual difference which must be bridged; but regardless of all that physically and spiritually separates us from God, stop and ponder the fact that God lives within you; he has in his own way already bridged that gulf. He has sent of himself, his spirit, to live within you and to toil with you as you pursue salvation and your eternal purpose.

God's presence remains with you in all disaster and through every sickness. But how unkind it is to knowingly defile or deliberately pollute the physical body, which must serve as the earthly tabernacle of this marvelous gift from God. All physical poisons, such as drugs, alcohol, sugar, and other physical addictions greatly retard the efforts of the spirit to guide us and help us. The mental poisons of fear, anger, envy, jealousy, suspicion, and intolerance tremendously interfere with the spiritual progress of our eternal soul. They tarnish this gift that God has given us.

When the development of our intellectual nature proceeds faster than our spiritual, when disease infiltrates the physical brain, communication with our Indwelling Spirit may become even more difficult and sometimes dangerous. Likewise, too rapid or over-spiritual development may produce a fanatical and perverted reaction to the spirits leadings. It is the mind of perfect poise, housed in a body of clean habits, stabilized physical energies, and balanced chemical functions—when the physical, mental, and spiritual powers are in harmony of development—that achieves the maximum capacity for light and truth. When we take shelter in the Most High, he conceals our defects from the universe. When we stand before God with a clean heart, we become fearless of all creation. A healthy mind and a healthy body prepare the way for spiritual fitness.

I find it easy and pleasant to worship one who is so great and at the same time so affectionately devoted to the uplifting ministry of all his children. It is natural to love one who is so powerful, and yet who is so perfectly good and so lovingly kind. I think I would love God just as much if he were not so great and powerful, as long as he is so good and merciful. We all love the Father more because of his nature—who he is—than in recognition of his amazing powers—what he is.

I think we love the heavenly Father because he first loves us. The experience of loving is very much a direct response to the experience of being loved. It is easy to love someone who loves us. Knowing that God loves me, I shall continue to love him with all my heart and all my soul, even if he should somehow lose all his power, infinity, and eternity.

The Father's love follows us now and throughout the endless circle of eternity. As we ponder the loving nature of God, there is only one reasonable and natural reaction to who God is: we will grow to love him more as our creator. We will grow to love God with an affection like that of a child for their earthly parent; for, as a father, a real father, a true father, loves his children, so does the heavenly Father love and care for all his sons and daughters.

But the love of God is an intelligent and farseeing parental affection. The divine love functions in unity and in association with divine wisdom and all other characteristics that make up the perfect nature of God the Father. God is love, but love is not God. The greatest proof of the Fathers love for us is this gift of our Indwelling Spirit; but the greatest revelation of the Father's love is seen in the life of Jesus—the Son of God—as he lived the ideal spiritual life on earth. It is the Indwelling Spirit who enables God to love us directly and personally as individuals. It is the revelation of God by Jesus that shows us how he loves us and how we should love each other.

I am almost pained to try to portray God's love by using the word "love". Even though the word "love" is used to describe the highest concept of the mortal relationships of respect and devotion, it is so frequently used to describe other things that are unfit to be known by any word which is also used to indicate the matchless affection of the living God for his children! I wish I could think up some beautiful word or exclusive term which would express the true nature and exquisitely beautiful divine affection of the Paradise Father. If we lose sight of the love of a personal God, the Kingdom of Heaven becomes merely a kingdom of good. Above all else, above all other aspects of God's nature, love is the dominant characteristic of all God's personal dealings with his children.

6. The Goodness of God

Our heavenly Father is true, beautiful, and good. In the physical world we may see the divine beauty, in the intellectual world we may discover eternal truth, but the goodness of God is found only in the spiritual world of personal religious experience. In its true essence, religion is a faith-trust in the goodness of God. In philosophy God could be great, perfect, and all-powerful, even intelligent and personal as the philosopher Rodan discovered, but in religion God must also be moral; he must be good. Man might fear a great God, but he trusts and loves only a good God. This goodness of God is part of the personality of God, and its full revelation appears only in the personal religious experience of the believing children of God; our own personal and unique relationship with God.

Religion implies that the spiritual world is aware of, and responsive to, the fundamental needs of the human world—often seen as the purpose of prayer. The old concept that God rules his children and his creations as a king was uplifted and replaced by Jesus who revealed to us that affectionately touching and intimate parent-child relationship that exists between God the Father and us—as his sons and daughters; a relationship of which there is none more tender and beautiful in all human experience.

The "goodness of God leads erring man to repentance." "Every good gift and every perfect gift comes down from the Father of lights." "God is good; he is the eternal refuge of the souls of men." "The Lord God is merciful and gracious. He is long-suffering and abundant in goodness and truth." "Taste and see that the Lord is good! Blessed is the man who trusts him." "The Lord is gracious and full of compassion. He is the God of salvation." "He heals the brokenhearted and binds up the wounds of the soul. He is man's all-powerful benefactor."

The ancient concept of God as a king or judge fostered a high moral standard and created a law-abiding people as a group. However, such a concept of God left the individual believer in the sad position of insecurity concerning his own personal status and standing in time, eternity, and before God. The early Hebrew prophets proclaimed God to be the Father of Israel; Jesus revealed God as the Father of each and every human being. The entire mortal concept of God is transcendently illuminated by the life of Jesus. Unselfishness, putting the needs of our children before ours, is a basic part of parental love. God loves not *like* a father, but *as* a father. He is the Paradise Father of every one of us and creator of all things. And, remember that love is the desire to do good for others.

Love gives and craves affection. Love seeks a personal relationship such as that which exists between a parent and child, husbands and wives, brothers and sisters, families and friends. Righteousness may be the divine thought, but love is the Father's attitude. It is a mistake to believe that the righteousness of God is not compatible with the unselfish love of the heavenly Father—that God cannot be both righteous and loving and merciful at the same time. This error would have us believe that God is not unified in his nature—that he is somehow a split personality. However, Jesus told us that "he who has seen me has seen the Father." His life shows us that God the Father is both righteous and loving at the same time. To believe that God must be either a just God or a loving God and cannot be both is an insult to God's personality and loving nature. To believe that God is an angry and vengeful God that demands payment for his love, mercy, or forgiveness is our own error in understanding who God is. Such a belief is not consistent with the loving Father that Jesus revealed. It is a great travesty upon the character of God to believe that his cold hard heart is so uncaring of the misfortunes and sorrows of his children that his love and mercy need to be bought or bargained for. God gives his love to you freely because he is your father and you are his child. You need not beg or negotiate for it. All of us have said, "you cannot buy love" and that is true with God as well.

The loving heavenly Father is not a divided personality—one of justice and one of mercy—Jesus taught that we do not need a mediator to secure the Father's favor or forgiveness. True that Jesus is the bridge between man and God but the way is open and even welcoming to all who choose to come. Jesus is not there to block the path but to shine a light on the way we should go. The Spirit of Truth that Jesus poured out upon all mankind at Pentecost said, "This is the way." Jesus said, "Follow me." God's righteousness is not dominated by a need for retribution or justice. An "eye for an eye" is man's way; not God's. God as a father is greater than God as a judge.

God is never wrathful, vengeful, or angry. Those are human traits unfit to be called human much less associated with God. I try not to become wrathful, vengeful, and angry when I hear people say such things about my Father. It is true that wisdom often restrains his love, and justice conditions his mercy but God is first and foremost a loving person. The goodness of God is the foundation of his divine nature to love, show mercy, have patience, and grant forgiveness. His love of righteousness might be seen as hatred for sin.

We have heard that "God loves the sinner and *hates* the sin"; philosophically that is true, but as we learned in a previous lesson, God is a personality, and persons can only love or hate other persons. Sin is not a person or even a thing. It is a choice. God loves the sinning person because God is also a person and the sinner is still his child. God has no personal opinion about sin itself because sin is not a spiritual reality to God. God does not know sin; only the justice of God is aware of the existence of sin. The love of God saves the sinner; the law of God destroys the sin.

In our personal search for God, he is discovered to be a loving person; in the spiritual world, he is a personal love; in religious experience he is both. Love identifies the will of God. The goodness of God is the foundation of his tendency to love, show mercy, manifest patience, and minister forgiveness.

7. Divine Forgiveness

During their time with the Master, one day Peter and James were engaged in discussing their differences of opinion about the Master's teaching regarding the forgiveness of sin. They had both agreed to lay the matter before Jesus, and Peter embraced this occasion as a fitting opportunity for securing the Master's counsel. Accordingly, Simon Peter asked: "Master, James and I are not in accord regarding your teachings having to do with the forgiveness of sin. James claims you teach that the Father forgives us even before we ask him, and I maintain that repentance and confession must precede the forgiveness. Which of us is right? What do you say?"

After a short silence Jesus looked up and answered: "My brethren, you err in your opinions because you do not comprehend the nature of those intimate and loving relations between the creature and the Creator, between man and God. You fail to grasp that understanding sympathy which the wise parent entertains for his immature and sometimes erring child. It is indeed doubtful whether intelligent and affectionate parents are ever called upon to forgive an average and normal child. Understanding relationships associated with attitudes of love effectively prevent all those estrangements which later necessitate the readjustment of repentance by the child with forgiveness by the parent.

"A part of every father lives in the child. The father enjoys priority and superiority of understanding in all matters connected with the child-parent relationship. The parent is able to view the immaturity of the child in the light of the more advanced parental maturity, the riper experience of the older partner. With the earthly child and the heavenly Father, the divine parent possesses infinity and divinity of sympathy and capacity for loving understanding. Divine forgiveness is inevitable; it is inherent and inalienable in God's infinite understanding, in his perfect knowledge of all that concerns the mistaken judgment and erroneous choosing of the child. Divine justice is so eternally fair that it unfailingly embodies understanding mercy.

"When a wise man understands the inner impulses of his fellows, he will love them. And when you love your brother, you have already forgiven him. This capacity to understand man's nature and forgive his apparent wrongdoing is Godlike. If you are wise parents, this is the way you will love and understand your children, even forgive them when transient misunderstanding has apparently separated you. The child, being immature and lacking in the fuller understanding of the depth of the child-father relationship, must frequently feel a sense of guilty separation from a father's full approval, but the true father is never conscious of any such separation. Sin is an experience of creature consciousness; it is not a part of God's consciousness.

"Your inability or unwillingness to forgive your fellows is the measure of your immaturity; your failure to attain adult sympathy, understanding, and love. You hold grudges and nurse vengefulness in direct proportion to your ignorance of the inner nature and true longings of your children and your fellow beings. Love is the outworking of the divine and inner urge of life. It is founded on understanding, nurtured by unselfish service, and perfected in wisdom."

8. Divine Truth and Beauty

God is good but he is also true and beautiful. Truth, our ability to comprehend truth, is determined by our current location in the long journey from this mortal life to the day we stand before God. We shall not know complete absolute truth until that day. In this life we can know only a certain amount of truth. We have been given the amount of truth we are able to understand and as we progress spiritually, when our pint becomes a quart, more truth is revealed to us. Have you ever been reading about God, Heaven, or Jesus and find that something you have read many times before but never understood is now suddenly clear to you? That, I think, is revealed truth. The truth was there all the time but you were not ready for it. When you are ready to discover expanded truth, it is then revealed to you—much as the brothers who walked with the resurrected Jesus at Emmaus. The truth was with them, walking right beside them, but they did not know it until, when they were ready, their eyes were opened to it. In our schools we don't teach calculus to kindergarteners because they cannot comprehend it. First we teach them to add and subtract. Only when they are ready can we teach them calculus. Religion and revelation are the same way. Just because we don't know the truth doesn't mean the truth does not exist, or is not true. We are kindergarteners in the school of spiritual education. Our greatest task, perhaps our greatest joy, and certainly the greatest of all human knowledge is to know the religious life of Jesus and how he lived it. The more you learn, the more truth is revealed to you. The more truth you know the more truth you want to know. Yes, truth is absolute but we who must work with a mortal mind are only capable of absorbing so much today. Tomorrow we can absorb more. So, in that sense truth is dynamic or changing but only because we cannot grasp it all in one short lifetime. That is why previously I said that a pint can never hold a quart. We must expand our knowledge and experience in order to have the capacity to hold more truth. When you get to that point I will tell you that a quart can never hold a gallon. And so it goes.

There is a difference between facts and truth. Physical facts are fairly uniform, but truth is living and flexible. We are only partially wise and true in our communications with others. We cannot always tell the truth, the whole truth, and nothing but the truth because we don't yet know all the truth. Is there anyone here who claims to know everything there is to know about God or about anything for that matter? Stagnant truth is dead truth—meaning that once we become so arrogant to think we know it all, we stop learning and we stop growing and therefore we stop progressing. Everything that is not growing is either dead or dying; materially, intellectually, or spiritually. We speak from the level of truth that we know. We can be certain about anything only as far as our own personal experience takes us. I like to say that we only believe that which we convince ourselves is true. Nobody else can make us truly believe anything. That which may seem wholly true today may be only somewhat true tomorrow after we have more experience. This is why it is so important to study God's word and communicate with him in prayer and to share the fellowship of other believers as we are doing here now.

Truth is beautiful because it is complete, repeatable, and symmetrical. Philosophers commit their greatest mistake when they focus upon one aspect of reality and then pronounce it to be the whole truth. The teachings of Aristotle are an example of this. The wise philosopher will always look for the intelligent design which is behind all creation; the creator behind the creation. I used to carry in my wallet a quote from Albert Einstein that said something like, "The true scientist will eventually come to the realization of God as the only possible source of everything". That isn't a direct quote because my wallet went through the washing machine.

Happiness comes from the recognition of truth because it can be *acted out*; it can be lived. Disappointment and sorrow result from a lack of truth. Divine truth is best known by its *spiritual flavor*. True religion makes the religionist *socially fragrant* and creates insights into human fellowship and happiness.

Our eternal quest is to find God and become like him, to love one another as he loves us, to do his will, to become perfect even as he is perfect, and to find our way to the Father in Heaven. Indeed, that is also the desire of the spirit that lives within us. That spirit came from God and seeks to return to God and take us with him. The eternal soul is made up of you, your personality—the "who" that is you—and this spirit fragment of God bonded together for eternity. The only reason we can someday enter into the very presence of God is because of this spirit that dwells within us. This spirit within us is what transforms us from a material caterpillar into a beautiful spiritual butterfly that can soar to Heaven.

Our failure to associate the goodness of God with the facts of science and the beauty of art is a great mistake. Religion, I think, is the study of God and science is the study of God's creations. Art is the honoring of the beauty of God and his creations by imitation. Truth, beauty, and goodness should not be considered separately. Taking them all together unifies our understanding of the universe—both physical and spiritual—and of God himself. All three are necessary for us to have any hope of completely understanding who God is and what he is—even to understand who we are and what we are. As civilization progresses, if we continue to overemphasize the goodness of God while excluding the truth and beauty of God, many people turn away from this incomplete picture of God that is so stubbornly dogmatic in some religions.

Scientists such as Stephen Hawking search for the theory of everything but that theory can only be found when they include everything in their theory. Scientists only consider the material world to be real and ignore the truth and beauty of everything else and deny the existence of the spiritual world—even as they speculate on the existence of other dimensions. Therefore, they fail to produce the theory they are searching for. They try to draw it in mathematical formulas on a chalkboard but such a theory must include all truth, beauty, and goodness. When scientists discover the reality of God the theory of everything will become obvious.

I sent an email to Stephen Hawking that said, "You cannot discover a theory of everything unless you include everything in your theory. The study of science is meaningless unless it recognizes the *scientist*. No appreciation of art is genuine unless it gives recognition to the artist. No evaluation of morals is worthwhile unless it includes the *moralist*. No recognition of philosophy is enlightening if it ignores the *philosopher*, and religion cannot exist without the real experience of the *religionist*. Likewise the universe is without significance apart from the I AM, the infinite God who created it and unceasingly manages it." Three days later Professor Hawking died.

Modern religion fails to hold the devotion and loyalty of many twenty first-century men and women but that would all change if religions would give equal consideration to the truths of science, philosophy, and spiritual experience, and to the beauties of the physical creation, the appeal of art, and the grandeur of genuine character achievement in addition to the moral inspirations of true religion.

The religious challenge of this age is to those farseeing and forward-looking men and women of spiritual insight who will dare to construct a new and appealing philosophy of living out of the enlarged concepts of truth, beauty, and divine goodness. This is much of the reason why we are here today. Such a new and righteous vision of morality will attract all that is good in the mind of man and challenge that which is best in the human soul. Truth, beauty, and goodness are divine realities, and as man ascends the scale of spiritual living, these supreme qualities of the Eternal God become increasingly part of the person and the person becomes more in tune and unified with the will of God, the way of God.

All truth is both beautiful and good. All real beauty is both true and good. All genuine goodness is equally true and beautiful. Happiness comes from the integration or unifying of truth, beauty, and goodness into our daily life. When truth, beauty, and goodness are made part of our lives the result is love, wisdom, and faith. The real purpose of all our efforts to study religious and spiritual things, to know the religious life of Jesus and how he lived it, to know God and become more like him, is to bring each of us to a greater knowledge of God and to actually experience his glory and grandeur. Our adventure in discovering God brings us a closer personal relationship with him. This journey of discovery leads us to realize that this life is only the beginning of an endless career of adventure, an everlasting life of anticipation, and an eternal voyage of discovery.

Truth is coherent, beauty attractive, and goodness stabilizing. And when these values of that which is real are co-ordinated in personality experience, the result is a high order of love conditioned by wisdom and qualified by loyalty. The real purpose of all universe education—life—is to effect the better co-ordination of the isolated child of the worlds with the larger realities of his expanding experience. Reality is finite on our level but infinite and eternal on the higher and divine spiritual levels.

God, Paradise, Heaven, and all of our Father's creations are much grander and more true, beautiful, and good than we can begin to imagine.

So, no matter how important or unimportant you think you are; no matter how important or unimportant those around you seem to think you are, you are supremely important to God because you ARE his child and he loves YOU unconditionally. The creator of this vast universe of universes IS your Father. He loves you and he wants you to love him in return; love him for WHO he is rather than WHAT he is. God loves you and wants you to succeed and find salvation after mortal death. He created you. He loves you so much that he sent his son to show you the way home. He loves you so much that he gave you an Indwelling Spirit to guide you through this life and the next. He loves you so much that he assigned legions of angels to watch over you, to walk with you as teachers and facilitators for your education and training in your eternal career and prepare you for your ultimate purpose in service to God and to mankind. He loves you so much that he has prepared many mansions for you to dwell in during the next life. They are already built and waiting for you. God is expecting you to survive. If you take nothing else away from this lesson, please take this: God loves you and would never do anything to hurt you.

Make note of your thoughts, questions, comments here:

Lesson Seven
The Attributes of God

Who is God? Does God love me? Where does God live? Why isn't God here with us? Is God angry with me? Why does God let evil things happen?

Why is it important for us to ask these questions? I think they are important because the more we know about God the more we will know about ourselves. The more we know about God the more we can witness and tell others about God in an informed way. The more we know about God the stronger our faith in God will become. The more we know about God the closer we will be to God and the closer we will become to being like God in the way we do things. And that is the mandate God has given us: to be perfect even as he is perfect.

This means that in our lives we should strive to do things and interact with people the way we believe God would do. We have all heard the saying, "What would Jesus do?" This is the same as saying, "Be you perfect even as God is perfect." When we ask: "What would Jesus do?" and then choose to do that, we are in fact choosing to become more perfect in what we do and more like God in our actions and reactions because Jesus is the perfect revelation of God to mankind. So, that is why I think it is important to take this time to get to know God personally.

We should take time each day in prayer and worship to spend quality time with God. Each day we should spend quality time with our loved ones and our Father in heaven. I like to do this in the morning when it's quiet and the first hints of the day are seeping through the windows. We should take time to give our Father our undivided attention for at least a few minutes each day through prayer, meditation, worship, and praise. However, God is with us all through the day. We should strive to be in constant communion with God—that is, constantly communicating with God.

Rely on God. Ask him questions. Ask for his guidance. Ask for his leadership. Ask his advice. Ask his direction. Take advantage of your relationship with God as you would with your best friend or someone you trust. Rely on his love, guidance, and wisdom because your heavenly Father is the one person other than yourself who truly has your best interest at heart. God is literally right there with you all through the day. So the more you know God the more you can communicate with God. The more you communicate with God the more you know God; the more you will become like God in the way you interact with other people and the choices you make.

God is everywhere present; our heavenly Father rules the circle of eternity. But he rules our universe in and through his son, Jesus. "God has given us eternal life, and this life is in his Sons." Jesus is the personal expression of God to his children of this world.

Nature can be described by the question: "God is...." Attributes can be answered by the statement: "God can...." The ability to create is not an attribute of God but rather an action of his divine nature. And this function of being a creator is conditioned and controlled by all the combined attributes of God who is the creator—the source—and center of everything. If ever there was "the first thing God ever did" it probably was some act of creation. And the creatorship of God is fulfilled in the truth of the Fatherhood of

God. The Universal Father is the God of all creation, the First Source and Center of all things and beings. First think of God as a creator, then as a controller, and lastly as an infinite upholder. The truth about the Universal Father had begun to dawn upon mankind when the prophet said: "You, God, are alone; there is none beside you. You have created the heaven and the heaven of heavens, with all their hosts; you preserve and control them. By the Sons of God were the universes made. The Creator covers himself with light as with a garment and stretches out the heavens as a curtain." Only the concept of the Universal Father—one God in the place of many gods—enabled mortal man to realize the Father as the divine creator and infinite controller.

1. God's Everywhereness

The Father's presence unceasingly fills the grand universe. "His going forth is from the end of heaven, and his circuit to the ends of it; and there is nothing hidden from the light thereof." With God, his circuit is infinite but whatever goes out from God comes back to God. God pours out his spirit and this spirit merges with personality and returns home. God spreads personality through living beings throughout the universes and those personalities long to return home to the Father of personality. God projects his love upon all his children and that love returns to the Father. This is the circuit of God.

The ability of the heavenly Father to be everywhere present, and at the same time, is called omnipresence. God alone can be in two places, in numberless places, at the same time. God is simultaneously present "in heaven above and on the earth beneath"; as the Psalmist exclaimed: "Whither shall I go from your spirit? or whither shall I flee from your presence?"

"'I am a God at hand as well as afar off,' says the Lord. 'Do not I fill heaven and earth?'" The heavenly Father is all the time present in all parts and in all hearts of his far-flung creation. He is "the fullness of him who fills all and in all," and "who works all in all," and further, the concept of his personality is such that "the heavens (universe) and heaven of heavens (universe of universes) cannot contain him." It is literally true that God is all and in all. But even that is not *all* of God. The cause can never be fully understood by an examination of its effects; the living God is immeasurably greater than the sum total of his creation. God is revealed throughout the cosmos, but the cosmos can never contain or encompass the whole being of God. All things exist within God and God exists in all things.

Think of this as one of your hobbies. One of mine is doing stained glass. I create a piece of stained glass but that piece cannot be greater than me the creator. A child cannot create their parent. The creator must always be greater than the thing created. So when we look at God's creation and all its immense grandeur and beauty and magnificent functioning, all the material and spiritual beings that live within it, all the love and personality, and all that it contains from the lowest to the highest, God must be more than all that and cannot be anything less. God is the creator. God's material creations are "things." The living organisms he creates give meaning and value to creation.

The child that is created not only exists in God, but God also lives in the child. "We know we dwell in him because he lives in us; he has given us his Indwelling Spirit. This gift from the heavenly Father is our inseparable companion." "He is the ever-present and all-pervading God." "The spirit of the everlasting Father is concealed in the mind of every mortal child." "Man goes forth searching for a friend while that very friend lives within his own heart." "The true God is not afar off; he is a part of us; his spirit speaks from within us." "The Father lives in the child. God is always with us. He is the guiding spirit of eternal destiny."

Truly, of the human race it has been said, "You are of God" because "he who dwells in love dwells in God, and God in him because God is love." Even in wrongdoing you torment the indwelling gift of God, for the spirit within must go through the consequences of evil thinking and erroneous actions along with the human mind of its incarceration.

The omnipresence of God is in reality a part of his infinite nature; space constitutes no barrier to this infinite spiritual being. God can only be seen in his home on Paradise. We cannot see him because he has limited his direct and actual presence here on earth. However, his divine presence is seen and felt through his manifestations in his Son Jesus, our Indwelling Spirit, and his mortal children that share this world we live in. It is not always possible to distinguish between the presence of the heavenly Father and the actions of his son because the actions of the son so perfectly match God's unchanging purpose—his will. But this is not so with the spirit of God within you; here God acts uniquely, directly, and exclusively.

The actions of our heavenly Father are coordinated with the functions of his son and his spirit who fulfill the trinity but this does not exclude the direct action of God himself in our lives. Such cooperation between the Father, Son, Spirit, and legions of angels does not diminish the Father's presence in our lives, on our planet, or in our universe. God's presence is measured by the degree of our recognition of him and our loyalty to him. Have you ever said, "I don't want to bother God with this." and then later wondered why God hasn't helped you? This is what I mean. The more you depend on God, the more you turn to God, the more present he will be in your life. The more our nation looks to God the more present he will be. The more our world seeks God the more present he will be. But if we don't invite God into our lives and have a personal relationship with him, he is not going to force himself upon us or impose his will upon us.

In this day and age it is all but certain that life exists beyond our planet—we just haven't found it yet. I am also certain that a parallel universe does exist. It is the spiritual realm but we cannot communicate with it directly. I often wonder if that is because God has isolated us from everyone else because of the sin and rebellion on this world and he does not want us to contaminate his other creations. Are the good people of this world suffering the isolating consequences of the sinful acts of a headstrong, wicked, and rebellious minority? Is this world so bad that he sent his son to try to straighten things out only to have that help rejected by the religious authorities of that day?

We belong to our mortal family, our planetary family, and to God's cosmic family. God does not punish a nation for the sin of an individual; neither will the Father in heaven punish one of his believing children for the sins of a nation. The individual member of any family must often suffer the natural consequences of family mistakes and group transgressions but the family often suffers from the actions of one of its erring members. Do you not realize that the hope of a better nation—or a better world—is bound up in the progress and enlightenment of the individual?"

Previously I spoke about how God down-steps his self, his being, through the Son and the Indwelling Spirit making it possible to have a direct personal relationship with us as much as an infinite spiritual being can have a relationship with a material mortal being. On the other hand, we must uplift ourselves to make us more like him in order to have a personal relationship with him. His influence on our actions and his effective presence in our lives is determined by the degree of cooperation we give to the leading of our Indwelling Spirit. Our efforts to study and learn about the life and teachings of Jesus and our choice to follow Jesus is another great influence upon the level of peace, security, and happiness we enjoy.

The fluctuations of the Father's presence that we feel from time to time are not due to the changeableness of God. God is not moody nor does he pout. The Father does not retire in seclusion because he has been slighted. The Father has freely bestowed himself upon us without limit and without favor. He is no respecter of persons, planets, systems, or universes. God does not love Billy Graham or the Pope any more than he loves you nor any less. In God's eyes there are only two types of people: those who choose to do his will and those who do not. Otherwise, all people truly are created equal in the eyes of God. His affections are not alienated because of any of our wrongdoings. Rather, it is our efforts and choices that directly determine the degree and the limitations of the Father's divine presence and influence in our own hearts and minds.

2. God's Infinite Power

All the universes know that "the Lord God omnipotent reigns." The affairs of this world and other worlds are divinely supervised. "He does all according to his will in the army of heaven and among the inhabitants of the earth." It is eternally true, "there is no power but of God."

It is literally true that "with God all things are possible." The long-drawn-out progressive evolutionary processes of peoples, planets, and universes are under the perfect control of the universe creators and administrators. The never-ending creation and maintenance of all of God's realm unfolds in accordance with the eternal purpose of the heavenly Father, proceeding in harmony and order and in keeping with the all-wise plan of God. There is only one lawgiver. He upholds the worlds in space and swings the universes around the endless circle of space.

Of all the divine attributes, God's all-powerfulness, what is called "omnipotence", is the best understood. As material mortals, we are most familiar with power in the material world. Viewed from a nonspiritual or perhaps scientific viewpoint, God is energy. This fact is based on the truth that God is the original source and center, the cause or creator and geographic center, of the material physical phenomena of all space. From this divine activity all physical energy and matter come; even light is a physical manifestation created by God.

At this point, let me ask you to expand your vision and concept of God. Consider the vastness of space and the uncountable number of universes, galaxies, systems, planets and beings, both spiritual and material, and everything else that our space telescopes, such as the Hubble space telescope, have revealed to us. All of these things God created. Our vision of God one hundred years ago must be exponentially expanded to include all this if we believe that God created everything. And in fact, he did. How anyone can see these pictures of things so immensely huge that they are beyond any measurement that we can possibly relate to and then view the birth of a child and see the simple complexity of God's creation in a microscope and not know there must be a God is beyond me. In the past the religious leaders were the scientists of their day. Today, with all the vast knowledge of mankind in our pocket in the form of a cell phone—I would think that scientists should be the religious leaders of today.

God controls all power; he has made "a way for the lightning"; he has ordained the circuits of all energy; light, heat, electricity, magnetism, gravity, and nuclear. All these are part of God's creation. He has decreed the time and manner of the manifestation of all forms of energy and matter. Everything did not come from nothing as some of today's supposedly brilliant scientists try to tell us. Everything came from something and that something is God.

Our telescopes and space probes are discovering thousands of planets circling hundreds of stars and it is projected that there are trillions of planets circling billions of stars. These myriads of planetary systems were all made to be inhabited by many different intelligent creatures who could know God, receive his divine affection, and love him in return. The universe of universes is the work of God and the dwelling place of all his diverse children and creatures of the realms. "God created the heavens and formed the earth; he established the universe and created this world not in vain; he formed it to be inhabited."

In lesson three we read about Melchizedek. He preached a God of creation and universal upholding. Speaking for the Lord God of Israel, this prophet, Melchizedek, said: "I have made the earth and put man upon it. I have created it not in vain; I formed it to be inhabited."

It says in Isaiah 40:12: "Who has measured the waters in the hollow of his hand, or with the breadth of his hand marked off the heavens? Who has held the dust of the earth in a basket, or weighed the mountains on the scales and the hills on a balance?"

All these things are held forever in his grasp by the gravitational control emanating from Paradise. Light, energy, and the endless but orderly procession of the starry realms that make up this grand universe swings forever around Paradise which is at the center of all things and beings. God, Paradise, Heaven, and the mansions that await all of us are very real.

The omnipotence of the Father pertains to the three forms of energy: physical, intellectual, and spiritual. And because our mortal minds are not directly responsive to the heavenly Father, he must adjust his perfect mind to our imperfect mind by the presence of our Indwelling Spirit in order to have a relationship with us. This is kind of like our technology today where we can convert light into sound and vice versa using a DVD or CD player which uses a laser light to produce sound. Imagine that God is speaking with light but we can only hear sound. God must convert his language of light into our language of sound so that we can detect his presence. God uses our Indwelling Spirit and Jesus to convert his spiritual language into something we can perceive if not hear. Jesus is the bridge between the spiritual Father and the material child.

The heavenly Father is not a transient force, a shifting power, or a fluctuating energy. The power and wisdom of the Father are wholly adequate to cope with any and all universe exigencies. As the emergencies of human experience arise, he has foreseen them all, and therefore he does not react to the affairs of the universe in a detached way but rather in accordance with the dictates of eternal wisdom and in consonance with the mandates of his infinite and perfectly wise judgment. Regardless of appearances, the power of God is not functioning in the universe as a blind force.

Situations do arise in which it appears that emergency action has been taken, that natural laws have been suspended, or that unanticipated problems arise and that an effort is being made to rectify the situation; but such is not the case. Such concepts of God have their origin in our limited vision and understanding. Such misunderstanding of God is due to our lack of first-hand knowledge of the higher laws that govern all of God's creations, the magnitude of our Father's character, the infinity of his love and personality, or the grand plan that God has in place that governs his actions.

God's mortal children are scattered hither and yon throughout the vast universes of space. Like the stars and planets created for them to live on, they are nearly infinite in number and order. Their intellects are so diverse, their minds are so limited and sometimes so gross, their vision is so limited both materially and spiritually that it is almost impossible to make generalizations about God's plans and laws that can adequately describe or explain the Father's infinite characteristics—his love, wisdom, power, mercy, and fairness—that could be understandable to any of these mortal children; to any of us. Therefore, to us, many of the acts of the all-powerful Creator seem to be arbitrary, detached, and often heartless and cruel. But again I assure you that this is not true. God's doings are all purposeful, intelligent, wise, kind, and eternally considerate of the best good, not always of an individual person, an individual race, an individual planet, or even an individual universe; but they are always perfectly best for the welfare and good of all concerned. Sometimes the good of the one may appear to outweigh the good of the whole in our minds, but in the mind of God there is no difference between the two.

We are all a part of the family of God, therefore we must sometimes share in the family discipline. Many of the acts of God which so disturb and confuse us are the result of the wisdom, power, and plans of God that require choices that embrace the highest and eternal welfare of all his vast and far-flung creation.

It is our detached, limited, and highly materialistic viewpoint and the limitations of this current form we live in that handicaps our ability to see, understand, or know the wisdom and kindness of many of the divine acts which to us may seem to deliver crushing cruelty, or utter indifference to the comfort and welfare, to the happiness and prosperity of our fellow man or even ourselves. It is because of the limitations of human vision, our limited understanding and comprehension, that we misunderstand the motives and pervert the purposes of God. But many things occur in our lives and in this world which are not the personal doings of the heavenly Father. Often, we reap what we sow and frequently we reap what others around us sow. The choices we make affect everyone around us. We tend to say, "It must be God's will" or "the devil made me do it". But God has given us free will to choose between truth and falseness, between good and evil, between right and wrong. Our lives are the result of our own personal choices and the choices of those around us—not always or only from the mandates of God. The freedom to choose includes the freedom to fail or succeed.

God's power, his omnipotence, is perfectly coordinated and balanced with the other attributes of his personality—such as his love, wisdom, and mercy. The power of God is, ordinarily, only limited by three conditions or situations:

1. By the nature of God, by truth, beauty, and goodness and especially by his infinite love. Even God cannot be something he's not.

2. By the will of God, by his mercy and fatherly relationship with all his children.

3. By the law of God, by the righteousness and justice that governs the plans and the actions of God and his creations.

God is unlimited in power, divine in nature, final in will, infinite in attributes, eternal in wisdom, and absolute in reality. All these characteristics of the heavenly Father are unified in and expressed through his Son and Spirit that complete the Paradise Trinity. Remember that it has been said that Jesus is the Word of God, the Word of God made flesh, meaning that Jesus' life is the expression of God's will and the revelation of who God is. God is not finished creating and I doubt that he ever will be. And God's presence, his power, is limited only because such is the will of God and the nature of God.

≈ The God of Jesus ≈

3. God's Universal Knowledge

"God knows all things." The divine mind is conscious of, and conversant with, the thoughts of all creation. His knowledge of events is universal and perfect. The divine spiritual beings going out from him are a part of him; he who "balances the clouds" is also "perfect in knowledge." "The eyes of the Lord are in every place." Said our great teacher of the insignificant sparrow, "One of them shall not fall to the ground without my Father's knowledge," and also, "The very hairs of your head are numbered." "He tells the number of the stars; he calls them all by their names." I wonder what his name is for our world and what our number is?

The heavenly Father is the only personality in all the universe who does actually know the number of the stars and planets of space. All the worlds of every universe are constantly within the consciousness, the awareness, of God. He also says: "I have surely seen the affliction of my people, I have heard their cry, and I know their sorrows." "For the Lord looks from heaven; he beholds all the sons of men; from the place of his habitation he looks upon all the inhabitants of the earth." Every creature child may truly say: "He knows the way I take, and when he has tried me, I shall come forth as gold." "God knows our downsittings and our uprisings; he understands our thoughts afar off and is acquainted with all our ways." "All things are naked and open to the eyes of him with whom we have to do." And it should be a real comfort to every human being to understand that "he knows your frame; he remembers that you are dust." Jesus, speaking of the living God, said, "Your Father knows what you have need of even before you ask him."

God has unlimited power to know all things; his consciousness and awareness is universal. His personality encompasses all personalities, and his knowledge of even the lowly creatures is supplemented indirectly through the presence of his divine Son, his spiritual helpers, and directly through the Indwelling Spirit that lives within us giving God total access 24/7 to everything we think, do and say. God is all the time everywhere present. He never sleeps or takes a break from his duties and responsibilities—to put it in terms we can understand.

I don't know whether or not God chooses to have foreknowledge of acts of sin. But even if God should know the future freewill acts of his children, such foreknowledge does not in the least limit our freedom of choice. But one thing is certain: God is never surprised.

The nature of God's power does not imply the power to do the non-doable, the ungodlike act. Neither does omniscience, his complete knowledge, imply the knowing of the unknowable. But we can hardly understand such statements. The creature, the thing created, can hardly understand the nature, attributes, and limitations of the Creator.

≈The God of Jesus≈

4. God's Limitlessness

God is limitless. He is limitless or unlimited in all that he is and all that he does. As the universe expands and the number of his children grows, God is in no way lessened in power or wisdom. In force, wisdom, and love, the Father has never been reduced or become smaller in any attribute of his glorious personality as the result of the bestowal of himself upon his children or his other creations. This is the infinity of God: no matter how much he gives out of himself, there is no less of him than before. This is the circuit of God: everything that goes out from God returns to the Father, not one is lost.

The creation of every new universe calls for a new adjustment of gravity; but even if creation should continue indefinitely, eternally, even to infinity, so that eventually the number of material creations would exist without limitations, still God's power of control and coordination would be found equal to, and fully adequate for, the mastery, control, and coordination of such an infinite universe. And even after creating such a limitless universe, the Infinite Father would still possess the same degree of force and energy; his power and presence would still be undiminished; God would still possess the same infinite potential, just as if force, energy, and power had never been poured forth for the creation of universe upon universe.

And this is true with wisdom as well: The fact that the mind of God is so freely distributed and shared with each and every one of his spiritual and mortal children in no way reduces the divine wisdom of our heavenly Father. As the universes multiply, and beings of the realms increase in number to the limits of our comprehension and beyond, still will God's personality and being continue to function in perfect coordination with the same eternal, infinite, and all-wise mind—the mind of God.

The fact that he sends forth spirit messengers from himself to indwell the minds of all men and women of our world and other worlds in no way lessens his ability to function as a divine and all-powerful spirit personality. This giving of himself to his children creates a boundless, almost inconceivable future of infinite progress and eternal life for each and every one of us. And this giving of himself does not diminish the all-wise, all-knowing, and all-powerful Father any more than having children diminishes us. We do not become less of a person because we have more children and neither does God.

We are creatures of time and space. We react to and are fully aware of time. We live in space and know east from west and up from down. To us there is a future, but God inhabits eternity and infinity so time and space have no effect upon God or his actions. I'm not sure even Einstein could explain that to us.

We cannot possibly know the infinity of the heavenly Father. Our minds cannot think through such an absolute truth or fact. But we can *feel*—literally experience—the full and loving embrace of such an infinite Father's LOVE. Such a love can be truly experienced. And while the quality of this experience of God's love is unlimited, the quantity of such an experience is only limited by our capacity and willingness to receive it and by our capacity and willingness to return it; to love the Father in return. I believe this is why we exist; this is our purpose. Why did God create us and everything around us? What is the meaning of life and what is my purpose? It is to love God and to be loved by him.

Our Father's mind, personality, and love is far greater than our logical mind can appreciate. We cannot prove God is real but we know that he is because we FEEL him within us and see him all around us. And this is because of the fact that mortal man is made in the image of God—there lives within us a fragment of divinity, a piece of God himself. Our physical body and intellectual mind are the temple of this fraction of our heavenly Father. Therefore our nearest approach to God is not "out there" or "up there" but within us, "in here", by and through love, for God is love. And this unique relationship is an actual experience of the Creator-creature relationship—the affection of a true Father for his child—a parental affection shared by every mother and father of all mortal children.

5. The Father's Supreme Rule

In his contact with his children, the heavenly Father does not assert his infinite power and final authority by direct contact but rather he communicates directly through his Son and the many subordinate personalities that we generalize as angels. Angels are certainly real but so are many other types of spiritual beings. And God does all this sharing of his divine power and authority of his own free will. Any and all power that God has delegated, if need should arise, could be exercised directly if God should choose to do so; but, as a rule, such action only takes place as a result of the failure of the delegated personality to fulfill the divine trust; a failure to do God's will. At such times and within the self-imposed limits of his divine power and supreme rule, the Father does act independently and in a manner of his own choosing; and that choice is always one of unfailing perfection and infinite wisdom. Perhaps when Lucifer and Satan rebelled against God and perhaps when Adam and Eve went astray God may have intervened in our world directly but I suspect that he delegated to his son the task of trying to set things right on this world. He sent Jesus to show us the way; and our world was changed forever.

The Father's rule is supreme. Even though he may delegate action to his Son and the myriads of his spiritual helpers, even to mortals, it is no mere poetic expression that exclaims: "The earth is the Lord's and the fullness thereof." "He removes kings and sets up kings." "The Most Highs rule in the kingdoms of men."

In the affairs of men's hearts the heavenly Father may not always have his way; but in the conduct and destiny of a world or universe the divine plan always prevails; the eternal purpose of wisdom and love triumphs.

Said Jesus: "My Father, who gave them to me, is greater than all; and no one is able to pluck them out of my Father's hand." As you glimpse the many functions and view the staggering immensity of God's almost limitless creation, you may question how such things are possible, but you should not fail to accept him as the creator of all things and as the merciful loving Father of all spiritual and mortal beings. There is but "one God and Father of all, who is above all and in all," "and he is before all things, and in him all things consist."

The uncertainties, trials, and tribulations of life do not in any way contradict the concept of the universal sovereignty of God. All life, our life, is beset by certain *inevitabilities*. Consider the following:

1. Is *courage*—strength of character—desirable? Then must man live in an environment which requires grappling with hardships and reacting to disappointments.

2. Is *altruism*—service of one's fellows—desirable? Then our life experience must provide for encountering situations of social inequality.

3. Is *hope*—the grandeur of trust—desirable? Then we must constantly be confronted with insecurity and uncertainty.

4. Is *faith*—the supreme achievement of human thought—desirable? Then must we find ourselves in that troublesome predicament where we know less than we can believe.

5. Is the *love of truth* and the willingness to go wherever it leads, desirable? Then we must grow up in a world where error is present and falsehood always possible.

6. Is *idealism*—the desire for divine perfection—desirable? Then we must struggle in an environment of relative goodness and beauty, surroundings that stimulate our desire to make things better.

7. Is *loyalty*—devotion to highest duty—desirable? Then we must carry on amid the possibilities of betrayal and desertion. The valor of devotion to duty consists in the implied danger of desertion.

8. Is *unselfishness*—the spirit of self-forgetfulness—desirable? Then we must live with an inescapable ego clamoring for recognition and honor. We cannot choose the divine and righteous life if there were no "self" to forsake. People could never live a life of righteousness if there was no real choice between good and evil.

9. Is *pleasure*—the satisfaction of happiness—desirable? Then we must live in a world where the alternative of pain and the likelihood of suffering are ever-present experiential possibilities. It is the experience of the bad that makes us appreciate the joy of the good.

From individual family members and throughout the universe, every "one" is regarded as a part of the whole. A single child is part of the whole family. A single family is part of a whole community. A single nation is part of a whole world and a single world is part of a whole universe. From that we can see that, not only are each of us a child of God, but also citizens of the whole universe—I like the term cosmic citizens because each of us lives in a part of the cosmic universe.

Survival of the one is dependent upon its cooperation with the plan and purpose of the whole. For us "cosmic citizens," this means that our survival is dependent upon our wholehearted desire and perfect willingness to do the Father's divine will—to follow the plan that is in the mind of God. The only world without error or the potential of sin would be a world without *free will* choice. In Heaven there must be billions of perfect inhabitants, but mortal man here on earth must have the ability to fail, to choose between right and wrong, if he is to be free. Free and inexperienced people cannot possibly, at first, be wise in everything they do. The possibility of mistaken judgment (evil) becomes sin only when the person **consciously chooses and knowingly embraces** a deliberate immoral action.

The full appreciation of truth, beauty, and goodness is inherent in the perfection of Paradise. Perfect or perfected individuals of Heaven do not require the ability to choose the good in contrast to the bad. But all such perfect beings are, in moral nature and spiritual status, what they are by virtue of the fact that they are created perfect even as God is perfect. Mortal man earns his status and standing before the heavenly judges by his own faith and hope. Everything divine which the human mind grasps and the human soul acquires through experience is a *reality* of personal experience and is therefore a unique possession that has been earned. In contrast, the inherent goodness and righteousness and perfection of the angels of Paradise is a birthright. We mortals must strive to be perfect. The native citizens of heaven can be nothing less.

The angels of Heaven are naturally brave, but they are not courageous in the human sense. They are innately kind and considerate, but hardly altruistic in the human way. They are expectant of a pleasant future, but not hopeful in the exquisite manner of the trusting mortal from a world of uncertainty. They have faith in the stability of the universe, but they are complete strangers to that saving faith whereby mortal man climbs from the status of an animal up to the gates of Paradise. They love the truth, but they do not know its soul-saving qualities. They are idealists, but they were born that way; they are wholly ignorant of the ecstasy of becoming perfected beings by choices they make. They are loyal, but they have never experienced the thrill of wholehearted and intelligent devotion to duty in the face of temptation to abandon a cause or purpose. They are unselfish, but they never gained such levels of experience by the magnificent conquest of their own belligerent selfish ego. They enjoy pleasure, but they do not experience the sweetness of pleasure as an escape from the potential of pain.

6. The Father's Primacy

With divine selflessness, consummate generosity, the heavenly Father relinquishes authority and delegates power, but he is still the lord of all with full sovereignty, authority and power; his hand is on the mighty lever of the events and activities of his universes; he has reserved all final decisions and he unerringly wields the all-powerful veto scepter of his eternal purpose with unchallengeable authority over the welfare and destiny of the outstretched, whirling, and ever-circling creation.

The sovereignty of God is unlimited; it is the fundamental fact of all creation. The universe was not inevitable. The universe is not an accident, neither is it self-creating. The universe is a work of creation and is therefore wholly subject to the will of the Creator. The will of God is divine truth, living love; therefore are the creations of the evolutionary universes, growing in perfection and expanding in purpose, characterized by goodness and the potential of evil.

I have absolute confidence in my heavenly Father's overcare; I am committed to doing the will of my Father in Heaven. I do not believe that real harm can befall me. I am absolutely assured that the entire universe is friendly to us because our Father built it to be a home for us to live in and enjoy life everlasting. This all-powerful truth I insist on believing with a wholehearted trust in spite of occasional appearances otherwise; in spite of the character building difficulties that either drive us upward toward perfection or temporarily drag us down in defeat.

All religious philosophy, sooner or later, arrives at the concept of universe rule unified in the one true God. Universe causes cannot be lower than universe effects. Things that create cannot be lower than the things they create. The source of all life and mind must be greater than the life and mind that flows from it. Our mortal mind cannot be explained in terms of the lower orders of mortal existence. The source of our mind comes from something greater than us, not less than us. Our mind can only be truly understood by recognizing the reality of higher levels of mind. Man as a moral being is unexplainable unless the reality of the heavenly Father is acknowledged.

The materialistic philosopher claims to reject the idea of a universal and sovereign God, the very sovereign whose universe laws the philosopher so deeply reveres. What a great compliment it is to our Father when the philosopher claims that such laws are self-creating and self-acting! The universe of God's creation runs like a well-oiled machine.

It is a great mistake to humanize God, to think that God acts like man, but even that is not so ignorant as completely to make God into some mechanical being. The eternal God is incapable of wrath and anger in the sense of these human emotions and as man understands such reactions. These sentiments are mean and despicable; they are hardly worthy of being called human, much less divine; and such attitudes are utterly foreign to the perfect nature and gracious character of the Universal Father.

As we grow in our knowledge and relationship with God and recognize that he is a personality who can love and be loved, some people ask "Does our heavenly Father ever feel pain or suffer?" I do not know. Jesus most certainly did suffer just as we often do. I suspect that our heavenly Father does too, but I cannot understand *how;* perhaps through our Indwelling Spirit he shares our sufferings and our joys. God has said that, "In all your afflictions I am afflicted." He unquestionably experiences a fatherly and sympathetic understanding of all that we experience. When we love someone, we share their joys and their sorrows. Since God loves us unconditionally, I suspect he too shares our triumphs and our defeats. Our Father may truly suffer, but I cannot explain or understand how. If so, I pray that he also shares our blessings and happiness. Perhaps this is the best reason for being happy, adventurous, and loving in this life that we share with God.

The infinite and eternal Ruler of the universe of universes is power, form, energy, process, pattern, principle, presence, and idealized reality. But he is more; he is personal; he exercises a sovereign will, experiences self-consciousness of divinity, executes the mandates of a creative mind, pursues the satisfaction of an eternal purpose, and enjoys a Father's love and affection for all of his universe children. And all these more personal traits of the Father can be better understood by observing them as they were revealed in the life of Jesus while he was here on earth living a life in the flesh as a mortal being. Jesus was and still is the ultimate revelation of God to man and our lord and savior.

In the Trinity, God the Father loves men; God the Son serves men; God the Spirit inspires all God's children to the ever-ascending adventure of finding God, being loved by God, and loving him in return.

In the theoretical beginning, the Father does everything but as the panorama of time and eternity unfolds, it becomes increasingly apparent that even mortal men and women are God's partners in the realization of purpose and destiny of all. Always must God provide the pattern universe, Heaven and Paradise; the perfect personalities, the Father, Son, and Spirit; and the origin of truth, beauty, and goodness for which all of us strive to achieve. Always must God first find man that man may later find God. Always must there be a Universal Father before there can ever be universal sonship and consequent universal brotherhood.

Make note of your thoughts, questions, comments here:

_____

_____

_____

_____

_____

_____

_____

_____

_____

_____

_____

_____

_____

_____

Lesson Eight

God's Relation to the Universe

In the past seven lessons we talked mostly about God himself. Now, let's get a little more specific and look at our Father's relationship with the universe. In these last lessons of our course together, we will discover his relationship to us, progress to our personal relationship to God as revealed in the life and teachings of Jesus, and finish up with how to use all his love and support to live our lives and deal with our daily problems. I hope I am giving you a lot to think about and that you are growing in your knowledge of God and finding stronger feelings of love and friendship and less fear of our heavenly Father.

Our heavenly Father has an eternal purpose pertaining to the material, intellectual, and spiritual activities of the universes, which he is executing throughout all time—from the eternity of the past to the eternity of the future. God created the universes of his own free and sovereign will, and he created them in accordance with his all-wise and eternal purpose. It is doubtful whether anyone except the other members of the Paradise Trinity really know very much about the eternal purpose of God. I suspect that even the angels hold very diverse opinions about the nature of the eternal purpose of God's plan and creations just as we do.

It is easy for us to understand that his purpose in creating heaven and Paradise, his perfect heavenly home, is for his own satisfaction. We create and decorate our home to satisfy us so it is safe to assume that a perfect being like God would create a perfect place in which to live. The existence of all creation must surely be primarily for the pleasure and satisfaction of the perfect and infinite creator of it. I am sure this is true for God's plan and purpose for each of us. I frequently tell people that God does have a plan for their life, but this is not it. Something much greater and more important than this mortal life awaits us in Paradise.

1. The Universe Attitude of the Father

For ages the people of this world have misunderstood the providence of God; providence meaning the protection and watchcare of God for us. Divine providence is not the childish, arbitrary, and material ministry many of us believe it to be. The providence of God consists in the coordinated activities of the celestial beings and the divine spirits who, in accordance with God's divine laws, unceasingly labor for the honor of God and for the spiritual advancement of his children.

We can only imagine and speculate on the vast number of spiritual and material beings who organize, administer, maintain, and connect all the vast domain of our Father's material and spiritual creations. I suspect that the number of entities, beings, and personalities that carry out the providence of God must be beyond our imagination in both types and numbers. We know of God the Father and the Son, the Spirit, Jesus, Gabriel, Melchizedek, the angels, and us but how many more magnificent beings must there be between us and God in order to carry out all the plans and purposes of an infinite God in his infinite realm? If this doesn't make the adventure of finding God exciting then nothing will.

Our purpose here today and every day is to advance in our concept of God's dealing with man to that level where we recognize that the watchword of the universe is *progress.* Through long ages the human race has struggled to reach its present position. Throughout all these millenniums providence has been working out the plan of progressive evolution. The two thoughts are not opposed in practice, only in man's mistaken concepts. Divine providence is never arrayed in opposition to true human progress, either material or spiritual. Providence is always consistent with the unchanging and perfect nature of the supreme Lawmaker.

"God is faithful" and "all his commandments are just." "His faithfulness is established in the very skies." "Forever, O Lord, your word is settled in heaven. Your faithfulness is to all generations; you have established the earth and it abides." "He is a faithful Creator."

There is no limitation of the forces and personalities which the Father may use to uphold his purpose and sustain his creations. "The eternal God is our refuge, and underneath are the everlasting arms." "He who dwells in the secret place of the Most High shall abide under the shadow of the Almighty." "Behold, he who keeps us shall neither slumber nor sleep." "We know that all things work together for good to those who love God," "for the eyes of the Lord are over the righteous, and his ears are open to their prayers."

God upholds "all things by the word of his power." And when new worlds are born, he "sends forth his Sons and they are created." God not only creates, but he "preserves them all." God constantly upholds all material things and all spiritual beings—including us. We are both material and spiritual. The universes are eternally stable. There is stability in the midst of the apparent instability of creation. The universes are still in the making and therefore in the pangs of birth. There is an underlying order and security of the plan in the midst of the creative energy upheavals and the physical cataclysms of the starry realms.

The heavenly Father has not withdrawn from the management of the universes; he is not an inactive god or a lazy father. If God should retire as the present upholder of all creation, there would immediately occur a universal collapse. Except for God, there would be no such thing as *reality.* At this very moment, as during the remote ages of the past and in the eternal future, God continues to uphold all things. His reach extends around the circle of eternity. The universe is not wound up like a clock to run just so long and then cease to function as some scientists predict; all things are constantly being renewed. Scientists even have a "law" for this called "The First Law of Thermodynamics" in which matter or energy cannot be created or destroyed—only converted from one form to another. Claiming that everything came from nothing or that someday everything will cease to exist goes against the very scientific principles scientists proclaim to be fact. The Father unceasingly pours forth energy, light, and life. The work of God is literal as well as spiritual. "He stretches out the north over the empty space and hangs the earth upon nothing."

There is harmony and profound co-ordination in the routine affairs of universe administration. Much that seems disjointed and haphazard to our minds appears orderly and constructive to God and angels. There are many phenomena of the universes that we could never understand and many amazing and beneficial "coincidences" of interactions between the forces, energies, intelligences, and spirits, which we cannot satisfactorily explain. It is the vastness of creation and the interaction of the spiritual with the material that we cannot perceive that makes it impossible for physicists, philosophers, or even religionists to predict with certainty as to just how the primordial forces, concepts, or spirits will respond to each other or to any given situation.

However, there is a basic unity in the universes of time and space which underlies the whole fabric of cosmic events. The living presence of the Supreme Being is the only explanation for the wonderous and amazingly fortunate co-ordination of what we may see as apparently unrelated universe events.

I am inclined to believe that it is this far-flung and generally unrecognizable divine control and co-ordination of all phases and forms of universe activity that causes such a hopelessly confused mixture of physical, mental, moral, and spiritual events to so unerringly work out to the glory of God and for the good of men and angels. But in the larger sense the apparent "accidents" of time—the constant creation, renewal, and metamorphosis of the physical realm—are undoubtedly a part of God's master plan for this universe of universes.

2. God and Nature

What we refer to as nature is the physical creations of God. The actions of God are probably different based on where we look in the universe. God acts in accordance with a well-defined, unchanging, immutable law throughout the wide-spread physical universe. When we speak of scientific laws such as the "Law of Conservation of Energy", "Boyle's law", the "Law of Gravity', and such, these are really God's laws. People will claim that they discovered this or that scientific law as if it is something new but in reality those laws are as old as creation itself: eternal.

Nature presents the underlying foundation and fundamental background of a changeless Deity and his immutable laws. God's laws have been ordained in Heaven.

Nature is a result of two factors: the perfection of God and the imperfection of some of his creations that includes the mistakes, blunders, errors, incompleteness, and imperfection of wisdom on the part of the growing and maturing children of God, from the highest to the lowest. Nature therefore carries a uniform, unchanging, majestic, and marvelous thread of perfection from the circle of eternity; but in each universe, on each planet, and in each individual life, this nature is modified, qualified, and sometimes marred by the acts, the mistakes, and the disloyalties of God's children. Therefore, must nature ever be of a changing mood, whimsical, and though stable underneath; varied in accordance with the nature of all of us and all of God's creatures and creations.

Nature is the perfection of Paradise divided by the incompletion, evil, and sin of the unfinished creations. This quotient is thus expressive of both the perfect and the incomplete, of both the eternal and the earthly. Progressing and continuing evolution modifies nature by augmenting the content of Paradise perfection and by diminishing the content of the error, evil, and disharmony of reality. We see this evolution all around us in the chaos and harmony, immorality and faith, destruction and construction of this world, our society and civilization. We are promised that someday all this will be finished and this world will be like paradise on earth.

God is not personally present in nature or in any of the forces of nature. The phenomenon of nature is the imposition of the imperfections of progressive evolution and, sometimes, the consequences of rebellion, error, evil, and sin upon the foundations of God's natural laws. Nature can never be the full expression, the true representation, the faithful portrayal, of an all-wise and infinite God.

What a travesty to worship nature because it is in a limited sense pervaded by God; because it is a phase of God's creation! Nature is also characterized by the unfinished, the incomplete, and the imperfect outworking of material progress, growth, and evolution.

The apparent defects of the natural world do not indicate any such corresponding defects in the character of God. Such observed imperfections are like the stop-moments between the picture frames of the movie reel of time. It is these very defects that make it possible for us to catch a fleeting glimpse of divine reality in time and space. The material manifestations of God appear defective to our minds only because we persist in viewing the phenomena of nature through natural eyes; human vision without the aid of spiritual wisdom or religious revelation; the counterpart or balance wheel of nature on our material world.

Nature is marred, her beautiful face is scarred, her features are seared, by the rebellion, the misconduct, the erroneous thinking of some of the children of God who are a part of nature. Nature is not God. Nature may be admired and enjoyed but it has no spiritual content. It is not an object to be worshiped.

3. God's Unchanging Character

All too long has man thought of God as one like himself. God is not, never was, and never will be jealous of man or any other being in the universe. Knowing that the Creator Son intended man to be the masterpiece of creation, to be the ruler of all the earth, the sight of man being dominated by his own baser passions, the spectacle of his bowing down before idols of wood, stone, gold, and selfish ambition—these sordid scenes stir God and his Sons to be jealous *for* man, but never of him.

Much, very much, of the difficulty which we have in understanding God is due to the far-reaching consequences of the rebellious Lucifer, Satan, and the one we refer to as the devil. And yes, they are real distinct and separate beings. Describing them as fallen angels may be accurate but it is an insult to angels. These wicked ones rebelled against

God. In Revelations 12:7 it says: "Then war broke out in heaven. Michael and his angels fought against the dragon, and the dragon and his angels fought back." There truly was an actual war in Heaven, but in this spiritual war the casualties were immortal souls, not merely flesh and blood. So while the carnage was not as gruesome as our wars here on earth, the death toll was far more severe. In earthly wars, souls of the dead are saved in heaven. In spiritual war, eternal life is lost and lost forever. While Jesus ended this war when he faced the iniquitous trio here on earth, I believe, we are still fighting a war between good and evil on this planet even today.

Let me interject here some information about this situation where Lucifer and Satan have rebelled against God. Have you ever wondered why supposedly brilliant and experienced spiritual beings like these have a problem with God and Jesus? I mean, what is their problem really?

It is very difficult to point out the exact cause of their prideful rebellious attitude and their objections but it is all well documented for us to discover. No doubt they probably believed that their actions are really for the good of the universe and everyone in it. However, their evil thoughts evolved into deliberate sin and iniquity. They were long offered opportunity for repentance. Just as he would later do with Judas Iscariot, Jesus offered his mercy and forgiveness to these traitors but always was this kindness rejected and rejected with increasing contempt and disdain. Even before his life on earth, Jesus was demonstrating the level God's love for all his children even to the point of loving his enemies. Notice the parallels with Judas' betrayal of Jesus before the crucifixion.

Lucifer questioned the reality of God claiming that the Universal Father does not really exist; that the Father is a myth. He even intimated that there is no proof of the Father's actual existence. Lucifer argued that in our lives unbridled personal liberty should rule. He exhorted his followers to believe that men and angels can rule themselves if only they have the courage to boldly claim their rights. He claimed that salvation is inherent in personalities, that resurrection is natural and automatic and that all beings will live forever without the need for faith in some fictional god. He suggested that we have been enslaved by too much discipline and moral requirements. He advocated that everyone should enjoy the liberty of individual self-determination. With such a declarations of liberty, Lucifer launched his orgy of darkness and death.

Throughout history conquerors first dehumanize and devalue their enemy in order to make it okay to kill them. As Hitler proclaimed that Jews were subhuman, the Japanese of World War II claimed that white people were subhuman, as the white people believed the red man was subhuman, as slave owners believe black people were subhuman, the evil forces, led by Lucifer, in our world today want us to believe that all of us are subhuman, merely animals in nature; that we are of no lasting value. Even our religions teach us that we are born sinners and not worthy of God's love; that only by the unjust sacrifice of an innocent Son of God are we worthy of redemption. In Isaiah 64:6 we are told: "But we are all as an unclean thing, and all our righteousnesses are as filthy rags; and we all do fade as a leaf; and our iniquities, like the wind, have taken us away."

But, the truth is that we are all children of a heavenly Father who loves us and values us so much that he sent his Son to lead us to salvation and eternal life. He gave us the ultimate gift of our Indwelling Spirit—even a part of himself. He created us as the masterpiece of his creation, to be the ruler of all the earth. The Father loves us and wants us to love him.

If we were not separated from the cosmic society by the sins of these wicked ones, we would have far better ideas of the Universal Father and suffer less confusion, distortion, and perversion of concepts of who God is and what God is. This situation causes us to feel that we are separated from God himself when we are not. This is why we need to learn about the God of Jesus. But, as we discussed previously, as a member of the family of God, while we are not contributors to or parties in the sinfulness of Lucifer, we do suffer from the consequences of the acts of all our family members. Even Lucifer is a child of God although a rebellious and iniquitous one. His rejection of God and his attempt to take all of us with him into that rebellion has caused us to be separated from our Father in many ways.

Had Lucifer and Satan not turned against God, we would today experience a much more open and normal experience with God and probably a greater presence of God's helpers here on earth. However, like all bad things, good things came from this. Probably the greatest benefit for us is that Jesus came to our world in an effort to set things right. But, there are many other benefits. Here, he confronted Lucifer and Satan, ended their rebellion and ended the ability of demons to possess mortal minds or lead us astray against our will. Since Pentecost, there has never been another true demon possession. It is only through our own choices that evil and sin can invade our life.

Let me get back on topic . . .

God repents of nothing he has ever done, now does, or ever will do. He is all-wise as well as all-powerful. Man's wisdom grows out of the trials and errors of human experience; God's wisdom consists in the absolute perfection of knowledge and insight effectively directs the creative free will actions of God.

The Universal Father never does anything that causes sorrow or regret, but the children of God, both mortal and spiritual, by their unfortunate choosing, sometimes cause divine sorrow in their Creator Father. The Father neither makes mistakes, harbors regrets, nor experiences sorrows of his own making. However, he is a being with a father's affection, and his heart is undoubtedly grieved when his children suffer, sorrow, and fail to attain the spiritual levels they are capable of reaching with the assistance of his own spirit which he so freely provides for their safety and security.

The infinite goodness of the Father is beyond the comprehension of our finite mind. Therefore, to see and appreciate the goodness of God, or even goodness among ourselves, there must always be a contrast between evil and goodness. It is this contrast that provides us with the ability to recognize and have the freedom to choose between right and wrong, good and evil.

4. The Realization of God

God is the only stationary, self-contained, and changeless being in the whole universe of universes, having no outside, no beyond, no past, and no future. God is creative spirit and absolute will, and these are self-existent and universal.

Since God is self-existent, meaning that nothing created him, he is absolutely independent. He is not dependent upon or indebted to anyone or anything. The very identity of God is unchangeable. "I, the Lord, change not." But his changelessness does not prevent God from making decisions, creating things, or manifesting himself in various forms—such as the Son, the Spirit, all the beings of providence, and our Indwelling Spirit. His absoluteness and perfection does not imply immobility through these manifestations; God has will—he *is* will.

God is the only being of absolute self-determination; there are no limits to what God can do other than those limits which are self-imposed, and his freewill acts are conditioned only by those divine qualities and perfect attributes which inherently characterize his eternal nature. Therefore, is God related to the universe as the being of final goodness plus an infinite free will of creativity.

Our Father is the creator of Paradise, Heaven, the universes and the Father of all other creators—from his Paradise Son down to mortal fathers and mothers. God shares personality, goodness, and many other characteristics with man and other spiritual beings, but infinity of will, absolute freedom of choice, is his alone. God is limited in his creative acts only by the desires of his eternal nature and by his infinite wisdom. As mortals, we have limited freewill choice. We cannot choose to become an Eagle just because we want to fly. God's freedom of choice is absolute in that whatever he desires and wills is.

God's nature is subject to the relationship of the Creator to his universe family. In all his vast family relationships with his children, God is governed only by his own *divine sentiment*; his own feelings and emotions. Remember, we have already proven that God is or has personality. First and last—eternally—the infinite God is a *Father*. Of all the possible titles by which he might correctly be known, to portray the God of all creation as the Universal Father is the most true of all possible descriptions.

In God the Father, freewill choices are not ruled by power, nor are they guided by intellect alone. The divine personality is defined as spirit and demonstrated by love. Therefore, in all his personal relationships with the children of the universes, God is always and consistently a loving Father. God is a Father in the highest sense of the term. He is eternally motivated by the perfect idealism of divine love, and that tender nature finds its strongest expression and greatest satisfaction in loving and being loved.

In science, God is the First Cause; in religion, he is the universal and loving Father; in philosophy, he is the one being who exists by himself, not dependent on any other being for his existence but creating unity of existence for all things and upon all other beings. The First Cause of science and the self-existent unity of philosophy are the God of religion, full of mercy and goodness and pledged to effect the eternal survival of his earthly children.

A victorious human life on earth is born of that personal faith which dares to challenge each recurring episode of existence when confronted with the awful spectacle of human limitations, by the unfailing declaration: "Even if I cannot do this, there lives in me a part of the heavenly Father of the universe of universes who can and will do it." That is "the victory which overcomes the world, even your faith."

5. Erroneous Ideas of God

Many religions suffer from the influence of primitive concepts of God; old truths that are hard to let go of even in the face of new and inspiring truth. We should not reject truth just because it is old but neither should we reject new truth only because of its source. This is the mistake the Pharisees made.

Many primitive religious concepts are preserved in the doctrines of our religious organizations. They are preserved in things like membership applications or church doctrines that require everyone to agree to the exact same concepts of God in order to enter the kingdom of God. Sometimes these are preserved in documents and sometimes literally carved in stone. Such documents welcome people to the temple of the family of God with a message of intolerance for others, the exclusivity of a chosen people, restrictions of belief, and the perception of spiritual arrogance.

It is all too true that such a church cannot survive unless there are people who preferred such a style of worship. Many spiritually indolent souls crave an ancient and authoritative religion of ritual and sacred traditions. They are spiritually lazy and what I call: Sunday morning believers. Human intellectual and spiritual progress are hardly sufficient to enable us to dispense with religious authority. The invisible brotherhood of the Kingdom of Heaven may well include these family groups of various social and temperamental classes. But in the brotherhood of Jesus there is no place for sectarian rivalry, group bitterness, nor assertions of moral superiority and spiritual infallibility.

The God who goes on a rampage in the storm; who shakes the earth in his wrath and strikes down men in anger; who inflicts his judgments of displeasure in times of famine and flood, who requires a human sacrifice to appease his anger, a God of the tribe or nation rather than the person—these are the gods of primitive religions. These are gods made in the image of man before man was told that he is created in the image of God. This is not the God who actually lives and rules the universes. Such concepts are a relic of the times when men supposed that the universe was under the guidance and domination of the whims of such imaginary gods. But people are beginning to realize that the real God lives in a realm of law and order as far as concerns the creation, controlling, upholding and uplifting of the universes.

The barbarous idea of appeasing an angry God, of placating an offended Lord, of winning the favor of Deity through sacrifices and penance and even by the shedding of blood, represents a primitive and immature religion, a philosophy unworthy of an enlightened age of science and truth. This type of religion is rejected more and more by educated and enlightened people. Such beliefs are utterly repulsive to God and all the celestial hosts who serve and reign in the universes. It is an affront to God to believe, hold or teach that innocent blood must be shed in order to win his favor or to divert the fictitious divine wrath. We cannot buy his love and mercy or purchase forgiveness and salvation. These are the religions of man, not of God.

The Hebrews believed that "without the shedding of blood there could be no remission of sin." They had not found deliverance from the old and pagan idea that the gods could not be appeased except by the sight of blood, though Moses made a great advance by forbidding human sacrifices and substituted in the primitive minds of his childlike Bedouin followers, the ceremonial sacrifice of animals. Later on, Jesus replaced even this abhorrent practice with the concept of service rather than sacrifice. The young Jesus was sickened by the sight of the slaughtering of hundreds of animals in the name of his heavenly Father. When he attended Passover as a man, he drove the sacrificial animals and their merchants from the temple.

Jesus taught that it is better to obey the will of God than to offer sacrifices. It is loyalty, not sacrifice, that Jesus demands. The Master said that God is one and there is none beside him. He is quoted in Mark 12:33 telling us: "To love him [God] with all your heart, with all your understanding and with all your strength, and to love your neighbor as yourself is more important than all burnt offerings and sacrifices."

What a travesty upon the true, beautiful, and good character of God to suggest that his fatherly heart in all its austere coldness and hardness was so untouched by the misfortunes and sorrows of his children that his love and tender mercies were not poured out upon mankind until he saw his blameless Son bleeding and dying upon the cross of Calvary! But, do not doubt that in the cross there is greatness and wisdom and demonstration of the truth about God's love for us, how we should love each other, and what lies ahead for all of us. If you want to know God, look to the messages and meanings of the cross. The real meaning of the cross is so much more important, true, beautiful, and good than we have been previously taught.

6. The Part and the Whole

Mercy characterizes God's attitude of love for the individual; equality motivates God's attitude toward the whole. The will of God does not necessarily prevail the heart of any one person but his will does actually rule the whole universe. The individual part of the whole may accept or reject God's will but God's will rules the whole of his creation

In all his dealings with all his children it is true that the laws of God are not arbitrary. They are not without purpose or planning; they are not "make it up as you go" laws. To our limited vision and finite viewpoint, the acts of God often appear to be dictatorial and arbitrary. The laws of God are merely the habits of God, his way of repeatedly doing things; and he always does all things well. We observe that God does the same thing in the same way, repeatedly, simply because that is the best way to do that particular thing in a given circumstance; and the best way is the right way, and therefore always does his infinite wisdom order it done in that same precise and perfect manner.

It is repugnant to the divine nature of God to allow any sort of deterioration or permit the execution of any of his purely personal acts in an inferior way. He always does the best thing in the best way. He is never half-hearted or inept in anything he does. If, in any situation, in an extreme circumstance, the course of supreme wisdom might indicate the need for a different way of doing something—if the demands of perfection dictate another method of action, a better one, then and there would the all-wise God function in that better and more suitable way. That would be the expression of a higher law, not the reversal of a lower law. It would be the fulfillment of God's perfection in all things.

God is not a habit-bound slave to the repetition of his own voluntary acts. There is no conflict among the laws of the Infinite; they are all perfections of his infallible nature; they are all the unquestioned acts expressive of perfect decisions. Law is the unchanging reaction of an infinite, perfect and divine mind. In God there "is no variableness neither shadow of changing." Because God is changeless, you can depend on his doing the same thing in the same identical and ordinary way. God is the assurance of stability for all created things and beings. He is God; therefore he changes not.

The great God is not a helpless slave to his own perfection and infinity. God is not a self-acting automatic force; he is not a slave to his law-bound power. God is neither a mathematical equation nor a chemical formula. He is a freewill personality. He is the Universal Father, a being with personality and the source of all other personality.

The will of God does not uniformly prevail in the heart of the God-seeking mortal, but if the time frame is enlarged beyond the moment to embrace the whole time period of the first life, then does God's will become increasingly visible in the spiritual fruits which are demonstrated in the lives of spirit-led children of God. And then, if human life is further enlarged to include the future spiritual experience of our next life, the glory of actually doing God's will shines brighter and brighter.

The Fatherhood of God and the brotherhood of man present the paradox of the part with the whole on the level of personality. God loves each one of us as an individual child in the heavenly family, yet, God is no respecter of persons. God loves every individual equally and his love for all of his children creates the family relationship, the brotherhood of man.

The love of the Father absolutely individualizes each personality as a unique child of the Universal Father, a child without duplicate in infinity, irreplaceable in all eternity. The Father's love glorifies each child of God, illuminating each member of the celestial family, sharply silhouetting the unique nature of each person against the material levels that lie outside the family of the Father of all. The love of God strikingly portrays the supreme value of each of his children, unmistakably reveals the high value which the Universal Father has placed upon each and every one of us from the highest creator personality of Paradise (the Son) to the lowest personality among the savage tribes of man from the dawn of civilization.

This very love of God for the individual brings into being the divine family of all individuals, the universal brotherhood of all children of the Paradise Father. And this brotherhood, being universal, is a relationship of the individual with the whole and the whole with the individual. Brotherhood, when universal, discloses not the **each** relationship, but the **all** relationship. Brotherhood is a reality of the total and that has qualities not seen in the part. The Brotherhood of man is not just a sum total of the individuals in it but an exponential multiplication of the attributes, talents, and value of the individuals. As individuals, four plus four equals eight but as a unified brotherhood working together then four times four equals sixteen. The larger the family of individuals, the greater the difference. As individuals we are the sum of our parts but as the brotherhood of man we multiply our spiritual power.

Brotherhood is the relationship between every personality in existence. No person can escape the benefits or the penalties that may come as a result of our relationship to other persons. The part profits or suffers to some degree with the whole. The good effort of each person benefits all people; the error or evil of each person brings tribulation to all people. As moves the part, so moves the whole. As the progress of the whole, so the progress of the part. The progress of part and whole determine whether the part is retarded by the stagnation of the whole or carried forward by the momentum of brotherhood.

It is a mystery that God is a highly personal self-conscious being with residential headquarters on Paradise, and at the same time personally present in such a vast universe and personally in contact with us and probably with an almost infinite number of beings throughout all creation. And, while this mystery is beyond human understanding, it should not in the least lessen our faith. Do not allow the magnitude of the infinity, the immensity of the eternity, and the grandeur and glory of the matchless character of God to overawe, stagger, or discourage you; for the Father is not very far from any one of us; he dwells within us, and in him do we all literally move, actually live, and have our being.

Even though the Paradise Father functions through his divine sons and his spiritual and angelic children, he also enjoys the most intimate inner contact with each of us. Knowing what we now know about this indwelling gift of God, we also know that the Father is in intimate touch not only with all his divine associates but also with all of his mortal children. The Father indeed lives on Paradise in Heaven, but his divine presence also dwells in the minds of men. This is probably one of the few instances in which "God works in mysterious ways." How God came to live among us as Jesus is another one of those few mysteries. So, you see, there is some mystery of God but it is a mystery of how he does certain things rather than any mystery of God himself.

Even though the spirit of the Son (Jesus) was poured out upon all flesh at Pentecost as the Spirit of Truth, even though the Son once dwelt with us in the likeness of mortal flesh, even though the angels and seraphim personally guard and guide us, how can any of these divine beings ever hope to come as near to us or to understand us as fully as does the Father, who has given a part of himself to be in us, to be our real and spiritual, even eternal, self?

Make note of your thoughts, questions, comments here:

_____

_____

_____

_____

_____

_____

_____

_____

_____

_____

_____

_____

_____

_____

Lesson Nine

God's Relation to the Individual

For us, probably the most important relationship we have is with God. We have many important relationships However, there is no relationship more important, more intimate, more personal, more complete, or more long lasting than the relationship of God with the individual. So, let's go even deeper into discovering how to develop this relationship and how to benefit from it.

If our finite mortal mind is unable to comprehend how so great and so majestic a God as the Universal Father can descend from his eternal abode in infinite perfection to associate with individual humans, then we must rest assurance of divine fellowship upon the truth of the fact that an actual fragment of the living God resides within the intellect of every normal-minded and morally conscious person. The Indwelling Spirit is part of the eternal Paradise Father. We do not have to go farther than our own inner experience to find God and attempt communion with him.

Have you ever thought about that word "communion"? I think communion is a form of the word communication. In order to have a relationship with someone, some other personality, we must have some communication with that person. Communion with the Father is communicating with the Father. Prayer, worship, and meditation are forms of communication; communing with the Father. The ultimate prayer, in my opinion, is when we get to that point where we are in constant communion with God. We preface everything we think and do by asking for God's guidance and help. We should frequently reaffirm our willingness and choice to do God's will.

God has distributed the infinity of his eternal nature throughout the grand universe of his creation, but he may, at any time, make direct personal contact with any part or person of that creation through his fragments that indwell us. And the eternal God has reserved to himself the bestowing of personality upon all his children, while he further reserves the direct and parental contact with all his children solely for himself and through this Indwelling Spirit, his personal presence within us.

Think about what this means to you here today and every day. God is with you always. Therefore, you are never alone, never without guidance, and never without love; never without a legion of angels and God Almighty himself watching over you and only a whisper away. Life is hard and has it's challenges. Life itself is a mystery. The purposes for our difficulties and the rewards of our joys are a mystery to us. But, remember what I said earlier, in the mind of God there is a plan. If you get nothing else from this course, please know that through all the inevitabilities of life, God loves you and you are never ever alone.

1. The Approach to God

Our difficulty as finite mortal beings in approaching the infinite spiritual Father is not caused by the Father's aloofness, but in the material limitations of our being. The magnitude of the spiritual difference between the highest personality of the universe and the lowest created intelligence—us—is inconceivable. Were it possible for us to be instantly transported into the presence of the Father himself, we would not know we were there.

We would be just as oblivious of the presence of the Universal Father as where we are now. There is a long, long road ahead of us before we can stand in the Paradise presence of the Universal Father.

Our Father is not in hiding; he is not in arbitrary seclusion. He has mobilized the resources of his divine wisdom in a never-ending effort to reveal himself to his children. There is an infinite grandeur and an inexpressible generosity connected with the majesty of his love which causes him to yearn for the association of every one of his children who can comprehend, love, or approach him.

When you love someone, you want to be near them. When you have children you long for them to come home. God loves you and longs for the day when you will be home with him. Think of our Indwelling Spirit as God's cell phone. He is with there with you giving you directions to find your way home through the dark and stormy night of life. And on that day, when the sun breaks through on a new spring day, our Father shall say to you: "Welcome home." Then to all those gathered around he shall say: "This is my beloved son in whom I am well pleased." This is the real beginning of our eternal career of Paradise service.

It is no attribute or fault of God that creates distance between us and God. The choices of our mind allow us to grow closer to or farther from God. Our physical limitations, that is, the current inseparability of our personality from our material body, determine the time, place and circumstances in which we may achieve the supreme goal of life and stand in the very presence of the Father at the center of all things. At some point we must shed this physical body in order to continue our journey to Paradise.

Although the approach to the Paradise presence of the Father must await our attainment of the highest levels of our spirit progression, we should rejoice in the recognition of the ever-present possibility of immediate communion with the spirit of the Father so intimately associated with our inner soul and our spiritualizing self.

We mortals may differ greatly in our abilities and intellectual endowment, we may enjoy environments exceptionally favorable to social advancement and moral progress, or we may suffer from the lack of almost every human aid to culture and civilization. We may come from good loving homes or totally dysfunctional families, but the possibilities for progress in our spiritual ascension career are equal for all. Increasing levels of spiritual insight and cosmic meanings are acquired quite independently of all such social and moral differences of material environments.

However we mortals may differ in our intellectual, social, economic, and even moral opportunities and endowments, our spiritual endowment is uniform and unique. We all enjoy the same divine presence of the gift from the Father, and we are all equally privileged to seek intimate personal communion with this Indwelling Spirit of divine origin, while we may all equally choose to accept their spiritual leading to the fullness of our capacity to do so.

If we are wholeheartedly motivated, unreservedly loyal and dedicated to doing the Father's will, then, since we are so certainly and so effectively spiritually endowed by the indwelling and divine spirit, we cannot fail to know God and have complete assurance of surviving physical death and finding God through the experience of becoming more and more like him; of progressively becoming perfect in our life as God is in his.

We are indwelt by a spirit fragment of God. If we are sincerely and spiritually motivated, if we desire to know God and become like him, honestly want to do the Father's will, there exists no negative influence of mortal deprivation, no power of interference which can prevent such a divinely motivated soul from securely ascending to the gates of Paradise. The Father desires for all his children to be in personal communion with him. He has on Paradise a place to receive all those who have gained salvation.

The Father is not in spiritual hiding, but so many of his children have hidden themselves away in the mists of their own willful decisions and for the time being have separated themselves from the communion of his spirit and the spirit of his Son by the choosing of their own perverse ways and by the indulgence of the self-assertiveness of their intolerant minds and unspiritual natures.

Mortal man may draw near God and may repeatedly forsake the divine will so long as the power of choice remains. Man's final doom is not sealed until he has lost the power to choose the Father's will. There is never a closure of the Father's heart to the need and the petition of his children. Only do his offspring close their hearts forever to the Father's love when they finally and forever lose the desire to do his divine will—to know him and to be like him. Likewise is man's eternal destiny assured when a child of the universe has made the final and irrevocable choice to live the Father's will.

The great God makes direct contact with mortal man and gives a part of his infinite and eternal and incomprehensible self to live and dwell within him. God has embarked upon the eternal adventure with us. If you yield to the leadings of the spiritual forces within you and around you, you cannot fail to attain the high destiny established by a loving God as the universe goal of his ascendant children.

Therefore settle in your hearts and minds now and forever: To each of you and to all of us, God is approachable, the Father is attainable, the way is open; the forces of divine love and the ways and means of divine administration are all coordinated in an effort to facilitate the advancement of every worthy intelligence of every universe, every child of God, to the Paradise presence of the Universal Father.

2. The Presence of God

The physical presence of God is the material universe. The mind presence of God is determined by the depth of our individual intellectual experience and personality. The spiritual presence of God is determined by our spiritual capacity to receive it and by the degree of our commitment to doing of the Father's will.

God lives in every one of his spirit-born sons. The Son and the Spirit of the Paradise Trinity always have access to the presence of God, "the right hand of the Father," and all of his children have access to the "bosom of the Father."

The divine presence cannot, however, be discovered anywhere in nature or even in the lives of God-knowing mortals so fully and so certainly as in our attempted communion with the Indwelling Spirit. What a mistake to dream of God far off in the skies when the spirit of the Universal Father lives within our own mind!

It is because of this fragment of God that lives within us that we can hope, as we progress in harmonizing our will with the will of God, to be more aware of the wisdom, power, and love of the Father and to feel his presence. The fact that you are not conscious of this close and intimate contact with the Indwelling Spirit does not in the least disprove the reality of such an exalted experience. The proof of your relationship with the divine spirit consists wholly in the nature and extent of the fruits of the spirit, the good works you do, which are the result of your faith. "By their fruits you shall know them."

3. True Worship

Though the Paradise Deities of the Trinity are as one, in their spiritual relationship with us, they are also three distinct and separate persons. There is a difference between the gods of the Trinity, God the Father, God the Son, and God the Spirit. But in the matter of personal prayers, communion, and other intimate relations, we worship the Universal Father and him only. True, we can and do worship the Father as he is manifested in the life of his Son, but it is the Father, directly or indirectly, who is worshiped and adored.

Supplications of all kinds belong to the realm of the Eternal Son. That is, we pray in the name of Jesus. Prayers, all formal communications, everything except adoration and worship of the Universal Father, are matters that concern our creator, father, brother, and friend: Jesus. But worship is directly communicated to God the Father himself. The worship and adoration of a spirit-indwelt mortal is facilitated by the Father's spirit presence. Our Indwelling Spirit is the bridge that connects us and sends our worshipful thanksgiving directly to the Father. Worship is our expression of love and appreciation to the Father; prayer contains some element of self-interest in that we pray for something, something for ourselves or for others; that is the great difference between worship and prayer. There is absolutely no element of personal interest in true worship; we simply worship God for what we understand him to be. Worship asks nothing and expects nothing for the worshiper. We do not worship the Father because of anything we may derive from such praise and thanksgiving. We render such devotion and engage in such worship as a natural and spontaneous reaction to the recognition of the Father's matchless personality and because of his lovable nature and adorable attributes.

The moment the element of self-interest intrudes upon worship, in that instant devotion translates from worship to prayer and is more appropriately directed to the Son to be considered and addressed. But in practical religious experience there exists no reason why prayer should not be addressed to God the Father as a part of true worship. Either way, the Indwelling Spirit forwards your prayers and worship to the right person. And so it is: You worship God; pray to, and commune with the Son; and work out the details of your earthly life with the Spirit. This is why we often pray "in the name of the Father, the Son, and the Spirit."

The Son receives, in the name of the Father, the adoration of worship and gives ear to your pleas. Jesus is, to all practical intents and purposes, God. He is the personification of the Universal Father. The Spirit maintains personal contact with the children of God through the Indwelling Spirits.

I doubt that we can ever be aware of the real significance of true worship or its importance to God and the pleasure and joy that it gives him. Our ability to worship God the Father is chiefly determined by the status of our evolving immortal soul. The spiritual growth of the soul is also something we experience but are not intellectually conscious of.

The worship experience consists in the attempt of our Indwelling Spirit to communicate our inexpressible longings and aspirations to the divine Father. Worship is, therefore, the act of the material mind's attempt, under the guidance of the associated spirit, to communicate with God. The mortal mind consents to worship; the immortal soul craves and initiates worship; the divine spirit presence conducts such worship in behalf of the mortal mind and the evolving immortal soul. True worship is an experience of our mind, soul, and spirit, and in unity with our personality.

Worship is our highest privilege and first duty. Worship is the conscious and joyous act of recognizing and acknowledging the truth and fact of the intimate and personal relationship of the Creator Father with his children. The quality of our worship is determined by the depth of our perception; our knowledge of God, and our capacity to love him and be loved by him. The act of worship grows and expands until it attains the glory of the greatest delight and the most exquisite pleasure that we can know and experience. But you can only experience this by worshiping God yourself.

I imagine Paradise as one vast sanctuary of divine service and worship. Worship is the first and greatest passion of all who climb to its blissful shores—the spontaneous rejoicing and praise of God by all who have come to know and love him. During our inward journey from here to Heaven and Paradise, worship is a growing passion. Worship will be our greatest joy of Paradise but it acts as refreshing play for our spirit. What play does for our jaded minds on earth, worship will do for our perfected souls on Paradise.

Worship is the completion of God's eternal plan and purpose for each of us. It is the full satisfaction of his infinite love for us and the ultimate expression of our love for him even to the fullest satisfaction of his own craving to be loved! It may be more blessed to give love than to receive love but I imagine that receiving our love through worship is God's greatest joy, highest pleasure, and most satisfying reward. Never underestimate the value of your worship to your heavenly Father.

≈The God of Jesus≈

4. God in Religion

Religions of the past drive men forward in the quest for God by the motive of fear; often guilt and fear. True religion invites all people to seek for a God of love because they crave to become like him. But religion is not merely a passive feeling of "absolute dependence" and "surety of survival"; it is a living and dynamic experience of spiritual attainment based on faith and service.

The great and immediate service of true religion is the establishment of an enduring unity in human experience, a lasting peace and a profound assurance. The religion of primitive man, polytheism, believing in many gods, is monotheism in the making. Sooner or later, God is revealed as the reality of values, the substance of meanings, and the light of truth.

God not only determines our destiny; he is our destiny. All nonreligious human activities seek to bend the universe to the service of the self; the truly religious individual seeks to identify the self with the universe and then to dedicate his activities, his life, to the service of his universe family of fellow beings: both mortal and spiritual beings.

Philosophy and art intervene between the nonreligious and the religious activities of the human self. Through art and philosophy the material-minded man is led into the contemplation of the spiritual realities of meanings and values.

All religions teach the worship of a god and some doctrine of human salvation. The Buddhist religion promises salvation from suffering, unending peace; the Jewish religion promises salvation from difficulties, prosperity predicated on righteousness; the Greek religion promised salvation from disharmony, ugliness, by the realization of beauty; Christianity promises salvation from sin; Islam provides deliverance from the rigorous moral standards of Judaism and Christianity. The religion of Jesus is salvation from self, aloneness, the deliverance from the evils of isolation in time and in eternity.

The Hebrews based their religion on goodness; the Greeks on beauty; both religions sought truth. Jesus revealed a God of love, and love is all-embracing of truth, beauty, and goodness.

The Zoroastrians had a religion of morals; the Hindus a religion of metaphysics; the Confucianists a religion of ethics. Jesus lived a religion of service. All these religions are of value in that they are valid approaches to God. Religion is destined to become the reality of the spiritual unification of all that is good, beautiful, and true in human experience.

The Greek religion had a watchword "Know thy self"; the Hebrews centered their teaching on "Know thy God"; Christians preach a gospel aimed at a "knowing the Lord Jesus Christ"; Jesus proclaimed the good news of "knowing God, and yourself as a son of God." These differing concepts of the purpose of religion determine the individual's attitude in various life situations and reveal the depth of worship and the nature of his personal prayers. The spiritual status of any religion is determined by the nature of its prayers.

The concept of a human-like and jealous God is an inevitable transition between polytheism and the truth of monotheism. An exalted anthropomorphism, God in the image of man, is the highest attainment level of purely evolutionary religions. Christianity elevated the concept of anthropomorphism from the ideal of the human to the transcendent and divine concept of the person of the glorified Christ. And this is the highest level of anthropomorphism that man can ever conceive.

The Christian concept of God is an attempt to combine three separate teachings:

1. The Hebrew concept—God as a vindicator of moral values, a righteous God.

2. The Greek concept—God as a unifier, a God of wisdom.

3. Jesus' concept—God as a living friend, a loving Father, the divine presence.

This is why this composite Christian theology encounters great difficulty in attaining consistency in the minds of many who are struggling to believe. This difficulty is further aggravated by the fact that the doctrines of early Christianity were generally based on the personal religious experience of three different persons: Philo of Alexandria, Jesus of Nazareth, and Paul of Tarsus.

In the study of the religious life of Jesus, view him positively. Think not so much of his sinlessness as of his righteousness, his loving service. Jesus upstepped the passive love disclosed in the Hebrew concept of the heavenly Father to the higher active fatherly love and affection of a God who is the Father of every individual, even of the wrongdoer.

5. The Consciousness of God

Morality has its origin in the reasoning of the conscious mind. Morality does not deliver us from the real struggles of mortal living. Our physical environment is primarily the battle for existence and physical survival. Our social surroundings require ethical adjustments; the moral choices in the highest realms of reason. The spiritual experience, once we realize God, demands that we find him and sincerely strive to be like him.

Religion is not grounded in the facts of science, the obligations of society, the assumptions of philosophy, or the implied duties of morality. Religion is an independent realm of human response to the situations of life and is unfailingly demonstrated at all stages of our life after we make our first moral decision. Religion permeates all levels of meanings and values and creates the enjoyment of fellowship with others. The first level is the physical or material urge of self-preservation; then the social or emotional level of fellowship with others like us; the sense of morality or duty; and the spiritual level of the awareness of God and our desire for his love and friendship through worship.

The fact-seeking scientist conceives of God as the First Cause, a God of force. Although they cannot give a name to the first cause or the one uncaused cause most are loath to call it God or recognize our belief in his existence. The emotional artist sees God as the ideal of beauty, a God of aesthetics. The reasoning philosopher is sometimes inclined to suggest a God of universal unity, even a pantheistic Deity—a god without personality. The religionist of faith believes in a personal god who fosters survival, the Father in heaven, the God of love.

Moral conduct is always the prelude of religion and is even a part of revealed religion, but morality is never the whole of religious experience. Social service is the result of moral thinking and religious living. Morality does not biologically lead to the higher spiritual levels of religious experience. The adoration of the abstract beautiful is not the worship of God; neither is exaltation of nature nor the reverence of unity the worship of God.

True religion is the mother of the science, art, and philosophy which elevate man to the level of revealed religion, including the bestowal of Indwelling Spirits and the blessing of the Spirit of Truth and the Holy Spirit. Human existence begins and ends with religion, although very different qualities of religion exist from the beginning to the end. And so, while religion is normal and natural to man, it is also optional. Man does not have to be religious against his will. Even the all-powerful God refuses to force that choice upon anyone even though he could.

Religious experience, being essentially spiritual, can never be fully understood by the material mind; this is the function of theology, the psychology of religion. The realization of God creates a paradox in our minds. It is almost impossible for human logic and material reasoning to harmonize the concept of divine immanence, the idea of God within us, with the idea of God's omniscience or everywhere presence. How can God be everywhere in the universe but also personally present within me? These two essential concepts of God can only be unified through faith in the transcendence of a personal God and in the realization of the indwelling presence of a fragment of that God. This is the only way we can justify intelligent worship and validate our hope of personal salvation. The difficulties and paradoxes of religion are inherent in the fact that the realities of religion are utterly beyond our limited capacity for understanding it all.

Mortal man secures three great satisfactions from religious experience, even in the days of his temporal life on earth:

1. Intellectually he acquires the satisfactions of a more unified mind.

2. Philosophically he enjoys the validation of his ideals of moral values.

3. Spiritually he thrives in the experience of divine companionship, in the spiritual satisfactions of true worship.

By the unification of these three factors of the divine realization, no matter how incomplete, the mortal personality can at all times see the personality of God everywhere and in everybody.

The experience of God-consciousness remains the same from generation to generation, but with each advancing epoch in human knowledge the philosophic concept and the theologic definitions of God must change. God-knowingness, religious consciousness, is a reality, but no matter how valid (real) our religious experience is, it must be willing to subject itself to intelligent criticism and reasonable philosophic interpretation; it must not seek to be a thing apart in the totality of human experience. Religion is rather the whole of human experience.

Salvation, eternal survival, life after death, immortality—is wholly dependent on the choosing of the mortal mind, whose decisions determine the survival potential of the immortal soul. When the mind believes God and the soul knows God, and when, with the fostering Spirit, they all desire God, then is survival assured. Limitations of intellect, curtailment of education, deprivation of culture, impoverishment of social status, even inferiority of the human standards of morality resulting from the unfortunate lack of educational, cultural, and social advantages, cannot invalidate the presence of the divine spirit in such unfortunate and humanly handicapped but believing individuals. The arrival of the Indwelling Spirit is the birth of the immortal soul and insures the possibility of its growth and survival.

The ability of mortal parents to procreate is not based on their educational, cultural, social, or economic status. The union of the parental factors under natural conditions is quite sufficient to initiate offspring. A human mind discerning right and wrong and possessing the capacity to worship God, in union with a divine Spirit, is all that is required in any mortal to initiate and foster the production of his immortal soul if such a spirit-endowed individual seeks God and sincerely desires to become like him, honestly elects to do the will of the Father in heaven.

6. The God of Personality

The Universal Father is the God of personalities. He is the domain of universe personality, from the lowest mortal personality status to the highest personalities of the Trinity. All personality comes from God. God the Father gives personality and preserves all personality. The Paradise Father is not only the source of personality but also the destiny of all those personalities who wholeheartedly choose to do the divine will, those who love God and long to be like him.

Personality is one of the unsolved mysteries of the universes. We are able to recognize the behaviors that make-up various types of personalities, but we do not fully comprehend the real nature of personality itself. We clearly perceive the many factors which, when put together, constitute the human personality, but we do not fully comprehend the nature and significance of such a personality.

Personality is potential in all beings who possess a level of mind ranging from the minimum of self-consciousness to the maximum of God-consciousness. But mind alone is not personality, neither is spirit nor physical energy. Personality is that quality and value in cosmic reality which is exclusively bestowed by God the Father upon his children of matter, mind, and spirit. Personality is not a progressive achievement; it does not evolve or grow. There either is personality or there is no personality. The non-personal never gains personality, never becomes personal, except by the direct action of the Paradise Father. There is no personality apart from God the Father, and no personality exists except for God the Father.

Our Indwelling Spirit does not have personality as it is a fragment of God. But it is the potential merger of this immortal spirit with the mortal personality that insures that these same beings may survive mortal death. When they join together or fuse into one organism, much like the male and female elements combine to create a new child, the personality and the spirit combine to create the soul. This personality and this spirit fragment unite with each other to bring into existence the surviving immortal soul.

Having provided for the growth of the immortal soul and having liberated man by granting him freewill choice, the Father stands aside. Having been thus liberated, it remains for man himself to enable the creation or to inhibit the creation of this surviving and eternal self. It is up to us to choose. The way I see this is that God gives us life. He then patiently waits to see what we make of it. Like the parable of the talents, which we all know from Matthew 25:14-30, God gives us life and the freedom to make what we can of it. The more talents you are blessed with, the more is expected of you. And, in the end, each life is a beautiful thing. As pertains to our eternal survival, God has decreed the sovereignty of the material and mortal will, and that decree is absolute. No other being, force, or agency in all the wide universe of universes can interfere to any degree with the absolute sovereignty of our mortal free will as it operates within the arena of choice regarding the eternal destiny of our personality.

The bestowal of personality frees us from slavish mechanical responses to the situations of life. All personalities are ever drawn towards the ultimate personality of the Paradise Father as a member of the vast and universal family and fraternity of God. Our personality comes from God and is drawn to God. God himself is personally aware of and in direct personal contact with each of us. There is spontaneity and creativity in all personality.

7. Who did Jesus say that God is?

Jesus taught that we are not legal subjects of an all-powerful king but rather we are privileged sons and daughters of a loving and divine Father. He taught that when the Father's will is your law, you are hardly in the kingdom. But when the Father's will becomes truly your will, then are you truly in the kingdom because the kingdom has become an absolute experience in you. When God's will is your law, you are noble slave subjects; but when you believe in this new gospel of divine sonship, our Father's will becomes your will, and you are elevated to the high position of the free children of God, liberated sons of the kingdom.

We read in the old Testament that God is a jealous God, a God of great wrath and fierce anger. The old prophets say he hates evildoers and takes vengeance on those who obey not his law. However, the new revelation of God that Jesus taught is that God is a kind and compassionate Father who so loves all men that he welcomes everyone into the kingdom of heaven. Our Father in Paradise is changeless. But our relation with God and our understanding of the nature of God has enlarged and grown from the days of Moses down through the generations of the prophet Isaiah and to this revelation of God by and through the life of Jesus. Jesus came, among other reasons, to reveal the Father in new glory and to show forth his love and mercy to all men on this world and all the worlds of his creation. As the gospel of this kingdom spreads over all the earth with its message of good cheer and good will to all men, there will grow up improved and better relations among the families of all nations. As time passes, fathers and mothers and their children will love each other more, and thus will be brought about a better understanding of the love of the heavenly parent for his children on earth. Remember, that a good and true father not only loves his family as a whole but he also truly loves and affectionately cares for each individual member of that family; not only his children but his children's children.

When our children are very young and immature, and when we must chastise them, they may reflect that their parent is angry and filled with resentful wrath. Their immaturity cannot penetrate beyond the punishment to discern the parent's farseeing and corrective affection. But when these same children become grown-up men and women, would it not be folly for them to cling to these earlier and misconceived notions regarding their father?

As men and women they should now discern their parent's love in all these early disciplines. And should not mankind, as the centuries pass, come to understand better the true nature and loving character of the Father in heaven? What profit have you from successive generations of spiritual illumination if you persist in viewing God as Moses and the prophets saw him? I say to you, under the bright light of this hour you should see the Father as none of those who have gone before ever beheld him. And thus seeing him, you should rejoice to enter the kingdom wherein such a merciful Father rules, and you should seek to have his will and love dominate your life forever more."

And now we know God as our Father in heaven. Jesus' teaching provides a religion wherein the believer *is* a son of God. That is the good news of the gospel of the kingdom of heaven. The Gospel is: the Fatherhood of God and the brotherhood of mankind.

Jesus came not to reveal the Father of the children of Israel, but rather to bring this knowledge of God and the revelation of his love and mercy to the individual believer—all individual believers—as a genuine personal religious experience. The prophets taught that Yahweh cares for his people, that God loves Israel and that is true. But Jesus taught a greater truth, that God loves us—every one of us—as individuals. In the past and even today we have all these national or racial religions but Jesus gave us a personal religion—a close personal relationship with our Father in Heaven.

Jesus always had trouble trying to explain to the apostles that, while they proclaimed the establishment of the kingdom of God, the Father in heaven *is not a king*. At the time Jesus lived on earth and taught in the flesh, the people knew mostly of kings and emperors in the governments of the nations, and the Jews had long contemplated the coming of the kingdom of God. For these and other reasons, the Master designated the spiritual brotherhood of man as the kingdom of heaven and the spirit head of this brotherhood as the *Father in heaven*. Never did Jesus refer to his Father as a king. After the feeding of the 5000 Jesus himself rejected the opportunity to become a king.

Jesus never gave his apostles a systematic lesson concerning the personality and attributes of the Father in heaven. He never asked men to believe in his Father; he took it for granted they did. Jesus never belittled himself by offering arguments in proof of the reality of the Father. His teaching regarding the Father all centered in the declaration that he and the Father are one; that he who has seen the Son has seen the Father; that the Father, like the Son, knows all things; that only the Son really knows the Father, and also those to whom the Son has revealed the Father; that he who knows the Son also knows the Father; and that the Father sent him (Jesus) into the world to reveal their combined natures and to show forth their joint efforts. He never made other pronouncements about his Father except to the woman of Samaria at Jacob's well, when he declared, "God is spirit."

You learn about God from Jesus by observing the divinity of his life; you learn about life by depending on his teachings. From the life of the Master we may each absorb a concept of God that matches our current capacity to perceive spiritual and divine realities. We as mortals on a material world can never hope to comprehend the Infinite Spirit God except as it was revealed to us in the human life of Jesus of Nazareth.

God can only be truly known by the realities of our own personal experience; never can God be understood by the mere intellectual teaching of the mind. Jesus taught his apostles that, while they can never fully understand God, they can most certainly *know* him, even as they knew Jesus himself. We can know God, not by understanding what Jesus said, but by knowing what Jesus taught and even more by what he did. Jesus *was* a new revelation of God.

Jesus only referred to Deity by two names: God and Father. Jesus never called the Father a king. Jesus employed the word "God" to designate the *idea* of Deity and the word "Father" to designate the *experience* of knowing God. We cannot really define the word "God" because it stands for the infinite concept of the Father. We often use it as his name. The word "Father," which we can define and understand, represents our highest human concept of the divine Father and our relationship with him. We often use the word "god" as a designation of all the many spiritual beings.

Jesus introduced the idea of the fatherhood of God and the world-wide brotherhood of man. He exalted the Yahweh concept of a racial God to the idea of a Father of all the children of men, a divine Father of the individual believer. And he further taught that this God of universes and this Father of all men were one and the same.

Jesus proclaimed himself as the revelation of the Father in the flesh, and he did say that he who has seen him has seen the Father.

Although Jesus revealed the true nature of the heavenly Father in his earth life, he taught little about him. In fact, he taught only two things: that God is spirit, and that, in all matters of relationship with his children, he is a Father.

Jesus is the spiritual lens in human form that makes visible he who is invisible. Jesus is our elder brother who, in the flesh, makes *known* to us a Father of infinite attributes. But all of this must consist in the personal experience of the *individual believer*. God who is spirit can be known only as and through a spiritual experience. God can be revealed to us by the divine Son only as a *Father*. We can know the Eternal as a Father; we can worship him as the God of universes, the infinite Creator of all things and beings.

And so the decision awaits each of us as it awaits all of us: Will you fail God who is so dependent upon your personal freewill decisions? Will you fail the supreme personality of the universes by slothfulness or animalistic behavior? Will you fail Jesus, the great brother of all men and women, who is so dependent on each us in his mission to bring peace on earth and goodwill to all mankind? Can you allow yourself to pass into oblivion when before you lies the enchanting horizon of the eternal universe career— participation in the search for and the discovery of the Paradise Father?

The world is filled with hungry souls who famish in the very presence of the bread of life; men die searching for the very God who lives within them. Men seek for the treasures of the kingdom with yearning hearts and weary feet when they are all within the immediate grasp of living faith. Faith is to religion what sails are to a ship; it is an addition of power, not an added burden of life. There is but one struggle for those who enter the kingdom, and that is to fight the good fight of faith. The believer has only one battle, and that is against doubt—unbelief.

Make note of your thoughts, questions, comments here:

Lesson Ten
Our Relationship with God

1. The I AM

I am certain that God is so much more than I am presenting here but I know too that we have eternity to get to know God and someday we will certainly stand in his presence.

Let me offer some further ideas about who God is with a list of seven ways that God functions and how these functions enable us to know him better.

1. God is the Universal Father, that is, the father of all. The existence of the Son makes God a father. The creation of all of us by the Son makes God our father and the father of all. All things are a part of the Universal Father. The Father is living love, and this life of the Father is in his Son. And the spirit of the Father is in his Son's sons—mortal men. When all is said and done, the Father idea is the highest human concept of God.

2. God is the Universal Controller. God **manages** all and everything of both the spiritual and material realms.

3. God is the Universal Creator. God **creates** all and everything of both the spiritual and material realms.

4. God is Infinite Potential. God has the power and potential to create and manage the all and everything of both the spiritual and material realms now and all that may come into existence in the eternal future. With God, all things are possible. The potential of God's actions is infinite and eternal—unlimited and everlasting.

5. God has Infinite Capacity. Because God is infinite and all things exist within and for God, he has virtually unlimited capacity to create as much of anything he wishes to create. I once sent out a Christmas letter about "What do you get the person who truly has everything?" (meaning God) God has everything already. In fact, he created it. If he wants something or more of something he has the capacity and power to create it himself. So think about this: "What gift can you give to God that he doesn't already have?" There is one thing that you have that God truly wants.

6. God is Infinity. In him we all live and move and have our being, from the mortals of this world to the spiritual citizens of Paradise; and this is just as true of the master universe as of the infinitesimal electron, just as true of what has been, which now is, and that which will be.

It is the spirit within us who creates our unquenchable yearning and incessant longing to find God and be like him and achieve Paradise. There we shall worship the source of our divine spiritual gift and discover the ultimate purpose God has for our life. The spiritual presence within us acts like gravity, spiritual gravity, to draw us nearer; "nearer my God to thee." The Indwelling Spirit fills the gap between our Father in heaven and us here on earth so that God is always and instantly present and we are never removed from God's presence. Do not make the fatal mistake, of looking for the kingdom of heaven far off in the cosmos, when in fact it is here today within your own soul.

Previously we talked about how God is simultaneously present "in heaven above and on the earth beneath"; as the Psalmist exclaimed: "Whither shall I go from your spirit? or whither shall I flee from your presence?"

"I am a God at hand as well as afar off." says the Lord. "Do I not fill heaven and earth?" The Universal Father is all the time present in all parts and in all hearts of his far-flung creation. He is "the fullness of him who fills all and in all, who works all in all."

When we are told that we are created in the "image of God", this does not refer to physical likeness nor to our mind, skills, or talents but rather to the gift of the spirit presence of the Universal Father that lives within us. God is spirit and we are spiritually created in his image or likeness. God does not have a physical body. Our physical body is not eternal; it returns to the dust from whence it came. So our physical being is not the image of God but rather it is our potential eternal spiritual being that is. Our physical body usually lasts about 80-90 years but our spirit has the potential to be eternal; immortal.

It is this spiritual gift, the spiritual presence, that distinguishes us from mere animal creatures. While our bodies are material, even animalistic with animalistic desires and reactions, we are spiritual personalities created in the image of God. Our challenge in this dual life of material and spiritual is to overcome the one and advance the other.

Our faithful spiritual guides are slowly changing us from being purely materialistic to being wholly spiritual—to be born again. This spiritual birth is necessary to prepare us for resurrection and residence in one of the many mansions Jesus told us about.

These heavenly helpers are dedicated to the stupendous task of guiding you safely inward and upward to Paradise, the celestial haven of happiness. These tireless toilers are the watchful workers who pilot the God-conscious human mind away from the shoals of evil while expertly guiding our growing soul toward the divine harbors of perfection on far-distant and eternal shores. They are loving leaders, our safe and sure guides through the dark and uncertain maze of our short earthly career; they are the patient teachers who so constantly urge their students forward in the progressive path of perfection. We should strive to love them more, co-operate with them more fully, and cherish them more affectionately.

Perhaps in this experience of being born again we can see ourselves as the human parent, and our Indwelling Spirit as the spiritual parent, of our higher and advancing self, our immortal soul. Perhaps in this way we can discover another of the truths and examples of Jesus' life in that materially we are sons of man and spiritually we are sons of God. I think one of the great failures of all religions and one of the reasons why people today are so lost and life is so cheap is because we have failed to educate people about their spiritual nature and their spiritual value and the great and glorious potential they have for the future. Take that away from a person and all they have left is their material animal nature of no value, no meaning, no potential and no hope or accountability.

So, the Indwelling Spirit is leading us to become less material and more spiritual until that day when this spiritual embryo has matured to spiritual adulthood and the Father of all creation welcomes his prodigal child home. Oh! What a day that will be! The

Indwelling Spirit also allows the spiritual Father to know us, our life's hardships and blessings, and to extend his unconditional love and forgiving mercy to us.

We have begun an endless unfolding of an almost infinite panorama, a limitless expanding of never-ending, ever-widening spheres of opportunity for exhilarating service here and in the life to come; a matchless adventure of thrilling uncertainty, and boundless achievement. When the clouds gather overhead, remember the presence of the indwelling Spirit within you, and while we may not understand how or why God blesses us with this gift of himself, we should be able to look beyond the mists of uncertainty into the clear shining of the sunlight of the beckoning heights of Heaven and Paradise with our Father standing in the door waving us in for the welcoming feast.

What do you give someone who truly has everything? Yourself. God has given himself to you in hopes that you will give yourself to him. He has first loved you in hopes that you will love him too.

2. The Mind Arena of Choice

Our mind is the arena in which we live, are self-conscious, make decisions, choose God or forsake him, eternalize or destroy ourselves.

Material creation has provided us a life machine, our physical body; the Father himself has endowed us with the purest spirit reality, our Indwelling Spirit. But into our hands, subject to our own personal decisions, he has given us mind. It is by mind that we live or die. It is within our mind and with our mind that we make those moral decisions which enable us to achieve spiritual progress and progressively become more like God— or not.

In this struggle, it is not so important what our mind understands or knows as what our mind desires to know that insures our survival; it is not so much what our mind is like as what our mind is striving to become that produces spirit progress and maturity. It is not so much that we are conscious of God, as that we yearn for God, that results in our ascension to heaven. What we are today is not so important as what we are becoming day by day and in eternity.

Mind is the instrument on which we can play the discords of destruction, or upon which we can bring forth the exquisite melodies of God consciousness and eternal survival. The spirit gift in man is impervious to evil and incapable of sin, but mortal mind can actually be twisted, distorted, and rendered evil and ugly by the sinful actions of a perverse and self-seeking human will. However, this same mind can be made noble, beautiful, true, and good—actually great—in accordance with the spirit-illuminated choices of a God-knowing person.

We do not passively, slavishly, surrender our will to the doing of God's will. Rather do we actively, positively, and co-operatively CHOOSE to follow the spirit's leading when such leading differs from the desires and impulses of our natural mortal mind.

Mind is your ship; the Indwelling Spirit is your pilot; the human will is captain. The master of the mortal vessel should have the wisdom to trust the divine pilot to guide the ascending soul into the harbors of eternal survival. Only by selfishness, slothfulness, and sinfulness does man reject the guidance of such a loving pilot and eventually wreck their mortal life upon the evil shoals of rejected mercy and upon the rocks of embraced sin. With your consent, this faithful pilot will safely carry you across the barriers of time and the handicaps of space to the very source of the divine mind, the Paradise Father.

3. The Consecration of Choice

The doing of the will of God is nothing more or less than our willingness to share our inner life with God—with the very God who has made such a life possible. Sharing is Godlike—divine. God shares all with his Eternal Son and the Infinite Spirit, while they, in turn, share all things with us.

The imitation of God is key to the perfection we are commanded to seek; the doing of his will is the secret of survival and of perfection in survival. To put it in more human terms: I want to be like my Father when I grow up.

We, and all things, live in God, and so God has chosen to live in us. As men trust themselves to him, so has he—and first—trusted a part of himself to be with men. He has consented to live in men and to indwell men upon their invitation for him to do so. We love God because he first loves us.

Peace in this life, survival in death, perfection in the next life, service in eternity—all these are achieved now when we choose to submit our will to the Father's will. But the Father already has chosen to make a fragment of himself subject to our will; our choice to accept God, have faith in God, and the wholehearted desire to be like God. Such a choice is not a surrender of will. It is a consecration of will, a dedication of will, an expansion of will, a glorification of will, a perfecting of will; and such choosing raises our own freewill choice from the level of earthly material significance to that higher realm where we commune with the spirit Father through prayer and worship but even more so to that level of constant communion when we recognize that God is within us and always with us and that we are never alone or separated from his love and guidance.

This choosing is not a rejection of our will in favor of God's will—"Not my will but yours be done"—but rather our positive affirmation: "It is my will that your will be done." And if this choice is made, sooner or later the will of the God-choosing person will become perfectly in tune and in full agreement with the will of God. They will then find supreme personal peace, joy, and satisfaction in the worship of their Maker; the two wills become one and that result in the birth of the eternal partnership of man and God—our immortal soul.

≈The God of Jesus≈

4. The Human Paradox

Many of our daily troubles come from the fact of our dual nature. We are a part of nature and yet we are so much more than nature. We are finite, but we have a part that is infinite. This dual situation not only creates the potential for evil but also creates many social and moral situations filled with great uncertainty and much anxiety.

The courage required for our physical nature to rise above our self is a courage that could also fall victim to the temptations of self-pride. The person who can transcend self might yield to the temptation to deify his own self. Our dilemma consists in the double fact that we are in bondage to nature while at the same time we possess a unique freedom of spiritual choice and action. On material levels we find ourselves subservient to nature, while on spiritual levels we are triumphant over nature and over all things earthly and material. Such a paradox includes great spiritual rewards but it also allows for temptation, potential evil, mistakes to be made, and when our self becomes proud and arrogant, sin may evolve.

Lucifer was a glorious and beautiful angel, highly respected and well experienced, a child of God, and Jesus was his father-creator just as he is ours. Lucifer allowed his pride-filled nature to lead him into temptation, to potential evil. Mistakes were made, and when he was not able to overcome his proud and arrogant self, sin was the result. When Jesus confronted him here on earth, Jesus offered his forgiveness and mercy to both Lucifer and Satan. But they rejected their father's loving mercy and fell into iniquity. Someday, judgement will determine their fate. Only God's mercy is delaying their inevitable end until everyone agrees that they were dealt with fairly and justly. On that day, the heavens will open up to us and we will, as a planet, rejoin the heavenly family of cosmic citizenship.

5. Evil, Sin, and Iniquity

It was the habit of Jesus two evenings each week to hold special conversations with individuals who desired to talk with him, in a certain secluded and sheltered corner of the Zebedee garden. At one of these evening conversations in private, the Apostle Thomas asked the Master this question: "Why is it necessary for men to be born of the spirit in order to enter the kingdom? Is rebirth necessary to escape the control of the evil one? Master, what is evil?" When Jesus heard these questions, he said to Thomas:

"Do not make the mistake of confusing evil with error, or sin, or iniquity.

"Evil is the unconscious or unintended transgression of the divine law, the Father's will. Evil is likewise the measure of the imperfection of our obedience to the Father's will.

"Sin is the conscious, knowing, and deliberate transgression of the Father's will. Sin is the measure of unwillingness to be divinely led and spiritually directed.

"Iniquity is the willful, determined, and persistent transgression of the divine law, the Father's will. Iniquity is the measure of the continued rejection of the Father's loving plan and the Son's merciful ministry of salvation.

"By nature, before the rebirth of the spirit, mortal man is subject to inherent evil tendencies, but such natural imperfections of behaviour are neither sin nor iniquity. We are just beginning our long ascent to the perfection of the Father in Paradise. To be imperfect is not sinful. We are indeed subject to evil but we are in no sense children of the father of iniquity or captives of the prince of darkness unless we knowingly and deliberately choose the paths of sin and a life of iniquity.

Evil is a natural part of life on this world because we are intentionally created as imperfect beings. But sin is an attitude of conscious rebellion which was brought to this world by those evil ones who fell from spiritual light into gross darkness—Lucifer, Satan, and the devil,

"Men are, indeed, evil by nature, but not necessarily sinful. Remember our definitions of evil and sin. The new birth—the baptism of the spirit—is essential to deliverance from evil and necessary for entrance into the kingdom of heaven, but none of this detracts from the fact that man is a son of God. Neither does this presence of potential evil mean that man is in some mysterious way estranged or separated from the Father in heaven and his love for us.

Lucifer himself is powerless to steal away any of God's children unless that child chooses the path of sin. Remember that the thing created cannot be greater than the creator. Lucifer cannot be more powerful than his father Jesus. Lucifer has the freewill to reject the Father but he does not have the power to steal away any of God's children.

Lucifer cannot demand ransom for something he does not possess. We are children of God. Lucifer is not our owner and therefore we do not need to be ransomed from him. Jesus is our father-creator; not Lucifer. And since the day of Pentecost, demon possession was made impossible by the pouring out of the Spirit of Truth upon all people.

When a person wishes to modify his physical reality, be it themselves or their material environment, they succeed to the extent that they have discovered ways and means of controlling matter and directing energy. When we wish to modify our spiritual reality, we do it by discovering the spiritual nature and spiritual presence within us and then learning how to use it to grow and progress our spiritual reality. And our Indwelling Spirit stands ever ready to assist us in that effort.

6. The Indwelling Spirit's Problem

The Indwelling Spirit cannot stop or even change our mortal life struggles; the Spirit cannot lessen the hardships of life as we journey on through this world of toil. The divine indweller can only patiently wait while we fight the battles of this life; but you could, if you only would—as you work and worry, as you fight and toil—permit your valiant spiritual partner and life aid to fight with you and for you. You could be so comforted and inspired, so enthralled and intrigued, if you would only allow the spirit within you to bring forth the real motives, the final aim, and the eternal purpose of all this difficult, uphill struggle with the commonplace problems of our life.

Why do you not aid the Spirit in the task of showing you the spiritual counterpart of all these strenuous material efforts? Why do you not allow the Spirit to strengthen you with the spiritual truths of cosmic power while you wrestle with the everyday difficulties of existence? Why do you not encourage the heavenly helper to cheer you with the clear vision of the eternal outlook of life as you gaze in confusion at the problems of today? Why do you refuse to be enlightened and inspired by the universe viewpoint while you toil amidst the handicaps of time and flounder in the maze of uncertainties which plague your mortal life journey? Why not allow your indwelling partner to spiritualize your thinking, even though your feet must, for now, tread the material paths on your heavenly journey?

That which the enlightened and unselfish spiritually motivated person wants to do and be, comes about in accordance with the degree of dedication to the doing of the Father's will. When man goes in partnership with God, great things may, and do, happen.

7. The Finite God

God is so trusting, so loving, that he gives a portion of his divine nature into the hands of even human beings for safekeeping but also to help us progress, grow, and experience. I can imagine that God, being perfect all the time might get bored with his perfection. So maybe, he sends a part of himself to experience life with us so that by experiencing sorrow he can feel joy, by experiencing defeat he can know victory, by experiencing hate and anger he can feel love and peace. I don't really know, of course, but I know how bored and restless I get when there is nothing to do, nothing to build, or no problems to solve.

Mankind does not ascend effortlessly in the universe, neither does he progress without purposeful and intelligent action. We do not attain perfection by passively accepting it like some spiritual welfare check; we must earn it. At the end of the movie "Saving Private Ryan", Tom Hanks, as he lays dying after saving Private Ryan, tells Private Ryan to "Earn this." And, salvation is a gift from God but it is also something we must earn. We earn it not from our good works. We earn it by faith—our trust in God and the choosing to do his will. Good works are the fruits of the spirit—the results. We earn salvation from finding God and putting our faith trust in God, that is, choosing to do his will and striving to become like God in all that we think, do and say.

And so the decision awaits each of us: Will you fail God, our heavenly father who is so dependent upon the decisions and choices we make? Will you fail the Supreme personality of the universe by the laziness of an animalistic ease seeking nature? Will you fail the great father, brother, friend of all mankind? Will you allow your selfish ego to end your journey on the ultimate adventure—the divine discovery of the Paradise Father, the thrilling adventure of seeking God and finding him and the vast rewards of success that await you?

God does not separate himself from his creation. God as the creator of all that he creates is also part of all that he creates. God first loves man and gives him the potential of immortality—eternal life. And as man loves God, so does man become eternal. And here is some mystery for you: The more closely a person approaches God through love, the greater the reality of that person. Remember when I said that this material life is the shadow of the spiritual world, that the spiritual universe is the true reality? Material things come and go. Materially we blink into and out of existence but once we achieve our spiritual nature, we are forever. And that is the truth of reality. The more spiritual we are the more real we are. The more man withdraws from God, the more nearly he becomes unreal—the permanent end of existence. When man consecrates his will to the doing of the Father's will, when man gives God all that he has, then does God make that man more than he is.

The religion of Jesus transcends all our former concepts of the idea of worship in that he not only portrays his Father as the ideal of infinite reality but positively declares that this divine source of values and the eternal center of the universe is truly and personally attainable by every human being who chooses to enter the kingdom of heaven and acknowledge the acceptance of sonship with God and brotherhood with man. That is the highest concept of religion the world has ever known, and I believe that there can never be a higher religion because this gospel embraces the infinity of God's reality, the divinity of values, the meaning of his love, and the achievement of eternity.

I am not only intrigued by the consummate ideals of the religion of our Lord and Master Jesus Christ, but I am convinced that his announcement that these ideals of the reality of spirit are achievable; that you and I can enter upon this long and eternal adventure with his assurance of the certainty of our ultimate arrival at the portals of Paradise. I have embarked; I am on my way with you in the ultimate adventure of finding God. What could be more thrilling than that?

The Master says he came from the Father, and that he will show us the way. I am fully persuaded he speaks the truth. I am fully convinced that with God, all things are possible; even saving "a wretch like me." Our Father made that possible by sending his spiritual gift to guide me, strengthen me, encourage me, and tell me: "this is the way." He sent his Son who then said: "Follow me." How then can I claim to be lost when in reality I am found.

We should worship, not merely the God of the present, but the God of all existences; past, present, and future universes of things and beings; an infinite and great God, without beginning or end, with all power and glory in the heaven of heavens, yet who loves us, each and every one of us, individually and unconditionally. And there is no other God, for there cannot possibly be any other God so true, beautiful, and good. Because God, our Father, is perfect in all these ways and nothing is greater than perfection. God is infinite. There can be nothing larger than infinity. God is eternal. There is nothing more timeless than God.

≈The God of Jesus≈

8. The Acme of Religious Living

Although we cannot hope, in this life, to attain the high perfection of character which Jesus of Nazareth acquired during his short life in the flesh, it is completely possible for every believer to develop a strong and unified personality along the perfected lines of Jesus' personality. The unique feature of the Master's personality was not so much its perfection as its symmetry, its exquisite and balanced unification of all factors of life. The most effective presentation of Jesus was when Pontius Pilot said, as he gestured toward the Master standing before his accusers, "Behold the man!"

The unfailing kindness of Jesus touched the hearts of men, but his firm strength of character amazed his followers. He was truly sincere; there was nothing of the hypocrite in him. He was free from ego and arrogance; he was always so refreshingly genuine. He never stooped to pretense, and he never resorted to shamming. He lived the truth, even as he taught it. He is the truth. And even though such sincerity sometimes caused pain, he was unquestioningly loyal to all truth.

The Master was so reasonable, so approachable. He was so practical in all his ministry, while all his plans were characterized by common sense. He was so free from all freakish, erratic, and eccentric tendencies. He was never capricious, whimsical, or hysterical. In all his teaching and in everything he did there was always an exquisite sense of propriety and dignity.

The Son of Man was always a well-poised personality. Even his enemies maintained a wholesome respect for him; they even feared his presence. Jesus was unafraid. He was charged with divine enthusiasm, but he never became fanatical. He was emotionally active but never flighty. He was imaginative but always practical. He frankly faced the realities of life, but he was never dull or ordinary. He was courageous but never reckless; prudent but never cowardly. He was sympathetic but not sentimental; unique but not eccentric. He was pious but not sanctimonious. And he was so well-poised because he was so perfectly unified and balanced.

Jesus was not bound by tradition or handicapped by enslavement to dogma. He spoke with undoubted confidence and taught with absolute authority. His authority came from God, not man. But his superb originality did not cause him to overlook the gems of truth in the teachings of his predecessors and contemporaries. He often referred to the best parts of scripture and acknowledged truth even when it came from others. And the most original of his teachings was the emphasis of love and mercy in the place of fear and sacrifice; two things he tried to put a stop to.

Jesus was very broad in his outlook. He exhorted his followers to preach the gospel to all peoples. He was free from all narrow-mindedness. His sympathetic heart embraced all mankind, even a universe. Always his invitation was, "Whosoever will, let him come."

Of Jesus it was truly said, "He trusted God." As a man among men he most sublimely trusted the Father in heaven. He trusted his Father as a little child trusts his earthly parent. His faith was perfect but never presumptuous. No matter how cruel nature might appear to be or how indifferent to man's welfare on earth, Jesus never faltered in his faith. He was immune to disappointment and impervious to persecution. He was untouched by apparent failure.

He loved men as brothers, at the same time recognizing how they differed in innate endowments and acquired qualities. "He went about doing good."

Jesus was an unusually cheerful person, but he was not a blind and unreasoning optimist. His constant word of exhortation was, "Be of good cheer." He could maintain this confident attitude because of his unswerving trust in God and his unshakable confidence in man. He was always touchingly considerate of all men because he loved them and believed "in" them. Still he was always true to his convictions and magnificently firm in his devotion to the doing of his Father's will.

The Master was always generous. He never grew weary of saying, "It is more blessed to give than to receive." Said he, "Freely you have received, freely give." And yet, with all of his unbounded generosity, he was never wasteful or extravagant. He taught that you must believe to receive salvation. "For every one who seeks shall receive."

He was candid, but always kind. Said he, "If it were not so, I would have told you." He was frank, but always friendly. He was outspoken in his love for the sinner and in his intolerance of sin. But throughout all this amazing frankness he was unerringly fair.

Jesus was consistently cheerful, notwithstanding he sometimes drank deeply of the cup of human sorrow. He fearlessly faced the realities of existence, yet was he filled with enthusiasm for the gospel of the kingdom. But he controlled his enthusiasm; it never controlled him. He was unreservedly dedicated to "the Father's business." This divine enthusiasm led his unspiritual brethren, even some of his own family, to think he was beside himself, but the onlooking universe considered him the model of sanity and the pattern of supreme mortal devotion to the high standards of spiritual living. And his controlled enthusiasm was contagious; his apostles and disciples were led to share his divine optimism.

This man of Galilee was not a man of sorrows; he was a soul of gladness. Always was he saying, "Rejoice and be exceedingly glad." But when duty required, he was willing to walk courageously through the "valley of the shadow of death." He was joyful but at the same time humble.

His courage was equaled only by his patience. When pressed to act prematurely, he would only reply, "My hour has not yet come." He was never in a hurry; his composure was sublime. But he was often indignant at evil, intolerant of sin. He was often mightily moved to resist that which was detrimental to the welfare of his children on earth. But his indignation against sin NEVER led to anger at the sinner or reduced his love for them.

His courage was magnificent, but he was never foolhardy. His watchword was, "Fear not." His bravery was lofty and his courage often heroic. But his courage was linked with discretion and controlled by reason. It was courage born of faith, not the recklessness of blind presumption. He was truly brave but never foolhardy.

The Master was a pattern of reverence. The prayer of even his youth began, "Our Father who is in heaven, hallowed be your name." He was even respectful of the faulty worship of his fellows. But this did not deter him from making attacks on religious traditions or assaulting errors of human belief. He was reverential of true holiness, and yet he could justly appeal to his fellows, saying, "Who among you convicts me of sin?"

Jesus was great because he was good, and yet he fraternized with the little children. He was gentle and unassuming in his personal life, and yet he was the perfected man of a universe. His associates, on their own choosing, called him Master.

Jesus was the perfectly unified human personality. He unifies life, ennobles character, and simplifies experience. Through the Spirit of Truth which he poured out upon all men and women the day of Pentecost, he enters the human mind to elevate, transform, and transfigure it. It is literally true: "If any man has Christ Jesus within him, he is a new creature; old things are passing away; behold, all things are becoming new."

If you want to know God, know who he is, what he is, and why we should love him and strive to do his will and to grow in spirit to become like God, then look first to Jesus because through his mortal life as the Son of Man, he showed us who God is and what God is. Jesus is the Son of God and he knows God personally just as you know your own father or son, even more so. After observing and studying the life and teachings of Jesus, can there be any mystery about God? As our understanding of God evolved from a tribal god to the Lord God of Israel, now for us taking this course, our God has been revealed as the God of Jesus and the God of each of us.

9. The Certainty of the Divine

You cannot be sure about God unless you know him; that being the purpose of this course. Being a child of God is the only experience which makes his fatherhood certain. God and the universe are not identical; one is cause, the other effect. The cause is absolute, infinite, eternal, and changeless; the effect, is ever changing, always growing.

God is the one and only un-caused fact in the universe. He always was, is, and will be; from the depths of eternity past and into the endless eternity of the future. He is the secret of the order, plan, and purpose of the whole creation of things and beings. The everywhere-changing universe is regulated and stabilized by his absolutely unchanging laws. The fact of God is changeless. The truth of God is dynamic truth and ever adaptable to the constantly evolving universe. Static truth is dead truth.

Those who would invent a religion without God are like those who would gather fruit without trees, have children without parents. You cannot have effects without causes; only the I AM is causeless. By this I mean that there was nothing before God that created him or caused him to exist. He is the only uncaused thing that is the cause of everything else. The fact of religious experience implies the fact of God, and such a God of personal experience must be a personal god. You cannot pray to a chemical formula or a mathematical equation. You cannot worship a hypothesis, confide in a postulate, commune with a process, serve an abstraction, or hold loving fellowship with a law. The intellectual earmark of religion is certainty; it's social fruits are love and service.

The God-knowing individual is not blind to the difficulties or unmindful of the obstacles which stand in the way of finding God in the maze of superstition, tradition, and materialistic tendencies of modern times. He has encountered all these deterrents and triumphed over them, surmounted them by living faith, and attained the highlands of spiritual experience in spite of them. But it is true that many who are inwardly sure about God fear to assert such feelings of certainty because of the superficial questions, arguments, and cleverness of those who raise objections and strain at gnats about believing in God. It requires no great depth of intellect to pick flaws, ask questions, or raise objections. But it does require forethought and planning to answer these questions; faith certainty is the greatest technique for dealing with all such difficulties.

We should reply to such questioning with the certainty of our own personal spiritual experience saying, "I know what I have personally experienced." Of God, the most inescapable of all presences, the most real of all facts, the most living of all truths, the most loving of all friends, and the most divine of all values, we have **the right** to be the most certain. You cannot prove to me that God does not exist because I know that he does.

10. Our Religion

The Lord our God is one Lord, and we should love him with all our mind and heart while we do our very best to love all his children not only as we love ourselves but rather as Jesus and God love us. God is our heavenly Father, in whom all things consist, and who dwells, by his spirit, in every sincere human soul, including mine and including yours. And we, as brothers and sisters, who are the children of God, should commit the safekeeping of our souls to him as our faithful Father-Creator. Before Jesus revealed the Father to us we could rightly say: "Do unto others as you would have others do unto you." But now that we know the God of Jesus we can say: "Do unto others as you believe God would do unto them."

With our heavenly Father all things are possible. Since he is the Creator, having made all things and all beings, it could not be otherwise. Though we cannot see God, we can know him. And by each day living the will of the Father in heaven, we can reveal him to our fellow man.

The divine riches of God's character must be infinitely deep and eternally wise. We cannot search out God by knowledge, but we can know him in our hearts by personal experience. While his justice may be hard to find or understand sometimes, his mercy may be received by even the humblest being on earth. While the Father fills the universe, he also lives in our hearts. The mind of man is human, mortal, but the spirit of man is divine, immortal. God is not only all-powerful but also all-wise. If our earth parents or we as parents ourselves know how to love our children and bless them with good gifts, how much more must the Supreme Universal Father in Heaven know how to wisely love his children on earth and desire to bestow suitable blessings upon them.

The Father in heaven will not allow a single child on earth to perish if that child has a desire to find the Father and truly longs to be like him. Our Father even loves the wicked and is always kind to the ungrateful. He returns goodness for evil. He makes the rain fall on the just and the unjust. He loves even his enemies. If more of us could only know about the goodness of God, come to really know God for who he is, we would certainly be led to repent of our evil ways and forsake all known sin, and love all people as our brothers or sisters. All good things come down from the Father, in whom there is "no variableness neither shadow of changing." The spirit of the true God is in our heart. He intends that all men should be brothers. When men begin to search for God, that is proof that God has already found them, and that they are truth-seekers in quest of knowledge about him. We live in God and God dwells in us.

God is the Father of all people but he is also **my** Father and **your** Father. Always will I worship God with the help of the Spirit of Truth and my Indwelling Spirit, who have been my helpers since the day I became really God-knowing. I practice worshiping God and it is my will to do the will of God in my life here on earth and beyond. When we do our best to treat each of our fellow human beings just as God would like to have them treated, when we desire to do all things the way God would do them, we may ask many things of God and he will give us the desire of our hearts so that we may better serve our fellow mortals. And all of this loving service of the children of God enlarges our capacity to receive and experience the joys of heaven, the pleasures of ministry, the ecstasy of worship, and the comforting love of God.

I thank God every day for his many gifts; I will praise him for his wonderful blessings to all his children and to all my children. To me, he is the Almighty, the Creator, the all-powerful, the merciful, the loving, the most true, beautiful, and good —but best of all, he is my spirit Father. As his child, I know that at the end of this mortal life I am going to see him. By getting to know God, I shall become like him which is my goal and my destiny. By faith in God I have attained peace with him and through him. My faith and my personal religion is full of joy, and it generates enduring happiness. I am confident that I shall be faithful even to death, and that I will surely receive the reward of eternal life.

I pledge to do to others as I believe God wants done to them and for them; as God himself would do. As I love God, so shall I serve man. This great and glorious God is my Father. I am his child and I recognize God within all my mortal brothers and sisters. I am certain in the fatherhood of God and that all men are my brothers. We cannot rejoice in the fatherhood of God but refuse to accept the brotherhood of man. "Whosoever calls upon the name of the Lord shall be saved." If that is true, then all men must be my brothers.

I have not even begun to master this practice of being Godlike but I am going to attempt to love my enemies; maybe not all of them today but at least one more each day. I will strive to be the most beautiful, loving, merciful, personal, and positive person I can be—like God. And by no other means than my honest sincere desire to be like him, shall I accomplish my goal to find him and eternally serve him and all his children. Our religion has a God, a marvelous God, an awesome God, and he is a God of eternal salvation.

11. The Faith of Jesus

Jesus enjoyed a sublime and wholehearted faith in God. He experienced the ordinary ups and downs of mortal existence, but he never religiously doubted the certainty of God's watchcare and guidance. His faith was the outgrowth of the insight born of the activity of the divine presence. His faith was neither traditional nor merely intellectual; it was wholly personal and purely spiritual.

The human Jesus saw God as being holy, just, and great, as well as being true, beautiful, and good. All these attributes of divinity he focused in his mind as the "will of the Father in heaven." The God of Jesus was at one and the same time "The Holy One of Israel" and "The living and loving Father in heaven." The concept of God as a Father was not original with Jesus, but he exalted and elevated the idea into a sublime experience by achieving a new revelation of God and by proclaiming that every mortal creature is a child of this Father of love, a son of God.

Jesus did not cling to faith in God as would a struggling soul at war with the universe and at death grips with a hostile and sinful world; he did not resort to faith merely as a consolation in the midst of difficulties or as a comfort in threatening despair. Faith was not just a compensation for the unpleasant realities and the sorrows of living. In the very face of all the natural difficulties and the earthly struggles of mortal existence, he experienced the peace of supreme and unquestioned trust in God and felt the tremendous thrill of living, by faith, in the very presence of the heavenly Father. And this triumphant faith was a living experience of actual spirit attainment. Jesus' great contribution to the values of human experience was not that he revealed so many new ideas about the Father in heaven, but rather that he so magnificently and humanly demonstrated a new and higher type of living faith in God. Never on all the worlds of this universe, in the life of any one mortal, did God ever become such a living reality as in the human experience of Jesus of Nazareth.

In the Master's life on earth, we discover a new and higher type of religion; religion based on personal spiritual relations with the Universal Father and wholly validated by the supreme authority of genuine personal experience. This living faith of Jesus was more than an intellectual reflection, and it was not a mystic meditation.

Theology may fix, formulate, define, and dogmatize faith, but in the human life of Jesus faith was personal, living, original, spontaneous, and purely spiritual. This faith was not reverence for tradition nor a mere intellectual belief which he held as a sacred creed, but rather a sublime experience and a profound conviction which securely held him. His faith was so real and all-encompassing that it absolutely swept away any spiritual doubts and effectively destroyed every conflicting desire. Nothing was able to tear him away from the spiritual anchorage of his fervent, sublime, and undaunted faith. Even in the face of apparent defeat or in the throes of disappointment and despair, he calmly stood in the divine presence free from fear and fully conscious of spiritual invincibility.

Jesus enjoyed the invigorating assurance of the possession of unflinching faith. In each of life's trying situations he unfailingly exhibited an unquestioning loyalty to the Father's will. And this superb faith was undaunted even by the cruel and crushing threat of a humiliating and pain-filled death.

As Jesus was dying upon the cross, amidst the increasing darkness of a fierce sandstorm, as his human consciousness began to fail, while his lips would often move, Jesus resorted to the repetition of many passages in the Hebrew scriptures, particularly the Psalms. He was too weak to utter the words of passages from scripture that he knew so well by heart. Only a few times did those standing by catch some utterance, such as, "I know the Lord will save his anointed," "Your hand shall find out all my enemies," and "My God, my God, why have you forsaken me?" Jesus did not for one moment feel that the Father had forsaken him; he was merely reciting in his vanishing consciousness from the twenty-second Psalm, which begins with "My God, my God, why have you forsaken me?" Jesus did not believe the Father would ever abandon him and neither should we.

Strong spiritual faith sometimes may lead directly to disastrous fanaticism, to exaggeration of the religious ego, but it was not so with Jesus. He was not unfavorably affected in his practical life by his extraordinary faith and spirit attainment because this spiritual exaltation was a wholly unconscious and spontaneous soul expression of his personal experience with God.

The all-consuming and indomitable spiritual faith of Jesus never became fanatical, for it never attempted to run away with his well-balanced intellectual judgments concerning the proportional values of practical and commonplace social, economic, and moral life situations. The Son of Man was a splendidly unified human personality; he was a perfectly endowed divine being; he was also magnificently co-ordinated as a combined human and divine being functioning on earth as a single personality. Always did the Master coordinate the faith of the soul with the wisdom of experience. Personal faith, spiritual hope, and moral devotion were always correlated in a matchless religious unity of harmonious association with the keen realization of the reality and sacredness of all human loyalties—personal honor, family love, religious obligation, social duty, and economic necessity.

The faith of Jesus visualized all spirit values as being found in the kingdom of God; therefore he said, "Seek first the kingdom of heaven." Jesus saw in the advanced and ideal fellowship of the kingdom the achievement and fulfillment of the "will of God." The very heart of the prayer which he taught his disciples was, "Your kingdom come; your will be done." Having thus conceived of the kingdom as comprising the will of God, he devoted himself to the cause of its realization with amazing self-forgetfulness and unbounded enthusiasm. But in all his intense mission and throughout his extraordinary life there never appeared the fury of the fanatic nor the phony sincerity of the religious egotist.

The Master's entire life was consistently conditioned by this living faith, this sublime religious experience. This spiritual attitude wholly dominated his thinking and feeling, his believing and praying, his teaching and preaching. This personal faith of a son in the certainty and security of the guidance and protection of the heavenly Father imparted to his unique life a profound endowment of spiritual reality. And yet, despite this very deep consciousness of close relationship with divinity, this Galilean, God's Galilean, when addressed as Good Teacher, instantly replied, "Why do you call me good?" When we stand confronted by such splendid self-forgetfulness, we begin to understand how the Universal Father found it possible to so fully manifest himself to Jesus and reveal himself through Jesus to the mortals of this world.

Jesus brought to God, as a man of the realm, the greatest of all offerings: the consecration and dedication of his own will to the majestic service of doing the divine will. Jesus always and consistently interpreted religion wholly in terms of the Father's will. When you study the career of the Master, as concerns prayer or any other feature of the religious life, look not so much for what he taught as for what he did.

Jesus never prayed as a religious duty. To him prayer was a sincere expression of spiritual attitude, a declaration of soul loyalty, a recital of personal devotion, an expression of thanksgiving, an avoidance of emotional tension, a prevention of conflict, an exaltation of intellect, an ennoblement of desire, a vindication of moral decision, an enrichment of thought, an invigoration of higher ideals, a consecration of impulse, a clarification of viewpoint, a declaration of faith, a transcendental surrender of will, a sublime assertion of confidence, a revelation of courage, the proclamation of discovery, a confession of supreme devotion, the validation of consecration, a technique for the adjustment of difficulties, and the mighty mobilization of the combined soul powers to withstand all human tendencies toward selfishness, evil, and sin.

Jesus lived just such a life of prayerful consecration to the doing of his Father's will and ended his life triumphantly with just such a prayer. The secret of his unparalleled religious life was this consciousness of the presence of God; and he attained it by intelligent prayer and sincere worship—unbroken communion with God—and not by leadings, voices, visions, fasting, or extraordinary religious practices.

In the earthly life of Jesus, religion was a living experience, a direct and personal movement from spiritual reverence to practical righteousness. The faith of Jesus bore the transcendent fruits of the divine spirit. His faith was not immature and credulous like that of a child, but in many ways it did resemble the unsuspecting trust of the child mind. Jesus trusted God much as the child trusts a parent. He had a profound confidence in the universe—just such a trust as the child has in the safety and security of their parent's home. Jesus' wholehearted faith in the fundamental goodness of the universe very much resembled the child's trust in the security of its earthly surroundings. He depended on the heavenly Father as a child leans upon its earthly parent, and his fervent faith never for one moment doubted the certainty of the heavenly Father's overcare. He was not disturbed seriously by fears, doubts, and skepticism. Unbelief did not inhibit the free and original expression of his life. He combined the stalwart and intelligent courage of a full-grown man with the sincere and trusting optimism of a believing child. His faith grew to such heights of trust that it was devoid of fear.

The faith of Jesus attained the purity of a child's trust. His faith was so absolute and undoubting that it responded to the charm of the contact of fellow beings and to the wonders of the universe. His sense of dependence on the divine was so complete and so confident that it yielded the joy and the assurance of absolute personal security. There was no hesitating pretense in his religious experience. In this giant intellect of the full-grown man the faith of the child reigned supreme in all matters relating to his religious awareness. It is not strange that he once said, "Except you become as a little child, you shall not enter the kingdom." Notwithstanding that Jesus' faith was childlike, it was in no sense childish.

Jesus does not require his disciples to believe **in** him but rather to believe **with** him, believe in the reality of the love of God and in full confidence accept the security of the assurance of sonship with the heavenly Father. The Master desires that all his followers should fully share his transcendent faith. Jesus most touchingly challenged his followers, not only to believe **what** he believed, but also to believe **as** he believed. This is the full significance of his one supreme requirement, "Follow me."

Jesus' earthly life was devoted to one great purpose—doing the Father's will, living the human life religiously and by faith. The faith of Jesus was trusting, like that of a child, but it was wholly free from presumption. He made robust and manly decisions, courageously faced many disappointments, resolutely overcame extraordinary difficulties, and unflinchingly confronted the stern requirements of duty. It required a strong will and an unfailing confidence to believe what Jesus believed and as he believed.

12. The Religion of Jesus

Today a reformation in the Christian church is beginning to get us back to the religious teachings of Jesus, the author and finisher of our faith. We preached a religion **about Jesus**, but, now we must live the religion **of Jesus**.

In the enthusiasm of Pentecost, Peter unintentionally inaugurated a new religion, the religion of the risen and glorified Christ. The Apostle Paul later transformed this new gospel into Christianity.

The gospel of the kingdom is founded on the personal religious experience of Jesus. Christianity is founded almost exclusively on the personal religious experience of the Apostle Paul. Almost the whole of the New Testament is devoted, not to the portrayal of the significant and inspiring religious life of Jesus, but to a discussion of Paul's religious experience and to a portrayal of his personal religious convictions embodying his own theologic views and portraying his own conversion experience with the Jesus of the Damascus road that he believed in.

. The only notable exceptions to this statement, aside from certain parts of Matthew, Mark, and Luke, are the Book of Hebrews and the Epistle of James. Even Peter, in his writing, only once reverted to the personal religious life of his Master. The New Testament, which uplifted and enlightened the Old Testament, is a superb Christian document, but it is only meagerly about Jesus himself or his teachings. This has been most unfortunate especially to those truth-seekers who are just beginning their journey to find God.

In our religion, it should be the words, actions, and teachings of Jesus, who is the Word of God made flesh, that reign supreme over all others. The little book, as foreseen in the "Book of Revelations," is now nearly 100 years old. It is meant to uplift and enlighten all religions, all people, and serve the future with the most complete, profound, and accurate spiritual, philosophical, and religious information available for us today. Much as in the days of Jesus, the very thing we have prayed for is now here with us ready to be the instrument for taking the gospel of Jesus to all the world.

Jesus' life in the flesh portrays a transcendent religious growth from the early ideas of primitive awe and human reverence up through years of personal spiritual communion until he finally arrived at that advanced and exalted status of the consciousness of his oneness with the Father. And thus, in one short life, Jesus demonstrated that experience of religious spiritual progression which man begins on earth and ordinarily achieves only at the conclusion of his long journey to Paradise. Jesus showed us the way from a dogmatic institutional religion, enslaved to ceremony, threatened by diversity, and frozen by tradition, to the sublime spiritual heights of an ever expanding faith in a loving, merciful, all-wise heavenly Father perfect in all truth, beauty, and goodness. He progressed from the humble status of mortal dependence which prompted him spontaneously to say to the one who called him Good Teacher, "Why do you call me good? None is good but God," to that sublime consciousness of achieved divinity which led him to exclaim, "Which one of you convicts me of sin?" And this progressing ascent from the human to the divine was an exclusively mortal achievement. And when he had thus attained divinity, he was still the same human Jesus, the Son of Man as well as the Son of God.

Mark, Matthew, and Luke retain some of the picture of the human Jesus as he engaged in the superb struggle to discover God's will and to do that will. John presents a picture of the triumphant Jesus as he walked on earth in the full consciousness of his divinity. The great mistake that has been made by those who have studied the Master's life is that some have conceived of him as entirely human, while others have thought of him as only divine. Throughout his entire experience he was truly both human and divine, even as he still is today. He was and is the Son of Man and the Son of God.

But the greatest mistake was made in that, while the human Jesus was recognized as having a religion, the divine Jesus (Christ) almost overnight became a religion. Paul's Christianity made sure of the adoration of the divine Christ, but it almost wholly lost sight of the struggling and valiant human Jesus of Galilee, who, by the valor of his personal religious faith and the heroism of his spirit, ascended from the lowly levels of humanity to become one with divinity, thus becoming the new and living way whereby all mortals may ascend from humanity to divinity. Mortals in all stages of spirituality and on all worlds may find in the personal life of Jesus that which will strengthen and inspire them as they progress from the lowest spiritual levels up to the highest divine values, from the beginning to the end of all personal religious experience.

It should be of great comfort and hope to all of us to know that the Holy Spirit, the Spirit of Truth, our Indwelling Spirit, and the angels lead, comfort, guide, and accompany us on this mortal journey. Having started out on the way of life everlasting, having accepted the assignment and received our orders to advance, we should not fear the dangers of human forgetfulness and mortal inconsistency. Do not be troubled with doubts of failure or by perplexing confusion. Do not falter and question your status and standing before God, for in every dark hour, at every crossroad in the forward struggle, the Spirit of Truth will always speak, saying, "This is the way." And, then Jesus leading the way says: "Follow me." Knowing this, never again can you claim to be lost or alone or forgotten or valueless. To God and Jesus, you are none of those things.

At the time of the writing of the New Testament, the authors not only most profoundly believed in the divinity of the risen Christ, but they also devotedly and sincerely believed in his immediate return to earth to initiate the Kingdom of Heaven. This strong faith in the Lord's immediate return had much to do with the tendency to omit from the record those references which portrayed the purely human experiences and attributes of the Master. The whole Christian movement tended away from the personally valuable picture of the human Jesus of Nazareth toward the exaltation of the risen Christ, the glorified and soon-returning Lord Jesus Christ.

Jesus founded the religion of personal experience in doing the will of God and serving the human brotherhood; Paul founded a religion in which the glorified Jesus became the object of worship and the brotherhood consisted of fellow believers in the divine Christ. In the mission of Jesus, these two concepts were potential in his divine-human life. It is indeed a pity that his followers failed to create a unified religion which might have given proper recognition to both his human and his divine natures as they were inseparably bound up in his earth life and so gloriously set forth in the original gospel of the kingdom as presented by Jesus.

You would be neither shocked nor disturbed by some of Jesus' strong pronouncements if you would only remember that he was the world's most wholehearted and devoted religionist. He was a wholly consecrated mortal, unreservedly dedicated to doing his Father's will. Many of his apparently hard sayings were more of a personal confession of faith and a pledge of devotion than commands to his followers. And it was this very singleness of purpose and unselfish devotion that enabled him to effect such extraordinary progress in the conquest of his human mind in one short life. Many of his declarations should be considered as a confession of what he demanded of himself rather than what he required of all his followers. In his devotion to the cause of the kingdom, Jesus burned all bridges behind him; he sacrificed all hindrances to the doing of his Father's will.

Jesus blessed the poor because they were usually sincere and pious; he condemned the rich because they were usually wanton and irreligious. He would equally condemn the irreligious pauper and commend the consecrated and worshipful man of wealth.

Jesus led men to feel at home in the world. His teachings led them to feel safe and secure in a friendly universe under the watchcare of their heavenly Father. He delivered them from the slavery of taboo and taught them that the world was not fundamentally evil. He did not long to escape from his earthly life; he mastered a technique of acceptably doing the Father's will while in the flesh. He attained an idealistic religious life in the very midst of a realistic world. Jesus did not share Paul's pessimistic view of humankind. The Master looked upon men as the sons of God and foresaw a magnificent and eternal future for those who choose salvation. He was not a moral skeptic; he viewed man positively, not negatively. He saw most men as weak rather than wicked, more distraught than depraved. But no matter what their status, they were all God's children and his brethren.

He taught men to place a high value upon themselves in time and in eternity. Because of this high estimate which Jesus placed upon men, he was willing to spend himself in the unremitting service of humankind. And it was this infinite value of the finite mortal that made the golden rule a vital factor in his religion. What person can fail to be uplifted and comforted by the extraordinary faith that Jesus has in them?

Jesus offered no rules for social advancement; his was a religious mission, and religion is an exclusively individual experience. The ultimate goal of society's most advanced achievement can never hope to transcend Jesus' brotherhood of men based on the recognition of the fatherhood of God. The ideal of all social attainment can be realized only in the coming of this divine kingdom.

13. True Religion

Jesus has called us to be born again, to be born of the spirit. He calls us out of the darkness of authority and the lethargy of tradition into the transcendent light of the realization of the possibility of making for yourselves the greatest discovery possible for the human soul to make—the supernal experience of finding God for yourself, in yourself, and of yourself, and of doing all this as a fact in your own personal experience. And so may you pass from death to life, from the authority of tradition to the experience of knowing God; thus will you pass from darkness to light, from a racial faith inherited to a personal faith achieved by actual experience; and thereby will you progress from a theology of mind handed down by your ancestors to a true religion of spirit which shall be built up in your souls as an eternal endowment.

Our religion shall change from the mere intellectual belief in traditional theologic authority to the actual experience of that living spiritual faith which is able to grasp the reality of God and all that relates to the divine Father in Heaven. The religion of the mind ties you hopelessly to the past; the religion of the spirit consists in progressive revelation of our heavenly Father and ever beckons you on toward higher and holier achievements in spiritual ideals and eternal realities.

While the religions of authority may offer a short term feeling of security, we pay for such fleeting satisfaction with the loss of our spiritual freedom and religious liberty. Our Father does not require as the price of entering the kingdom of heaven that we should force ourselves to subscribe to a belief in things which are spiritually repugnant, unholy, and untruthful. It is not required that our own sense of mercy, justice, and truth should be outraged by submission to an outworn system of religious forms and ceremonies. The religion of the spirit leaves you forever free to follow the truth wherever the leadings of the spirit may take you. And who can judge—perhaps this spirit may have something to impart to this generation which other generations have refused to hear?

Shame on those false religious teachers who drag hungry souls back into the dim and distant past and leave them there! And so are these unfortunate persons, these little children in spirit, doomed to be frightened by every new discovery and fearful of every new revelation of truth. The prophet who said, "He will be kept in perfect peace whose mind is stayed on God," was not a mere intellectual believer in authoritative theology. This truth-knowing human had discovered God; he was not merely talking about God.

May I suggest that we give up the practice of always quoting the prophets of old and praising the heroes of ancient Israel, and instead aspire to become living prophets of the Most High and spiritual heroes of the coming kingdom. To honor the God-knowing leaders of the past may indeed be worthwhile, but why, in so doing, should we sacrifice the supreme experience of human existence: finding God for ourselves and knowing him in our own souls? Discover God in your own mind and soul rather than being told what to believe by someone who only repeats what they read on the internet, or is too lazy to experience the truth, is enslaved to dogma, or paralysed by fear and guilt.

Every race of mankind has its own mental outlook upon human existence. Therefore, must religions of the mind ever run true to these various racial viewpoints. Never can the religions of authority come to unification because none of them can surrender their authority for the benefit of mankind; but honestly, they all believe they are doing the will of God so do not fault them for that. Unity and brotherhood can be achieved only by and through the religion of the spirit. Racial minds may differ, but all mankind is indwelt by the same divine and eternal spirit. All are equal in the eyes of God. The hope of human brotherhood can only be realized when, and as, the many different religions of authority become impregnated with, and overshadowed by, the unifying and ennobling religion of the spirit—the religion of individual personal spiritual experience.

The religions of authority can only divide men and set them in conscientious array against each other; the religion of the spirit will progressively draw men together and cause them to become understandingly sympathetic with one another. The religions of authority require uniformity of belief. We see this in the membership requirements of nearly every church, synagogue, or mosque. But this is impossible to realize in the present state of the world. The religion of the spirit requires only unity of experience—uniformity of destiny—making full allowance for diversity of belief. The religion of the spirit requires only uniformity of insight, not uniformity of viewpoint and outlook. The religion of the spirit does not demand uniformity of intellectual views, only unity of spiritual feeling. The religions of authority crystallize into lifeless creeds; the religion of the spirit grows into the increasing joy and liberty of ennobling deeds of loving service and merciful ministration.

But do not look with disdain upon the children of Abraham because they have fallen on these evil days of traditional barrenness. They gave themselves up to the persistent and passionate search for God, and they found him as no other whole race of men have ever known him since the times of Adam. Our Father has not failed to acknowledge the long and untiring struggle of Israel, ever since the days of Moses, to find God and to know God. For many generations, the Jews (and others) have not ceased to toil, sweat, groan, travail, endure the sufferings and experience the sorrows of a misunderstood and despised people all in order that they might come a little nearer the discovery of the truth about God. And, notwithstanding all the failures and setbacks of Israel, their ancestors, from Moses to the times of Amos and Hosea, increasingly revealed to the whole world an ever clearer and more truthful picture of the eternal God. And so the way was prepared for the still greater revelation of the Father which we have been called to share in this modern day and age.

Never forget there is only one adventure which is more satisfying and thrilling than the attempt to discover the will of the living God, and that is the supreme experience of honestly trying to do that divine will. Do not fail to remember that the will of God can be done in any earthly occupation. Some callings are not holy and others secular. All things are sacred in the lives of those who are spirit led. They are subordinated to truth, ennobled by love, dominated by mercy, and restrained by fairness—justice. The spirit which Jesus sent into the world is not only the Spirit of Truth but also the spirit of idealistic beauty.

You must cease to seek for the Word of God only on the pages of the olden records of theologic authority. Those who are born of the spirit of God from this day forward shall see and understand the Word of God regardless of its origin. New prophets are among us and new revelation has been given to us. Divine truth must not be discounted because its source may seem to be human or even unknown. Every person may be a modern day prophet because the gift of God, the Indwelling Spirit, and the gift of Jesus, the Spirit of Truth, are leading all of us to do God's will and to share his gospel; the gospel of the Fatherhood of God and the Brotherhood of Mankind.

Many of our siblings have minds which accept the theory of God while they spiritually fail to realize the presence of God. They believe in God but have not yet found faith in God. And that is just the reason why Jesus so often taught that the kingdom of heaven can best be realized by acquiring the spiritual attitude of a sincere little child. It is not the mental immaturity of the child but rather the spiritual simplicity of such an easy-believing and fully-trusting little one that is important. It is not so important that you should know about the fact of God as that you should increasingly grow in the ability to feel the presence of God.

When you begin to find God in your soul, you will begin to discover him in other men's souls and eventually in all the creations of a mighty universe. But what chance does the Father have to appear as a God of supreme loyalties and divine ideals in the souls of men who give little or no time to the thoughtful contemplation of such eternal realities? While the mind is not the seat of the spiritual nature, it is indeed the gateway thereto.

Do not make the mistake of trying to prove to other men that you have found God; you cannot consciously produce such proof, albeit there are two positive and powerful demonstrations of the fact that you are God-knowing, and they are:

1. The fruits of the spirit of God showing forth in your daily routine life.

2. The fact that your entire life plan furnishes positive proof that you have risked everything you are and everything you have on the adventure of survival after death of finding the God of eternity.

Now, mistake not, our Father will always feel and respond to the faintest flicker of faith. He takes note of the physical and superstitious emotions of the primitive man. And with those honest but fearful souls whose mustard seed of faith is so weak that it amounts to little more than passive agreement to religious authority, the Father will always honor and foster all such attempts to reach out for him no matter how feeble they may be. Do not be afraid to take one small step into the eternal adventure. But those of us who have already been called out of darkness into the light are expected to believe with a whole heart; our faith dominates the attitudes and desires of body, mind, and spirit.

Religion shall not become a theologic shelter to which you may flee in fear of facing the rugged realities of spiritual progress and idealistic adventure; but rather religion is the fact of real spiritual experience which testifies that God has found you, idealized, ennobled, and spiritualized you, and that you have enlisted in the eternal adventure of finding the God who has already found you.

14. Farewell and Conclusions

[This is an example. Instructor should create their own personal farewell and conclusions]

After several years of creating this compilation from the teachings of the world religions concerning our Paradise Father, let me give credit and offer a summary of my beliefs about God as a result of my study mainly of the Christian Bible and *The Urantia Book*. A great deal, if not everything, in this book came from these two books and my own personal experience with God.

As we come to the end of our time together, I hope that you have gotten as much out of this study as I have. I find that when creating and conducting courses of study it is the teacher who learns the most. Many times the pupils function as teachers by the questions they ask or the answers they give. Sometimes the investigation of a supposedly simple question, an erroneous response, or a contentious opinion leads to great discoveries of truth for everyone in the course. Jesus once said in this situation: "Let us be patient; the truth never suffers from honest examination."

If you consider giving this course yourself, which we certainly encourage you to do, remember this quote: "Even if I cannot do this, there lives in me one who can and will do it, a part of the heavenly Father. And that is the victory which overcomes the world, even your faith."

Let me recap a few thoughts from our earlier study and offer some conclusions:

There is in the mind of God a plan which embraces all of his vast domains, and this plan is an eternal purpose of boundless opportunity, unlimited progress, and endless life. And the infinite treasures of such a matchless career are yours for the striving!

The goal of eternity is ahead! The adventure of spiritual progress lies before you! The race for perfection is on! Whosoever will may enter, and certain victory will crown the efforts of every human being who will run the race of faith and trust, depending every step of the way on the leading of the Indwelling Spirit and the guidance of the Spirit of Truth.

To "follow Jesus" means to personally share his religious faith and to enter into the spirit of the Master's life of unselfish service for man. One of the most important things in our life is to find out what Jesus believed, to discover his ideals, and to strive for the achievement of his exalted life purpose. Of all human knowledge, that which is of greatest value is to know the religious life of Jesus and how he lived it.

Men all too often forget that God is the greatest experience in human existence. Other experiences are limited in their nature and content, but the experience of God has no limits other than our own capacity to learn and understand. When men search for God, they are searching for everything. When they find God, they have found everything. The search for God is the unstinted bestowal of love attended by amazing discoveries of new and greater love to be bestowed.

All true love is from God, and man receives the divine affection as he himself bestows this love upon his fellows. Love is dynamic. It can never be captured; it is alive, free, thrilling, and always moving. Man can never take the love of the Father and imprison it within his heart. The Father's love becomes real to us only when this love is given from us to our fellow mortals. Love is the one thing that must be given in order to be received. The great circle of love is from the Father, through his children to their brothers and sisters, and then back to the Father. The love of the Father is received by the ministry of the indwelling Spirit. Such a God-knowing person reveals this love to their family and friends, and this fraternal affection is the essence of the love of God and the meaning of Jesus' saying: "Love one another and I have loved you."

After our time together, I hope now you see God for who he really is. I hope that you have come to know the God of Jesus as your own personal God too. Don't take it lightly when someone tells you that God is this or God is that. Now, you know the truth about God and that truth has set you free to stand up boldly and defend the image and character of our Father in Heaven. Defend the character and honor of our heavenly Father as you would with your family or friends. God the Father is your family and your friend.

Always remember that your mission among men is to proclaim the gospel of the kingdom—the fatherhood of God, that you are a child of a living and loving God, and the brotherhood of man, and that you are saved by faith alone. Proclaim the whole truth of this good news, not just a part of this gospel. Go forth boldly and cheerfully preaching the love of God and service to mankind.

God changes not. God loves you. God wants you to love him. God wants you to succeed. So much so that he gave you a spirit helper and sent his Son Jesus to show you the way home to the shores of heaven and the destiny of Paradise. The Spirit of Truth says: "This is the way." Jesus says: "Follow me."

God wants you to be happy and healthy but he also wants you to be educated and experienced—ready for the ultimate purpose he has planned for you and what a glorious purpose that shall be. Do not neglect your daily worship. Spend quality time with your Father each day. Pray for more laborers to be sent forth into the gospel harvest. When you see something that you believe God wants done, pray and say: "Father, here am I; send me."

"Behold what manner of love the Father has bestowed upon us that we should be called the sons of God."

≈The God of Jesus≈

Please take the end of course survey. Compare your responses to the survey given to you at the beginning of the course.

[Return the beginning of course surveys to the students UNOPENED]

Thanks to God for his guidance. Thanks to my beloved Indwelling Spirit for leading me in this effort. Thanks to the angels watching over us and to all our friends seen and unseen. And with love and friendship, we thank you for participating in this course. To purchase additional copies of this course material visit us at:

Website: CosmicCreations.BIZ

Email: CosmicCreations606@gmail.com

It is also available on Amazon.com

For more information about *The Urantia Book* visit:

www.urantia.org.

I want to also give credit to my best friend, spiritual partner, and wife Susan for her unique study of the "Book of Revelations" and *The Urantia Book* that was used on page 162.

Make note of your thoughts, questions, comments here:

_____

_____

_____

_____

_____

_____

_____

_____

_____

_____

_____

_____

The God of Jesus

END OF COURSE SURVEY:

God is: _____

Who is God? _____

What is God?_____

_____

God should:_____

_____

I know why God:_____

_____

What has God done for me? _____

_____

What have I done for God?_____

_____

How have my thoughts changed about God? _____

_____

_____

The most important thing I learned is: _____

_____

My experience with this course was:_____